Limited Government

AND THE

Bill of Rights

Limited Government

AND THE

Bill of Rights

Patrick M. Garry

UNIVERSITY OF MISSOURI PRESS

COLUMBIA AND LONDON

Copyright © 2012 by
The Curators of the University of Missouri
University of Missouri Press, Columbia, Missouri 65201
Printed and bound in the United States of America
All rights reserved
5 4 3 2 1   16 15 14 13 12

Cataloging-in-Publication data available from the Library of Congress.
ISBN 978-0-8262-1971-8

♾™ This paper meets the requirements of the
American National Standard for Permanence of Paper
for Printed Library Materials, Z39.48, 1984.

Designer: Steph Foley
Typesetter: FoleyDesign
Printer and binder: Integrated Book Technology
Typeface: Minion

For Michael and Elizabeth

Contents

Acknowledgments

Without the reliably outstanding research assistance of Candice Spurlin and the excellent editing and manuscript-preparation work of Stephannie Bonaiuto, this book would not have been possible. To these friends and colleagues, the author extends his most sincere gratitude.

I would like to acknowledge the *SMU Law Review* and the *Quinnipiac Law Review* for giving me the opportunity to flesh out my initial thinking on some of the ideas and themes of this book.

Finally, I would like to very gratefully acknowledge the staff of the University of Missouri Press for all their diligent work in preparing the manuscript for publication. In particular, I thank Sara Davis and Gloria Thomas for their highly professional, insightful, and sensitive editorial contributions. I also thank Beth Chandler and John Brenner for their invaluable assistance in bringing the book to publication.

Limited Government

AND THE

Bill of Rights

Introduction

Under the leadership of Chief Justice Earl Warren in the 1950s and 1960s, the United States Supreme Court adopted an aggressive brand of individual-rights jurisprudence, interpreting the Bill of Rights as setting out mandates for achieving a certain vision of individual autonomy. But this individual autonomy was defined in isolation, apart from the larger social or political landscape occupied by individuals.

Under the modern view of the Bill of Rights, as taken by the Warren Court, individual autonomy has become a primary if not exclusive focus. According to this view, the Bill of Rights was included in the Constitution for the purpose of preserving individual autonomy through insulating the individual from various democratic outcomes. It is a view that has constitutional roots in the Court's New Deal period, reflected in the infamous footnote 4 of *United States v. Carolene Products Co.*, in which the Court suggested that it would no longer strictly scrutinize structural provisions of the Constitution, such as federalism and separation of powers, but would instead give heightened scrutiny to individual rights, such as those contained in the Bill of Rights.[1] Unfortunately, this change in the Court's orientation served to distort the meaning of the Bill of Rights. It cast the Bill of Rights as focused primarily or exclusively on individual autonomy. It also served to separate the Bill of Rights from the structural orientation of the Constitution as a whole. Both these effects contradicted the original intent behind the Bill of Rights.

During the New Deal constitutional revolution, the Court, in order to accommodate the New Deal legislation, retreated from enforcing the Constitution's structural provisions. In this retreat, the Court suggested that it would concentrate its attentions on individual-rights matters. However, since the Bill of Rights is essentially structural in itself, the Court was simply choosing one set of structural provisions to enforce while ignoring other structural provisions. The mistake was compounded when the Court began interpreting the Bill of Rights as exclusively concerned with individual rights and autonomy, rather than with providing structural limitations on government power and authority.

There is much debate among scholars as to the intent and purpose behind the Bill of Rights. One argument is that it serves to protect and nourish certain fundamental individual rights. Under this argument, the Bill of Rights seeks

1

first and foremost to identify particular individual freedoms and then to create a constitutional protection for those substantive freedoms, in a way that facilitates or preserves a judicially defined view of those freedoms.

Another argument looks at the Bill of Rights from a wholly different perspective. This argument sees the bill as a set of provisions designed primarily to better ensure the maintenance of limited government within the constitutional scheme. According to this argument, the Anti-Federalists, as the primary advocates for and shapers of the Bill of Rights, sought to achieve not a particular substantive protection of specific individual rights, but rather an assurance that the government being created through the new Constitution would indeed be a government of limited powers.[2] To further secure this limited government, the Bill of Rights specified certain explicit areas in which the government would have no power to act or intrude. Whereas the rest of the constitutional scheme set out structural provisions for the overall maintenance of limited government, the Bill of Rights articulated specific substantive areas in which the principle of limited government was to prevail. The Anti-Federalists were not so concerned about identifying and protecting a finite list of particular individual rights in the new democracy; they were more concerned about alleviating fears that the original Constitution had not adequately prevented the new government from overstepping its allotted powers.

Of course, under the first argument—the individual-autonomy argument—the Bill of Rights would also serve to limit government. Under an individual-autonomy model, the provisions in the Bill of Rights act as rights-bearing constitutional trump cards to be played whenever the courts find that individual freedom or autonomy has been impacted by state power. But the difference between this model and the limited-government model is that the former seeks primarily to serve individual-autonomy interests and only secondarily to limit the power of government, whereas the latter model focuses primarily on limiting government and thereby indirectly protecting individual freedom. However, as this book will argue, the limited-government model can be applied in a more workable, judicially restrained, and historically supported manner than the individual-autonomy model.

The impetus for the Bill of Rights arose from the same set of concerns that influenced the structural scheme of the original Constitution. These concerns involved creating the appropriate structures and checks to keep the new central government sufficiently limited. The bill was just one more facet to that endeavor, providing additional means through which to keep the new central government limited. The Bill of Rights reinforced the boundaries of power that were already set out, albeit more generally, in the original Constitution.

It should be noted that although the original Constitution was much concerned with limitations on government power, this was not the first and foremost aim of the constitutional framers. The Constitution first and foremost sought to create a strong central government, in contrast to the weak federal government existing under the Articles of Confederation. But once this strong central government was in fact created, the Constitution then sought to limit the powers of that government.

And in doing so, the Constitution employed an array of structural features aimed at ensuring a sufficiently limited federal government. In addition, and as an added assurance of such limited government, the Bill of Rights was proposed and ratified.

Aside from the desire for limited government, the framers of the Bill of Rights were very much concerned about individual freedom and the natural rights of the individual. Indeed, this concern had helped inspire the Declaration of Independence and America's break with England. However, the framers of the Bill of Rights were also leery of giving the judiciary the kind of unbounded power it would need to define and enforce individual natural rights. Moreover, the framers did not see the individual as living in a state of nature, nor in a state of conflict with democratic society. Individual liberty was not defined in isolation, nor was it seen as something that should automatically trump the wishes of a democratic society.

The Bill of Rights was not ratified so as to express or protect this view of individual autonomy. Instead, it sought to reinforce the general structural scheme of the Constitution—that is, the provision and maintenance of a system of limited government. What is often ignored about the Bill of Rights is that it was drafted and ratified with a view toward integrating it into the overall scheme of the original Constitution. This scheme or focus, according to near-unanimous historical opinion, was one of structure. The original Constitution set out to create certain types of governmental structures; it did not seek to dictate substantive values and norms. The most important structural aspect of the original Constitution was one of limited government. Indeed, the whole scheme of the Constitution focused on setting up structures ensuring that the new central government was a limited one. Moreover, the rights identified in the Bill of Rights were seen as vital in terms of their capacity, when freely exercised, to keep government limited.

This book does not intend to suggest that the framers and ratifiers of the Bill of Rights did not care about individual freedoms or the constitutional protection of those freedoms. As will be discussed at more length in Chapter 1, notions of natural rights were very prominent among the framers' political ideas. As Hadley Arkes explains in *Constitutional Illusions and Anchoring Truths: The Touchstone of the Natural Law,* the Founders believed that the right to free speech, for instance, comes not from the First Amendment but from nature. Indeed, the framers and ratifiers held passionate views about individual liberty. They also held an array of opinions on how to constitutionally protect that liberty in general and how the Bill of Rights in particular would serve the cause of liberty.

There is no historical dispute as to the desire of the framers for a political and constitutional system that protected liberty, and there is no dispute that the Bill of Rights served the goal of protecting liberty. What this book suggests, however, is that while the desire to protect liberty may have inspired it, the Bill of Rights tried to secure that goal through a means other than strictly a judicial protection of certain specific rights that in turn defined a particular notion of individual autonomy. This book will argue that the framers and ratifiers of the Bill of Rights did not intend the preservation of individual autonomy or dignity to be the direct or primary goal of the Bill of Rights. This was because the framers and ratifiers did not know exactly how to go about that goal. They did not have a sufficiently clear idea of the parameters and scope of those individual rights, nor of how to protect each of those specific rights. Instead, they went about trying to protect liberty in a slightly more indirect manner—that of striving to limit the power and reach of government, which in turn would serve the cause of liberty.

Over the past half century, the Court has often received much criticism for its individual-autonomy approach to the Bill of Rights. For instance, in trying to protect individual autonomy through an enforcement of the free speech clause of the First Amendment, the Court has ended up protecting much socially objectionable entertainment material. Moreover, despite all the First Amendment case law, there is still much disagreement over the scope and application of the free speech clause, reflecting the framers' fears that speech freedoms could not be adequately defined or expressed within one clause of the Constitution.

It is the goal of this book to propose a new approach to the Bill of Rights in general and the First Amendment in particular. Instead of focusing on the particular freedoms specified in each amendment and precisely defining the scope of each freedom, this book seeks to arrive at a simpler, more objective and comprehensive approach. It argues that each amendment within the Bill of Rights can be understood within and applied pursuant to the context of a larger goal— namely, limiting the power of government. The idealistic hope behind the Bill of Rights may have been to achieve a protection of individual liberty, but because the framers did not know how to specifically go about doing that, they crafted a bill that focused not on the substance of each right but on limiting the power of government in certain areas. Limited government thus became the means by which liberty would be preserved.

This book strives to understand the Bill of Rights through an application of this limited-government model. It is hoped that a more simple, consistent, and comprehensive jurisprudential model can be developed, one that is more in tune with the original intent of the framers and ratifiers of the Bill of Rights. A limited-government model of the free speech clause, for instance, may provide a better understanding and application of that clause than would a judicial approach aimed at protecting the kind of speech activities that might preserve and enhance individual autonomy.

The individual-autonomy or natural-rights view of the Bill of Rights is set forth in Chapter 1 of this book. Although this view has become prominent during the past half century, there are problems and difficulties with it in that it tends to put the Bill of Rights in conflict with the rest of the Constitution. Moreover, the judiciary is ill equipped for a number of reasons to enforce a natural-rights model of the Bill of Rights. Perhaps the main reason for this judicial shortcoming is that a natural-rights or individual-autonomy model requires judges, on their own, to formulate the definitions and parameters of whatever individual autonomy is to be immune from democratic lawmaking.

Chapters 2 through 4 of this book examine the general structural scheme of the Constitution and the principle of limited government. In particular, those structures include federalism and separation of powers. Chapter 2 discusses not only the limited-government focus of the Constitution, but also the values and purposes behind this limited-government focus. It argues that the Bill of Rights contains a similar structural focus aimed at limiting the new central government, and in this respect is consistent with the original Constitution. This consistency, as discussed in Chapter 3, is illustrated through the concerns and viewpoints of the Anti-Federalists, who were the prime instigators of and influences on the Bill of Rights. Indeed, the historical record reveals that the overriding motivation of the Anti-Federalists was to limit the power of the federal government, not to place all hopes for liberty in the hands of judges who would then have the power to define the nature and impact of various individual freedoms. Whereas the limited-government model is not original when applied to the philosophy or structure of the original Constitution, it is quite original when applied to the Bill of Rights— and this original theory is what is explored in this book.

Not only does the limited-government model coincide with the original intent underlying the Bill of Rights, but also it provides for a more objective and manageable application. Under an individual-autonomy view of the Bill of Rights, courts must define the ingredients necessary for a sufficient or acceptable degree of individual autonomy. However, as Chapter 4 reveals, this endeavor is fraught with ambiguity. Under the limited-government model, the judicial role is more objective. Instead of trying to define an ambiguous individual autonomy, courts only need to focus on whether a particular right is necessary for maintaining limited government. Furthermore, the limited-government model does not put the Bill of Rights in conflict with democratic society—it just uses the Bill of Rights to maintain a check on government and to ensure that government remains vibrant in energy yet limited in scope, just as the original Constitution seeks to do.

Of course, the claim that a particular constitutional model, and especially a new and untested model, will provide a simpler and more objective means of interpreting the Bill of Rights is itself an unproven and uncertain claim. Because this limited-government model of the Bill of Rights is a model of first impression, it cannot in its theoretical state be completely convincing. It has never been articulated or applied before, and its tangible consequences are obviously speculative. Nonetheless, the limited-government model is well positioned to provide a simpler and more objective model than the personal-autonomy model because the former has only one focus (and a historically documented focus), whereas the latter entails several layers of inquiries.

Under the limited-government model, judges need to look only at whether, in the case at hand, the law or regulation at issue jeopardizes the limited-government principle by giving too much power to the government in a way that will serve to entrench that power. Moreover, for a guide to the meaning of the limited-government principle, judges have a wealth of constitutional history to consult.

However, with the personal-autonomy model, a judge has to engage in numerous highly undefined inquiries. First the judge must identify which aspect of personal autonomy the subject law affects. Then the judge has to define the meaning of personal autonomy as it pertains to the law at issue. Then the judge has to identify the degree to which that aspect of personal autonomy is to be or can be balanced against other individuals' autonomy or the interests of the community. And finally, the judge has to determine the proper boundaries between democratic freedoms and individual-autonomy interests.

The framers did not intend the Bill of Rights to give open-ended, undefined powers to courts; yet that would be the case if the Bill of Rights were seen as primarily concerned with protecting individual natural rights or autonomy, since the courts would have to decide in each case where the boundary lines of individual autonomy occurred. It is more manageable for the courts to define limits on government than to define the parameters of individual natural rights or autonomy. Thus, with a limited-government focus, the courts could approach Bill of Rights issues more objectively and consistently.

The fear of unbounded judicial power represents but one of the problems with the individual-autonomy model of the Bill of Rights. These problems and drawbacks are discussed in Chapter 4. Because the parameters or elements of individual autonomy are not set out in the Constitution or in any Constitution-supportive document, any Bill of Rights jurisprudence based on individual-autonomy concerns ultimately devolves into a jurisprudence of judicial discretion, which jeopardizes rule-of-law notions. An individual-autonomy model of the Bill of Rights also results in a centralized imposition of uniform rules governing the complex relationship between individuals and their communities. A limited-government model, which focuses only on the issue of government power, helps courts avoid entanglement in these complex relationships.

Another problem with the individual-autonomy model is that it necessarily and consistently envisions an adversarial relationship between the individual and the democratic community, conferring rights-bearing trump cards to individuals against the workings of self-government. However, the limited-government model does not see the individual as being in constant conflict with the larger democratic community. Instead, it simply sees that the government has authority only to act in certain areas—but when it does act legitimately, the government and the individual are seen to be in harmony. Whereas the individual-autonomy model puts the Bill of Rights in contrast to the rest of the constitutional scheme, which is concerned not with individual rights but with government power, the limited-government model harmonizes the Bill of Rights with the original Constitution. Because of the autonomy model's envisioned inherent conflict between the Bill of Rights and the original Constitution, the judicial application of that model has distorted the meaning and purpose of the Bill of Rights in a host of ways.

In chapters 5 through 8, this book examines specific applications of the limited-government model of the Bill of Rights. Chapter 5 discusses how the various rights set out in the amendments were intended to act as a means of ensuring limited government. Chapters 6 and 7 focus particularly on the First Amendment, illustrating how a limited-government model would operate in that context and examining how the Court has already in many ways adopted a limited-government model in its First Amendment decisions. Under this model, First Amendment rights are interpreted in terms of their necessity for or contribution to the maintenance of limited government.

Because the limited-government model is an original one, it has never been expressly applied or even mentioned in judicial decisions. Therefore, an examination of previous case law cannot be undertaken for the purpose of finding direct references to the limited-government model; it has to be for the more subtle purposes of finding supportive arguments, similar effects, or consistent assumptions. Indeed, there is no direct support for the model in the existing case law, since it has never before been applied. Therefore, the examination of existing case law is for the purpose of determining whether the limited-government model would produce a radically different kind of jurisprudence or whether it might produce somewhat similar or predictable results but through a simpler and more straightforward approach.

Finally, this book discusses the methodology to be used in evaluating just how the Bill of Rights should be interpreted to protect individual freedom. As outlined in Chapter 8, an equal protection analysis provides a workable and consistent approach for sufficiently guarding the freedoms set out in the Bill of Rights. It also provides an approach that minimizes the opportunities for judicial policymaking. By adopting an equal protection approach to protecting individual rights, the courts can avoid making the kind of substantive values decisions that have subjected them to so much public criticism and derision in the past. The equal protection approach is not an interpretive model distinct from the limited-government model, but is simply a way of describing how the limited-government model of the Bill of Rights works to protect individual liberties.

In connection with the basic function of the Bill of Rights as a limited-government concern, the individual provisions of the Bill of Rights should not automatically be given greater weight than any other specific provision in the Constitution aimed at limiting government. Such an approach would highlight individual rights as extra special in a way that they are not. The provisions of the Bill of Rights, in the way they are integrated into the Constitution, are different means of limiting the power of government, just as are, for instance, the separation-of-powers and federalism provisions of the Constitution.

The limited-government model of the Bill of Rights, as set forth in this book, is not the same thing as the political campaign for limited government being waged by various political groups and that became so prominent during the 2010 election. The limited-government model of the Bill of Rights is not about the size of the government budget, nor does it involve any political judgment of what government should be doing. Instead, the limited-government model as presented here seeks to understand the Bill of Rights through a particular constitutional principle that greatly influenced and motivated the drafting of both the original Constitution and the Bill of Rights. The model is about the constitutional meaning of the Bill of Rights, not about the political boundaries of government action or the size of the government budget.

This book strives to do three things. First, it attempts to assert a constitutional case against the personal-autonomy or natural-rights model of the First Amendment. This case relies not only on looking at the original intent of the ratifiers, but also on how the personal-autonomy or natural-rights model functions in practice and how that functioning in many ways contradicts the intentions of the constitutional generation. Second, the book tries to lay the constitutional groundwork for the limited-government model. In doing so, it examines the pervasive influence of the principles of limited government throughout the constitutional period. It looks at both original intent and constitutional structure in its argument that the limited-government model provides the most accurate and consistent understanding of the Bill of Rights. Third, and finally, the book attempts to demonstrate and explain how the limited-government model would actually work in terms of its application to concrete constitutional litigation. For this purpose, the book has focused primarily on how the limited-government model would be applied with respect to the First Amendment. A wide array of cases has been discussed in terms of demonstrating how this model might be applied by the courts. However, as this model is a newly articulated model, and one that has never been recognized or applied by the courts, it obviously at this theoretical stage carries much uncertainty. And there are many criticisms that will inevitably be levied against it. But these criticisms in turn may very well lead to a stronger and better-defined model. It is only through such criticism that the model can be sufficiently examined and developed so as to address all the various contingencies and circumstances.

One criticism of the limited-government model is that the parameters of limited government may be as difficult to define as the parameters of individual autonomy. Although this is a valid criticism, during the constitutional period a much more detailed and tangible discussion of the application of limited-government principles occurred than did any discussion of natural-rights or individual-autonomy principles. Furthermore, with the limited-government model, judges can look to the whole scheme of the Constitution so as to define the nature and parameters of limited government. This should be of great help in terms of better defining the focus and application of the limited-government principle in the context of the Bill of Rights.

Another criticism is that, if the framers of the Bill of Rights simply wanted to more effectively provide for limited government, then why did they not strengthen or expand the limited-government provisions already in the original Constitution? In other words, why introduce a whole new subject matter area—i.e., individual rights—if the primary focus was limited government? There is no question that the framers and ratifiers of the Bill of Rights did value natural rights and individual freedom. They very much wanted to constitutionally protect such rights and freedoms. However, the question is how the framers and ratifiers sought to do so. The argument presented in this book is that they sought to do so through the means of limited government, not through the means of particular substantive-rights provisions directing future courts to craft doctrines protecting only those specified rights. Just as the signers of the Declaration of Independence used natural rights to justify and argue their case for independence, so too the drafters and ratifiers of the Bill of Rights used the subject matter area of individual freedom to obtain additional safeguards for limited government. The provisions in the Bill of Rights were extremely popular, and they were popular because there was very little disagreement among the public regarding the notion that government should be limited from interfering in those particular areas of individual and social life. Thus, it is logical that the framers would have chosen the subject matters of widest agreement or consensus so as to provide an additional anchor or framework for limited government.

A criticism might be made that the limited-government model has never been used to interpret the individual-rights provisions found in state constitutions that predated the ratification of the Bill of Rights. Indeed, there is no evidence that any-one thought the notion of limited government would supply the means or method for defining or applying the rights found in various state-constitution declarations of rights. Thus, the argument could be made that the limited-government model was never conceived as especially helpful in construing the rights provisions found in the various state declarations of rights. What this argument ignores, however, is the basic difference between state and federal constitutions. The state constitutions dealt with state governments of general powers, as opposed to a federal government of limited or enumerated powers. The notion of limited government was woven into the federal constitution in a way that was never incorporated into state constitutions. Thus, the individual-rights provisions in state constitutions had little connection with the limited-government structure that existed within the federal constitution.

Finally, the criticism can be made that the limited-government model gives inadequate importance or protection to fundamental freedoms and natural rights. However, the limited-government model in no way denies the existence or impor-tance of natural rights. It simply argues that the framework of natural rights cannot be used to constitutionally apply and enforce the Bill of Rights. The framing gen-eration did value natural rights, but it chose to protect human liberty through the means of limited government. It chose this method because to do otherwise would be to give courts too much unbounded power to cancel out democratic lawmaking decisions through judicially defined individual rights.

1

The Individual-Autonomy View
of the Bill of Rights

The Natural-Rights View

The founding generation adhered to a natural-rights philosophy. Their speeches and writings frequently contained references to a higher law, and they based their legal and political judgments on a moral grounding of "first principles."[1] This natural-law philosophy was supported by the writings of John Locke, who argued that government exists to protect natural rights.[2]

Eighteenth-century Americans often looked to notions of natural rights to outline their concepts of individual liberty.[3] The individual right to natural liberty was defined as the power to control one's person and actions without interference by others.[4] In the natural-rights tradition, liberty encompassed "the capacity to actively determine one's own thoughts and actions."[5] Freedoms of speech and religious belief, for instance, were considered to be among the natural rights of individuals. Natural law was considered the source of the rights listed in the First Amendment.[6] Patrick Henry, for instance, argued that freedom of press was one of the "rights of human nature," and Roger Sherman similarly argued that freedom of speech and press was a natural right.[7]

Underlying a natural-rights theory is the belief that each individual "possesses a profound, inherent, and equal dignity simply by virtue of his nature as a rational creature—a creature possessing, albeit in limited measure (and in the case of some human beings, merely in root or rudimentary form), the godlike powers of reason and freedom."[8] In his 1955 article *Are There Any Natural Rights?* H. L. A. Hart described natural rights as reflecting a sovereignty for individuals over certain aspects of their lives. This sovereignty in turn sets out a kind of individual moral autonomy that the state must honor.

The argument that the Bill of Rights serves to protect natural rights stems in part from the statement in the Declaration of Independence that all persons "are endowed by their creator with certain unalienable rights; that among these are life, liberty, and the pursuit of happiness."[9] According to scholars like Harry Jaffa, the rights referenced in the Declaration are not civil or political rights, which result from human or positive law, but natural rights that predate civil society.[10] Jaffa also argues that the natural-law doctrines embodied in the Declaration of Independence are fully incorporated in the United States Constitution.[11]

As articulated in the Declaration, a natural-rights theory was used to explain the American Revolution against Britain. According to the colonists, Britain's violation of their natural rights justified the American withdrawal from the British Empire.[12] Under the notion of natural rights prevailing at the time, individual natural rights preceded the formation or existence of any government.[13] John Locke posited that preceding government all persons lived in a state of nature, possessing the same natural rights.[14] When forming a society, individuals then agreed to relinquish only some, but not all, of their natural rights.[15] Consequently, natural rights operated as limits on the actions of government, including the British government.[16]

Randy Barnett argues that the Bill of Rights serves to protect individual natural rights.[17] According to Barnett, natural rights define a moral space or liberty in which individuals should be free to live their own lives, free from interference by other persons.[18] Such rights "are natural insofar as their necessity depends upon the nature of persons and the social and physical world in which persons reside."[19] John McGinnis likewise sees the free speech protections in the First Amendment, for instance, as protecting a natural right of the individual.[20]

Closely related to a natural-rights theory of the Bill of Rights is a view of the bill as protecting individual autonomy. According to Martin Redish, for instance, the First Amendment is all about "individual self-realization."[21] Indeed, the judiciary has often endorsed an individual-autonomy view of the First Amendment.[22] The Court's embrace of individual autonomy as the basis of its Bill of Rights jurisprudence reflects the "widespread appeal of autonomy-based conceptions of individual rights."[23] This conception mirrors Locke's description of natural rights as representing a kind of individual moral claim.

Another related theory is that the Bill of Rights serves to protect fundamental rights. As Justice Benjamin Cardozo stated in *Palko v. Connecticut* in 1937, there are certain rights "so rooted in the traditions and conscience of our people as to be ranked as fundamental."[24] Judicial recognition of a fundamental-rights theory in constitutional jurisprudence occurred in 1823 in *Corfield v. Coryell,* in which Justice Bushrod Washington spoke of certain "fundamental" rights that belong "to the citizens of all free governments."[25] Justice John Marshall Harlan II likewise referred to rights, particularly those included in the Bill of Rights, as stemming from those "fundamental principles of liberty and justice which lie at the base of all our civil and political institutions."[26]

Problems with the Individual-Autonomy View

Viewing the Bill of Rights as an expression of natural rights or as a protection of individual autonomy has been troublesome for the courts. To the framers, the concepts of natural and individual rights were vague and highly abstract.[27] Consequently, natural rights do not provide a workable guideline for constitutional rights.

As Philip Hamburger notes, theories of natural rights were not only so ambiguous and imprecise as to prevent broad consensus, but in fact were the subject of "substantial differences" among eighteenth-century Americans.[28] According to Hamburger, the principles of natural rights were so vague and general that the framers and ratifiers could not incorporate those norms into the Constitution.[29] Indeed, most of the first eight amendments were adopted with very little debate or discussion.[30] Therefore, it is unlikely that they intended each different amendment to be a constitutional protection for a different substantive natural right, which they neither defined nor even debated.

This is why contemporary efforts to uncover substantive meanings of liberties protected by the Bill of Rights may be "largely futile"—because the framers "consciously enumerated general principles whose practical applications they knew were contestable."[31] History provides little guide in using notions of natural rights or individual autonomy for purposes of constitutional interpretation, since the attitudes on natural rights of late-eighteenth-century Americans often appear "unsystematic, contradictory and even paradoxical."[32] Furthermore, according to Michael McConnell, the notions of "rights" under Lockean natural-rights theory carried different meanings in the eighteenth century than they do today.[33]

Aside from the difficulty in defining natural or fundamental rights, it is also impossible to list all such rights. As Supreme Court Justice James Iredell said to the North Carolina ratification convention, "Let any one make what collection or enumeration of rights he pleases, I will immediately mention twenty or thirty more rights not contained in it."[34] Of course, fundamental rights are not exhausted by the list set out in the Bill of Rights. According to Mark Graber, "[N]o proponent of the Bill of Rights asserted that the rights enumerated by Madison's proposed amendments were more important than the rights not enumerated."[35] Therefore, the question arises as to why certain specific rights were included within the Bill, if there were many other natural rights or aspects of individual autonomy that were omitted.

Even regarding rights explicitly mentioned in the Constitution, defining them in terms of "fundamental" or "natural" rights still causes problems.[36] Interpreting a right as a natural or fundamental right can allow courts to exercise almost unlimited power to define, apply, and enforce that right. It can also allow courts to expand and contract constitutional standards to conform to judicial conceptions of individual dignity and civilized decency.[37] And this unrestrained grant of judicial power may be "as likely to lead to injustice and the denial of basic rights as it is to advance those goals."[38] Thus, the question is whether the framers intended to convey to judges the power to determine the nature and boundaries of such rights. The Anti-Federalists, for instance, feared that the original Constitution conferred unlimited and uncontrolled power upon the Supreme Court.

Justice Iredell rejected judicial review based solely on the principles of natural law and natural rights.[39] Since the parameters of natural law and natural rights are undefined, they cannot form an adequate basis of constitutional adjudication. According to Iredell, "The ideas of natural justice are regulated by no fixed standard."[40] As McConnell notes, no judge possesses the "authority to second-guess the sovereign act of the people in drawing the line between power and rights" regarding the nature of the social compact in which individuals entering into society give up a share of their natural liberty so as to empower the state to preserve the rest.[41] And because courts are given the power, through judicial review, to strike down democratically enacted laws, it is "as important to freedom to confine the judiciary's power to its proper scope as it is to confine that of the President, Congress, or state and local governments; indeed, it is probably more important, for only courts may not be called to account by the public."[42]

The problems involved with judges applying and enforcing natural rights are such that even well-known believers in natural rights, such as Justice Clarence Thomas and Judge Robert Bork, do not believe that courts have the authority to enforce them.[43] According to Bork, natural law exists, but judges do not "have any greater access to that law than do the rest of us."[44] Consequently, if judges do try to enforce natural rights, they may end up striking down democratically enacted laws because those laws conflict with the judge's personal definition of natural rights. This prospect was surely one the constitutional framers would not have welcomed.

Furthermore, if the Bill of Rights sought to protect fundamental or natural rights, it would seem as if the Founders would certainly want to protect those rights in their entirety, from both the state and federal government.[45] When the framers did seek to protect a right or freedom on its own accord, rather than as a means of limiting power, they did so in a manner that would protect that right or freedom from all governments, including state governments.

In *Barron v. Baltimore*,[46] Chief Justice John Marshall wrote that the Bill of Rights acted as a restraint only on the actions of the federal government, not on the actions of the individual states. In explaining his decision in *Barron*, Marshall explained that the Bill of Rights was specifically designed as limitations on the power of the federal government. But if the Bill of Rights did not apply to the states, it cannot be seen as securing individual natural rights, since the states could still infringe on such rights.

Even more evidence that the Bill of Rights was never meant to apply to the states can be found in James Madison's initial effort to nationalize the Bill of Rights. He proposed in the First Congress of 1789 a version of the original Bill of Rights that included a clause stating, "No state shall infringe the right of trial by jury in criminal cases, nor the rights of conscience, nor the freedom of speech, or of the press."[47] Madison foresaw that the states could infringe on these rights just as much as the federal government could; however, his failure to nationalize the Bill of Rights reflects the overriding concern that the bill should apply as limits only on the federal government.[48]

Not only did the framers and ratifiers not apply the Bill of Rights to the states, but they tolerated rather significant regulations of those rights, thus further undermining the notion that the protection of individual autonomy was the primary purpose of the Bill. As Hamburger notes, freedom of speech and press during the constitutional period "was considerably less extensive than the liberty to speak and publish as one pleased."[49]

The individual-autonomy view of the First Amendment speech clause, which justifies free speech on the basis of its being an important means for personal fulfillment, is not supported by history and the highly restrictive laws that late-eighteenth-century Americans accepted on speech and press.[50] According to Leonard Levy, the framers were not libertarians and did not think people should have the right to say whatever they wanted.[51] Speech rights were limited to truthfulness, good taste, social peace, and public morals.

As Larry Eldridge illustrates in *A Distant Heritage: The Growth of Free Speech in Early America,* eighteenth-century Americans balanced their belief in free speech against their desire to maintain what they saw as a moral society. A Virginia statute, for instance, outlawed "swearing, cursing, profaning God's holy name, and Sabbath abusing," and a New Jersey law prohibited "all sorts of lewdness and profane behavior in word or action."[52] Believing that disrespectful language could lead to breaches of public order, early American authorities commonly punished individuals for slandering and defaming one another.[53] Thus, as Eldridge concludes, speech was regulated "in order to maintain moral society, social hierarchy, the public peace, and state institutions."[54]

Eighteenth-century Americans had a narrower view of fundamental rights than do many contemporary legal scholars, and that eighteenth-century view is not consistent with an individual-autonomy interpretation of the Bill of Rights. During the constitutional period, fundamental rights were seen as protections primarily against class legislation. The liberties the framers sought to protect were freedoms from "legislation directed at particular persons or classes."[55] They did not consider general laws aimed at safeguarding public welfare or safety "as violating fundamental rights."[56] To the framers, the crucial issue was that government pursue the common good, "not that government pursue the common good by means that did not interfere with individual autonomy."[57]

A further problem with a natural-rights interpretation of the Bill of Rights, according to Robert George, is that it is philosophically difficult to arrive at a sound theory of natural rights without arriving at some agreement on the existence of God and the role of God in human affairs.[58] Eighteenth-century political thought saw natural rights as the bestowal from a transcendent God.[59] James Otis, for instance, saw natural rights as God given. John Locke similarly believed that natural rights are founded in God's law—because when natural-rights theories are "fundamentally concerned with human well-being and fulfillment," the definitions of those rights can be somewhat fleeting and subjective.[60]

Still another drawback to an individual-autonomy view of the Bill of Rights is that it reflects and contributes to a therapeutic culture, in which the central moral question is individual fulfillment.[61] Such a culture does not ask whether individuals or society should conform to some external governance system, but simply whether individuals are happy or fulfilled in their internal lives. In a therapeutic culture, the self becomes the moral order, and the development of the self is among the highest goals of society. This kind of culture departs from the more traditional cultural models of classical republicanism or Lockean liberalism, which tend to treat the individual as less important than some higher authority or some larger moral or civil order existing outside of the individual.[62] Moreover, by ignoring the reality that human beings live not as isolated individuals but in various types of social communities, an individual-autonomy view often fails to consider the whole realm of human fulfillment and well-being.

The modern, individual-autonomy view of the Bill of Rights came into prominence during the Warren Court's rights revolution, which expanded the scope and reach of the provisions in the Bill of Rights, interpreting them as outlining a sphere of personal autonomy that the courts needed to protect.[63] This rights revolution both reflected and reinforced the therapeutic culture that was developing within society at large. It is within this culture that the Bill of Rights has taken on an individual-autonomy interpretation.[64]

According to Daniel Piar, the major rights decisions of the past half century have increasingly adopted the rhetoric of therapy in determining the content of individual constitutional liberties, with the boundaries of state power repeatedly set with reference to the emotional or psychic needs of the individual.[65] One example of this can be found in the Court's First Amendment establishment clause jurisprudence, where the endorsement test focuses on whether government action makes people feel like outsiders of the community, or whether they may feel isolated, offended, or affronted by certain government actions. Another example occurs in *Lee v. Weisman*,[66] where the Court applied a coercion test to strike down a nonsectarian prayer offered at a high school graduation ceremony, finding that the prayer could cause embarrassment, offense, or isolation among people in attendance.

The Problem of Using the Declaration of Independence to Interpret the Bill of Rights

As Randy Barnett observes in *Restoring the Lost Constitution,* the founding generation subscribed to the idea of natural rights, even though there was no universal agreement about the content of those rights or the remedies for their violations. It is often argued that this belief in natural rights was inscribed in the Declaration of

Independence and later incorporated into the Bill of Rights. But as historian Philip Detweiler explains, the Declaration of Independence was a document concerned primarily with justifying American independence from Britain, not with articulating a coherent theory on natural rights. Thus, during the revolutionary period, natural rights were employed not as an end in themselves, but as a means of justifying independence from Britain.[67] Furthermore, Americans at the time of the drafting of the Declaration of Independence and ratification of the U.S. Constitution were not well versed in theories of natural rights.[68] For most Americans during the founding era, natural rights were only vaguely known, in such general terms as "life, liberty and property, or life, liberty and the pursuit of happiness."[69]

Scholars like Scott Douglas Gerber argue that the Constitution reflects the philosophy of the Declaration of Independence and that the Constitution should be seen as striving to fulfill the goal declared by the Declaration: to secure individual natural rights.[70] However, regardless of whether the Declaration of Independence incorporates a natural-rights theory, it is doubtful that it can be used to interpret the Constitution, including the Bill of Rights. Because the Declaration of Independence served primarily to provide a moral and political rationale for independence from Britain, it was not intended as a document about individual rights or the parameters of those rights.[71] As John Hart Ely explains, any use of the Declaration of Independence to interpret the Constitution is unfounded, since there was a critical difference in function between the two documents. Whereas the Declaration was a document justifying independence from Britain, the Constitution provided a frame of operation for the new United States government.[72] It was not a document focused on the judicial protection of natural rights.

According to the historical research of Lee Strang, there were very few statements made during the framing and ratification of the Constitution that made even implicit reference to the Declaration.[73] Similarly, historian Pauline Maier found that participants in the debates over creation and ratification of the federal constitution barely even mentioned the Declaration of Independence.[74] Although scholars who argue for a role of the Declaration in constitutional interpretation focus almost exclusively on the first two sentences in the second paragraph—namely, the reference to the rights of "life, liberty, and the pursuit of happiness"—the vast bulk of the Declaration is not a rights document at all; instead, it is a list of violations by the king that justified American independence from Britain.[75] And as Detweiler argues, the Declaration of Independence's rights language played little role in public debate and discussion once independence was achieved.

An Unworkable Model of the Bill of Rights

Even if the rights contained within the Bill of Rights reflect notions of natural rights, eighteenth-century Americans believed that natural rights could be limited insofar as the exercise of those rights might cause injury to another.[76] To the eighteenth-century political philosophers, natural rights were limited by the duty to respect the rights of others and not to injure other people or society.[77] Some legal scholars and commentators even believed that natural rights could be limited by legislation aimed at achieving the common good.[78]

Although eighteenth-century Americans often spoke of certain rights as being natural rights, such as the free exercise of religion and freedom of speech, they actually used notions of natural rights to justify restrictions on individual freedoms.[79] This was because individual natural rights were subject to the implications of natural law, which meant they could not be exercised in a way that would infringe upon the rights or equal freedom of another person.[80] For instance, free speech was limited by the duty not to engage in blasphemous, obscene, or defamatory speech.

Almost everyone, from William Blackstone to Thomas Jefferson, believed that freedom of expression was bounded by law and could be limited if its exercise injured society.[81] Because of the natural-rights theory that free speech was limited by the fundamental rights of other persons and the community, the parameters of such a right were quite fluid and uncertain, since to determine the scope of any right a court had to not only define the nature of that right but also consider the rights of other persons with which the right might conflict.[82] As Locke theorized, courts would have to determine how much or which part of an individual's natural liberty is to be parted with "as the good, prosperity, and safety of society shall require."[83]

Barnett likewise argues that a natural-rights model does not preclude all necessary and proper regulations of those rights.[84] The model does not see natural rights as necessarily trumping all laws that may affect or regulate the exercise of those rights.[85] The natural-rights model "would not end all regulation, but would instead scrutinize a regulation of liberty to ensure that it is reasonable and necessary, rather than an improper attempt by government to restrict the exercise" of the particular right.[86]

While rightful exercises of liberty may only be regulated, wrongful acts that violate the rights of others may be prohibited outright.[87] Therefore, under this natural-rights model, judges must make determinations of when certain regulations of certain rights are appropriate so as to protect the rights of others.[88] And even under an originalist approach, this task becomes exceedingly difficult, as it is "fanciful to suppose that Americans would have had a clear understanding, in the late eighteenth century, about our twenty-first century world—a world that would have been, to them, in every way wildly hypothetical, and in some respects literally inconceivable."[89] Moreover, modern scholars who see the Bill of Rights as reflecting a strictly individual-autonomy view see only part of the natural-rights theory— they see only the natural right itself, without the duty aspect that limits the exercise of a right in a way that does not infringe on the rights of another.

Natural rights have been described as defining the "moral space" in which individuals are "free from the interference of other persons."[90] However, this individual "moral space" view of the Bill of Rights has distorted its meaning as it existed when it was adopted. In modern times, there is a tendency to see individual rights as the primary purpose of the constitutional scheme. But this viewpoint has taken the Bill of Rights out of the context of the larger constitutional scheme, seeing individual rights in isolation, as if the Constitution were primarily focused on protecting individual autonomy, not on creating a new system of government.

During the constitutional period, notions of rights encompassed the interrelationship between the individual and the community. In particular, under natural-law theories, individual rights were to be balanced against the needs of public order and the rights of the community. But over the past half century, rights have become increasingly focused solely on individual-autonomy concerns. As reflected in the philosophy of Ronald Dworkin, modern notions of rights see them as the exclusive property of individuals, to be used as trump cards against the community.[91]

A problem with this individual-autonomy view is that it sees the individual and the community as completely separate and even antagonistic to each other, whereas in truth most individuals are not completely self-defining, but instead see themselves as members of a community.[92] Indeed, a vital aspect of personal autonomy may be to define oneself within a larger community and to be a part of that larger community. However, the modern view of the Bill of Rights as focusing solely on individual autonomy may be a product of how American society and culture has changed over time. According to one scholar, "[L]iving in an apparently broken and fragmented culture, we are swayed far more easily by images of individualism and autonomy than by visions of unity; the fabric of relatedness seems dangerously threadbare and frayed."[93]

2

Limited Government in the
Overall Constitutional Scheme

The Purpose of Limited Government

To the framers, governmental structures were among the most important features of the United States Constitution. These structures, rather than any specific individual-rights provisions, were seen to provide the greatest protections for liberty.[1] (Of course, limiting the power of government was not the chief concern of the constitutional framers—the creation of a republican form of government, which included a stronger national government than had existed under the Articles of Confederation, was the chief concern—but once a stronger federal government had been created, a primary concern at that point was to build in structural limitations, preventing that government from overstepping its proper role and functions.)

A belief in limited government and the rule of law reflects the framers' opposition to the patterns of statism, absolutism, and totalitarianism existing in the eighteenth-century world. The framers of the Constitution created an array of checks and limitations on the new federal government. Those checks and limitations included a divided legislature, a presidential veto subject to override by legislative super majorities, judicial review by an independent judiciary, and a federal government of limited and enumerated powers. In addition, the framers mandated certain constitutional procedures governing the enactment of any law recognized by the supremacy clause. These procedures, such as bicameralism and presentment, are generally regarded as an integral part of the separation-of-powers scheme, but they also preserve federalism by making federal law more difficult to adopt.[2]

The government-checking role played by these constitutional lawmaking procedures is reflected by the fact that only a small number of bills introduced in Congress each year actually pass both houses and get signed into law by the president.[3] Thus, the requirements of bicameralism and presentment not only limit the power of government, but also make it difficult for the government to exercise the powers already given to it.[4] For instance, Congress may possess power under the commerce clause to regulate a certain activity, but it can only regulate that activity once it complies with all the various constitutional lawmaking procedures.

Within the constitutional scheme, federalism and separation of powers are prominent structural provisions aimed at ensuring limited government.[5] Just as the Constitution creates a system of checks and balances at the national level, it also creates a dual-sovereignty structure of state and federal governments.[6] Whereas separation of powers addresses the horizontal structure or division of power among the legislative, executive, and judicial branches of the federal government, federalism focuses on the vertical division between the national and state levels.[7]

Federalism and separation of powers reflect structural aspects of the constitutional scheme because they do not involve specific powers or rights of specific actors, but the organization of the political system and the relationship between governmental units. Both federalism and separation of powers act as a check on the power of the national government. Although there is no specific "separation of powers" provision in the Constitution, there is also no "federalism" clause.[8] Instead, both are features inherent within the scheme of the Constitution, reflecting constitutional structures and relationships.[9] And both were seen by the framers as a way to ensure and preserve individual liberty by checking the power of government.

Federalism and separation of powers are both intended to limit government by fostering a competition for power between various governmental entities.[10] They serve as structural restraints on government in general, not as substantive prohibitions on any one particular government action.[11] The doctrines of federalism and separation of powers, according to James Madison, empower the people "to conquer government power by dividing it."[12] Essentially, federalism and separation of powers accomplish a twofold dilution of governmental power. As Madison argued, "[T]he power surrendered by the people is first divided between two distinct governments, and then the portion allotted to each subdivided among distinct and separate departments."[13] Thus, federalism and separation of powers create a political system characterized by a two-tiered check on government.[14]

The Constitution relies on this structural limitation of power as the primary means by which to protect liberty.[15] To the framers of the original Constitution, this structural organization and scheme was even more important to the preservation of liberty than was the constitutional articulation of specific individual rights. While individual rights protect against particular acts of government abuse of power, structural rights protect against systemic and continuing government abuses of power that result from a lack of effective limits on that power. As Steven Gey points out,

> If we countenance government misconduct within the category of individual rights, an isolated injustice occurs, but this sort of violation usually does very little permanent damage to the social or political structure. If we countenance government misconduct within the category of structural rights, however, then

the entire structure of government is threatened in a way that could potentially exterminate all rights—individual as well as structural.[16]

Indeed, as Randy Barnett argues in his book *Restoring the Lost Constitution,* it is congressional abuses of the commerce clause that have been most often responsible for restrictions on liberty.

The U.S. Constitution did not just limit the federal government; it also included numerous limitations on state power. For instance, states cannot pass bills of attainder or ex post facto laws; they cannot coin money or emit bills of credit; they cannot deny the privileges and immunities of out-of-staters or impair the obligation of contract. Article I, Section 10 prohibits states from entering into treaties or alliances, imposing duties on imports and exports, and engaging in many foreign and military affairs. The Constitution also mandates that each state maintain a republican form of state government. But these limitations on the states also indicate something about the meaning of the Bill of Rights. If the Bill of Rights were meant to preserve individual freedom and autonomy, the question arises as to why its restrictions were not put on the states as well as the federal government, since the original Constitution did put some restrictions on the states.

By separating and dividing power, both horizontally and vertically, the constitutional framers established a governmental structure distributing power among different institutions that could in turn oversee and enforce the limitations on each other's powers.[17] The ability of the states to monitor abuses of the federal government, for instance, can be seen in state reactions to the Alien and Sedition Acts of 1798. The legislatures of Virginia and Kentucky both adopted resolutions declaring the Acts abusive and unconstitutional. In this way, the states served as useful political "instruments of redress" in alerting people to threats to their liberty.[18]

The Ninth and Tenth Amendments in particular reflect the limited-government structure of the original Constitution. The Tenth Amendment incorporated the doctrine of enumerated power, with all nondelegated power reserved to the states, whereas the Ninth Amendment limited the interpretation of the powers that were actually delegated to the federal government. As Madison explained, the Tenth Amendment prohibited the federal government from exercising any source of power not specified within the Constitution itself, and the Ninth Amendment prohibited any interpretations of enumerated federal powers that would unduly expand federal power.[19] According to Kurt Lash, the Ninth and Tenth Amendments reflected such a universal desire for limited government that they faced very little opposition.[20]

The Ninth Amendment was a necessary parallel to the Tenth Amendment, since a government of limited enumerated powers might still achieve unlimited power if its delegated powers were too broadly construed.[21] Indeed, for the first century and a half of the nation's history, courts and commentators cited both the Tenth and the Ninth Amendments as expressing rules of strict construction limiting federal power.[22] Thus, the Ninth and Tenth Amendments express the focus of the entire Bill of Rights as being limitation on the power of the federal government.

Separation of Powers

Although limited government is achieved primarily through the doctrine of enumerated powers, which prohibits the federal government from exercising any powers other than those granted by the Constitution, it is also served by the doctrine of separation of powers. Under this doctrine, the Constitution sets up a federal government consisting of three distinct branches, each possessing its own powers and functions. By design, each branch is empowered to check any abuses of the other branches.[23] This structural restraint on government power thus serves as a protection against governmental infringements on individual liberty.[24] The primary motivation underlying the constitutional scheme of separation of powers was the framers' fear of centralized power.

A fear of centralized power also underlay the framers' decision during the constitutional debates to reject the "federal negative"—a provision granting congressional power to veto state laws. Although this federal negative promised to prevent the kind of disunity and fragmentation experienced under the Articles of Incorporation, it was ultimately seen as something that would give the national government the power "to regulate areas of activity traditionally left to the states, effectively usurping powers the states had claimed ever since they were colonies chafing against parliamentary oversight."[25]

The framers also saw that a scheme of checks and balances was needed to combat the human hunger for power and the abuse of it; to the framers, the reality of human nature required strict controls on the use of power.[26] Consequently, there was never any real debate during the Constitutional Convention on whether the new constitution should incorporate the doctrine of separation of powers.[27] As Madison declared, "The accumulation of all powers, legislative, executive, and judiciary, in the same hands, whether of one, a few, or many, and whether hereditary, self-appointed, or elective, may justly be pronounced the very definition of tyranny."[28] And as John Adams put it in 1775, "[B]y balancing each of these powers against the other two, the efforts in human nature towards tyranny can alone be checked and restrained."[29]

The framers were influenced in this respect by the Protestant Reformation.[30] Given the nature of human failings, John Calvin had advocated a government in which "neither King nor judges had excessive power."[31] This fear of excessive power has been prevalent throughout American history. As Justice Hugo Black later explained, America's colonial history "provided ample reason for people to be afraid to vest too much power in the national government."[32]

One of the earliest advocates of the concept of separation of powers was Montesquieu, who wrote that "when the legislative and executive powers are united in the same person, or in the same body of magistrates, there can be not liberty."[33] On this issue, the framers were greatly influenced by Montesquieu.[34] Throughout their deliberations, the representatives at the Constitutional Convention remained steadfast in their belief that governmental power should be separated and balanced among the three branches of government, as recom-mended by Montesquieu.[35]

The framers foresaw that a separation-of-powers structure would guard against improvident and impetuous government action by placing impediments in the path of the political process. This structure essentially multiplies the veto points in the lawmaking process, which in turn makes excessive state action more difficult. And although this structural bias in favor of the status quo would naturally defeat "a few good laws," it would also prevent "a number of bad ones."[36] Furthermore, onto the classical notion of separation of powers the framers grafted a unique sys-tem of checks and balances. A rigid separation of functions in different hands was not itself seen as a sufficient safeguard. A system of checks and balances was also needed, with each branch sufficiently independent so as to be able to keep the oth-ers in check.[37] According to Thomas Jefferson, "[P]owers should be so divided and balanced as that no one could transcend their legal limits, without being checked and restrained by the others."[38] Thus, the two doctrines—separation of powers, and checks and balances—were combined into a single, uniquely American doc-trine designed to limit government power.[39]

Federalism

The doctrine of federalism refers to the sharing of power between two differ-ent levels of government, each representing the same people.[40] The Constitution establishes a dual-governmental structure consisting of state and national gov-ernments. Although its purpose was to create a strong national government, the Constitution also sought to preserve the independent integrity and lawmaking authority of the states.[41] This bifurcated system of power was codified in the Tenth Amendment, which divides sovereign power between that delegated to the federal government and that reserved to the states.[42] The Tenth Amendment forbids the federal government from exercising undelegated powers that would infringe on the autonomy of the states.[43]

Under the framers' view of federalism, the national government would exert supreme authority only within the limited scope of its enumerated powers; the states, meanwhile, would exercise the remainder of sovereign authority, subject to the restraint of interstate competition from other states.[44] Thus, by granting only limited powers to the national government, as well as by maintaining another level of competing governments, the framers sought to control the power of the national government.[45]

Similar to a separation of powers, federalism was employed by the framers to further achieve a limited government and the protection of individual liberty. By seeking to achieve a balancing of power between two different levels of govern-ment—state and national—federalism serves as a means of curtailing the power of each.[46] Federalism provides a type of safety valve against all the powers' being delegated to the national government, since the states can still serve as a check on the federal government's use of power.[47] Just as the colonial governments had mobilized opposition to abuses by Parliament, the state governments would serve as watchdogs against abuses by the federal government.[48] In this respect, federalism provides a check against overreaching by the federal government.[49] This "state/federal division of authority protects liberty both by restricting the burden that government can impose from a distance and by facilitating citizen participation in government that is closer to home."[50] Indeed, federalism concerns were so important to the Founders that nearly all the arguments opposing the new constitution involved the threat to state sovereignty.[51]

Although there is no specific "federalism" clause in the Constitution, the Tenth and Eleventh Amendments are often the focus of the Court's federalism decisions.[52] In addition to these two amendments, there are numerous references to federalism in the Constitution. Throughout the text, the framers use the term *states* to denote independent entities of sovereignty.[53] The term *states* is also used in a way that suggests the framers "intended that these governments possess some of the traditional immunities that states enjoyed" prior to adoption of the Constitution.[54]

The Constitution tends to treat states differently than the federal government. It explicitly lists the powers of the federal government; but to the extent it defines state powers, it does so primarily through negative implication, by setting out the limited constraints on those powers.[55] According to Madison, the "powers delegated by the proposed Constitution to the Federal Government are few and defined," while those retained by the states are "numerous and indefinite."[56]

By prohibiting the federal government from infringing on powers reserved to the states, the Constitution "split the atom of sovereignty" by designating two different political entities (federal and state governments), "each protected from incursion by the other."[57] This division of authority between the state and federal levels, with the latter enjoying only limited, enumerated powers, was not created for the benefit of the states, but for the benefit of the American people.[58] According to the framers, the principle of dual sovereignty would prevent any distortion of the balance of power that in turn would subject the people to a tyrannous federal government.[59] As Steven Calabresi explains, federalism is a vital ingredient of America's constitutional democracy:

> It prevents religious warfare, it prevents racial warfare. It is part of the reason why democratic majoritarianism in the United States has not produced violence or secession for 130 years, unlike the situations, for example, in England, France, Germany, Russia, Czechoslovakia, Yugoslavia, Cyprus, or Spain. There is nothing in the U.S. Constitution that is more important or that has done more to promote peace, prosperity, and freedom than the federal structure of that great document.[60]

Liberty and the Constitution

The Constitution's embodiment of the structural principles of federalism and separation of powers is designed not just to create a blueprint for government, but to create one that protects individual liberty.[61] This system reflects what Madison called the Constitution's "double security" for individual rights.[62] To the framers, the primary justification of federalism involved the role of the states as guardians against possible federal tyranny.[63] By diluting the power of the centralized national government, federalism restricts its ability to acquire and yield such power as to threaten the liberty of its citizens. Furthermore, by maintaining a separate governmental watchdog layer in the states, federalism provides a built-in mechanism to combat any overreaching by the national government.[64] The framers believed that the states could lead public uprisings against any tyrannical abuses by the national government. Alexander Hamilton argued that individuals who felt their rights violated by the central government could use the state governments "as the instrument of redress."[65]

In *The Federalist,* Hamilton distinguishes between a free government and a republican government.[66] Whereas free government focuses exclusively on securing specified individual rights, republican government tries to achieve political freedom as a means to securing individual freedom.[67] In choosing the latter, the framers saw the structure of government as the best protection of individual rights.[68] To the framers, "the primary safeguards against government tyranny were architectural."[69] And these architectural safeguards were found in the various limited-government provisions in the Constitution. As Gey states it,

> The category of structural rights is even more important to the preservation of constitutional democracy than the more familiar category of individual rights. Individual rights protect against isolated acts of government misconduct; structural rights protect against systematic and continuing government misconduct. Individual rights involve an abuse of power; structural rights involve an illegal aggrandizement of power. If we countenance government misconduct within the category of individual rights, then isolated injustice occurs, but this sort of violation usually does very little permanent damage to the social or political structure. If we countenance government misconduct within the category of structural rights, however, then the entire structure of government is threatened in a way that could potentially exterminate all rights—individual as well as structural.[70]

In forming a republican government, the framers and ratifiers of the Constitution believed that liberty was best achieved through limited government and through constitutional structures that checked, diffused, and divided government power.[71] For this reason, the Constitution's primary focus is not on providing a finite list of individual rights, but on creating a structure of government.[72] The genius of the American Constitution "lies in its use of structural devices to preserve individual liberty."[73] As Carl Esbeck notes, individual liberties were believed to be best protected "indirectly by this finely balanced diffusion of enumerated powers, thereby limiting the reach of government, which in turn left ample space for individuals to live in freedom and enter into independent-sector associations with others."[74]

A republican government scheme tries to provide a cultural freedom at large, rather than to just simply protect specific individual rights. Under such a scheme, liberty is incorporated into and reflected by a larger constitutional structure that encompasses more than just specific, isolated rights. By limiting government and restraining it from arbitrary interference into individual and social life, the constitutional structures enable an inherent and overall cultural freedom to exist in a society, without having to define that freedom by a written list of individual rights contained within the Constitution. Indeed, Madison recognized that liberty could best be protected not by a written list of certain individual rights, but by a structural scheme that limited government. Madison believed that "[t]he best chance for justice and security for rights would be to prevent the formation of unjust majorities. And to do that he recommended not a bill of rights but rather structural constitutional arrangements that would encourage the growth of a multiplicity of interests, and devices such as a congressional veto over state legislation."[75]

The debate surrounding the drafting of the Constitution, "with rare exceptions," was "limited to the structure of the national government," and did not involve the protection of substantive individual freedoms.[76] According to Mark Graber, the "desire to pacify political opponents better explains what liberties were specified by the Bill of Rights than do founding beliefs that the rights enumerated were more fundamental than the rights not explicitly mentioned."[77] What were most important to the framers were the structural arrangements in the Constitution that would be the primary guardian of liberty. Whenever amendments were proposed to alter these arrangements, Madison and his allies "responded aggressively and decisively."[78]

The Bill of Rights "was not designed to add rights to those that the original Constitution was expected to protect."[79] As Graber notes, the framers' reliance on the Constitution's structural provisions to protect liberty explains why they did not care that the specific rights mentioned in the Bill of Rights "lacked clear legal meanings."[80]

The Modern Decline of Government-Limiting Constitutional Provisions

For a century and a half, the framers' commitment to federalism and separation of powers was preserved in constitutional doctrine. But during the New Deal period, the notion of protecting liberty through the maintenance of limited and divided government gave way to the desire to ensure economic security through a powerful and activist central government.[81] The framers' view of political freedom requiring a limited government was largely abandoned by the New Deal reformers, who called upon an activist central government to combat the problems of the Great Depression. Although the framers had sought political freedom by setting up structural divisions within the government to prevent the concentration of government power, the New Dealers believed they could preserve liberty strictly through the judiciary's enforcement of specified individual freedoms.[82]

For the first century and a half of the nation's existence, courts and legal commentators acknowledged both the Ninth and Tenth Amendments as expressing strict limitations on federal power.[83] However, the two amendments met the same fate during the New Deal constitutional revolution. Because the New Deal sought to greatly expand federal power to address the social and economic crisis, the Supreme Court had to cease enforcing structural restrictions on federal power. For instance, the Tenth Amendment as a limitation on federal power was basically dismissed in *United States v. Darby*, where the Court upheld federal regulation of intrastate commerce as long as Congress had reasonably concluded that the activity in question would have some effect on interstate commerce.[84]

Up until the New Deal, both the Ninth and Tenth Amendments had continued to serve as twin guardians of state autonomy.[85] As Lash observes, federalism flourished in the period prior to the New Deal, with Ninth and Tenth Amendment challenges frequently and successfully brought against a host of federal regulations.[86] But with the New Deal constitutional revolution, the commands of the Ninth and Tenth Amendments, as well as a jurisprudence that had existed since the nation's founding, were swept away, allowing for a significant expansion of federal power to regulate many of the local matters that had been previously reserved to the states.[87]

As a result of the New Deal constitutional revolution, Congress was given great leeway to enact the kind of legislation that would have previously been judged a violation of the federalism and separation-of-powers provisions of the Constitution. However, this abandonment of limited-government provisions undercut a fundamental protection of individual liberty. To compensate for this loss of constitutional protection, the Court made a compromise: although it would retreat from reviewing structural issues, it would intensify its review of individual-rights issues. Larry Kramer calls this the New Deal "settlement," in which the Court decided to enforce rigorously a selective set of substantive individual rights while deferring to Congress on structural matters, such as federalism and separation of powers.[88] Thus, a deferential judicial posture in connection with federalism and separation of powers coincided with an increasingly intensive judicial scrutiny in individual-rights cases.

In 1937, the Court articulated a "preferred-freedoms" approach, calling for heightened constitutional protection of individual rights "so rooted in the traditions and conscience of our people as to be ranked as fundamental."[89] A year later, in footnote 4 to his opinion in *United States v. Carolene Products Co.*, Justice

Harlan Fiske Stone argued that the Court should protect the personal rights out-lined in the Bill of Rights more zealously than property or economic rights.[90] This heightened protection of individual rights provided a substitute for judicial review of structural issues, and led to a gradual incorporation of the Bill of Rights guarantees into the due process and equal protection clauses of the Fourteenth Amendment.[91]

The Warren Court era solidified the transformation in constitutional approaches to the preservation of liberty from relying on the limited-government provisions of the Constitution to focusing primarily on the judicial enforcement of substan-tive individual rights.[92] This practice of strict review of individual-rights cases and lenient review of structural cases came into full flower during the 1960s and 1970s.[93] It was during this period when the Warren and Burger Courts carried out a constitutional revolution in many areas of substantive individual rights, including criminal justice,[94] race,[95] the First Amendment,[96] abortion,[97] the rights of women,[98] the death penalty,[99] and procedural due process.[100] But this transformation essen-tially turned self-government and individual liberty into antagonists, making the protection of individual rights the main purpose of the U.S. Constitution.

Through this new reading of the Bill of Rights, the individual-rights revolution distorted the nature of the Bill of Rights and the way in which the Constitution protected liberty. Instead of taking a limited-government view of the Bill of Rights, this revolution looked on the Bill of Rights as an almost unlimited grant of power to the judiciary to pursue and enforce its view of individual autonomy. Forgotten was the rule that if government power is constrained it cannot repress liberty, that a limited government of checks and balances can provide a lasting and supportive environment for individual liberty. Instead, the Court relied for the protection of liberty exclusively on judicial enforcement of specific, individual substantive rights, casting them as rights-bearing trump cards against the democratic political process.

The bifurcated pattern of judicial review that resulted from the New Deal settlement was revealed in a 1978 study conducted by Arthur Hellman.[101] Hellman found that during the six terms from 1971 through 1976, 43 percent of the Supreme Court's cases involved as their principal issue individual rights.[102] Compared with the 383 decisions involving individual rights during this period, the Court handed down only 8 decisions in which the principal issue was a question of either federalism or whether Congress had exceeded its constitutionally delegated powers.[103]

Other scholars and commentators have similarly documented this skewed focus of the Court that greatly favors individual-rights cases over federalism or separation-of-powers cases.[104] Mary Ann Glendon argues that prior to the 1950s the principal focus of constitutional law was not individual rights but structural issues involving the allocation of governmental powers.[105] Seventy years ago, the Court heard far fewer cases involving individual-rights claims; currently, however, those kinds of cases make up the bulk of the Court's constitutional workload.[106]

In the legal culture of the late twentieth century, judicial review by an undemocratic court came to be seen as the only way to protect liberty.[107] But when the Court ceases to protect the kind of governmental structures designed to guard individual liberty, then only the judiciary is left to act as the guardian of liberty—and it does so by defining and strictly enforcing individual substantive rights. Individual liberty is seen to thrive only with activist courts defining and enforcing an array of specific individual rights, whereas the political process comes to be seen as an enemy to liberty. But it was only after the New Deal and the Warren Court eras that America came to rely exclusively on the judiciary and the various provisions of the Bill of Rights for the protection of liberty.[108]

Ever since the New Deal constitutional revolution, the connection between limited government and liberty has been ignored, replaced by a sense that it is the Bill of Rights that primarily serves to protect individual freedom and autonomy.[109] The vast expansion of federal power has overshadowed the framers' belief in limited government and the ways in which limited government is ingrained in the constitutional scheme. In the modern mentality, it is difficult to even see how limited government serves the cause of liberty. And yet, this was how the framers believed liberty would be procured.

The transformation of modern ideas on liberty and limited government is illustrated through the evolution of judicial interpretations of the Ninth Amendment. In *Griswold v. Connecticut* (1965), for instance, the Ninth Amendment was resuscitated after its decline during the New Deal constitutional revolution; but this resuscitation ended up distorting the true meaning of the Ninth Amendment. In *Griswold,* the Ninth Amendment was viewed as an individual-rights provision, rather than as a federalism provision aimed at limiting federal power.

According to Thomas McAffee, the historical evidence reveals that the purpose of the Ninth Amendment was to prevent a feared inference from the inclusion of the Bill of Rights—namely, that the scheme of limited, enumerated powers was being abandoned in favor of a government of general powers, subject only to the specific restrictions listed in the Constitution and the Bill of Rights. The intent behind the Ninth Amendment was to ensure that the Bill of Rights did not undermine the scheme of limited federal government established by the original Constitution.[110]

Although now the Supreme Court is widely viewed as the sole guarantor of individual liberties, during the constitutional period the protection of individual liberty through judicial review of substantive individual rights was rarely mentioned.[111] However, the exclusive reliance on judicial enforcement of substantive rights can foster the illusion that the rights in question are more secure than they in fact are. Consider, for instance, the history of property rights in constitutional law. To the framers, one of the primary purposes behind the new constitution was to develop a governmental structure for the protection of private property.[112] This was considered the right most vulnerable to government infringement.[113] But as it turned out, property rights were the first casualty of the New Deal transformation in constitutional law, going from being a fundamental freedom to being simply one of many social interests.

During the constitutional era, limited government was seen as the way to protect individual rights, and the enumeration of individual rights in the Bill of Rights was seen as another way to ensure limited government. As both Lash and McAffee have pointed out, the ratifiers were much more concerned with the allocation of power between state and federal governments than with the status of particular individual rights. Throughout the constitutional debates, the discussion was not so much about individual freedoms or rights as it was about how to maintain a sufficiently limited government.

The principle and value of limited government is so important to and ingrained in the constitutional scheme that it was revived by the Rehnquist Court in what came to be known as the Court's "federalism revolution."[114] Under the leadership of Chief Justice William Rehnquist, the Court issued a wide array of decisions reviving various limited-government provisions within the Constitution. As a reaction to the demise of these provisions during the New Deal constitutional revolution, the Rehnquist Court reinvigorated the Tenth Amendment as a limitation on federal power; it also revived pre–New Deal limits on the power of Congress under the commerce clause (invalidating a congressional statute on commerce clause grounds for the first time in almost sixty years), as well as curbing Congress's enforcement power under Section 5 of the Fourteenth Amendment. Finally, the Rehnquist Court placed limits on the ability of Congress to use its commerce power to abrogate state sovereign immunity as provided for in the Eleventh Amendment.[115] Thus, despite more than a half century of ignoring and abandoning the limited-government nature and provisions of the Constitution, the Rehnquist Court provided a strong and clear message that such provisions are vital and essential to the U.S. constitutional scheme.

3

The Impetus for the Bill of Rights

Limited-Government Concerns

With the rights revolution of the Warren Court era, judges and legal commentators began emphasizing an individual-autonomy view of the Bill of Rights. According to this view, the Bill of Rights served a primarily individualistic role—namely, the protection and facilitation of individual freedom and autonomy. But this view misrepresents the intent of the drafters and ratifiers of the Bill of Rights. The real motivation behind the Bill of Rights was not to strengthen individual autonomy in society; it was to address the Anti-Federalists' fear of a large, distant, and powerful central government. This is why the focus of the Bill of Rights was on the limits of government, not on the fulfillment or nature of individual rights.[1] The goal of the Bill of Rights was not to outline a comprehensive list of positive individual rights, but "to deny to the new national government the ability to later claim certain powers implied from the original 1787 Constitution."[2] Each of the first eight amendments was "designed to anticipate and negate a power wrongly imputed to the national government."[3] James Madison drafted the First Amendment in the negative language of restrictions on government power, not in the more positive language of defining the nature and value of particular individual rights. The language in the Bill of Rights was in stark contrast to the softer kind of language in state constitutions, which focused on the moral value of liberty and individual rights and which were phrased more as obligations than as prohibitions.[4] Neither the free speech clause nor the free exercise clause, for instance, conferred any new positive powers on the federal government to protect or enhance any speech or religious-exercise freedoms.

As American society has evolved into a more individualistic, rights-oriented society, the Bill of Rights has been given new meanings by modern generations. Historian Jack Rakove argues that the disputes over interpretations of the Bill of Rights characterizing contemporary constitutional law are part of a larger contemporary propensity to view the Constitution through the lens of absolute individual entitlement, rather than through the lens of governmental structure.[5]

Furthermore, an individual clause-by-clause approach to the Bill of Rights skews the intended meaning of it, since the ratifiers of the Bill of Rights were concerned not so much with specific individual rights as with larger ideas of where the dangers to liberty lie and how liberty is to be protected.[6]

The Bill of Rights is not about individual autonomy; it is about using the language of rights to limit the power of government.[7] The Bill of Rights was not intended to empower courts to enforce some judicially defined notions of individual autonomy. Instead, the Anti-Federalists and other supporters of the Bill of Rights feared that the structural provisions of the original Constitution aimed at limiting government might fail to adequately control the power of the new federal government, which they feared could perpetuate the kind of abuses experienced under the rule of George III. Thus, the Bill of Rights defines immunities from government power; it does not specify claims on the government. As Ervin Pollack explains it in *Jurisprudence*, "The indiscriminate use of the term rights to describe an immunity or a privilege has fostered confusion in the law. As has often been stated, our constitutional government was originally framed on a system of limited powers, reserving rights in individuals. However, what were reserved in this context were not actually rights but immunities—restraints on the government."[8]

Randy Barnett explains that the Constitution limits government in two complementary ways. The first way, as reflected by the "federalist constitution," limits government through structural provisions such as separation of powers and federalism. The second way, reflected by the "anti-federalist constitution," limits government by providing explicit areas in the Bill of Rights in which government cannot act or intrude.[9] But these two attempts at limited government reflect the same basic goal and purpose. Even though the Anti-Federalists obviously wanted to protect individual freedom as much as they could, they desired more than anything to implement structural limitations on federal power. This intent is reflected in a 1789 report by William Davie on the goals and attitudes of North Carolina Anti-Federalists: "Instead of a Bill of Rights attempting to enumerate the rights of the individual or the state governments, they seem to prefer some general negative confining Congress to the exercise of the powers particularly granted, with some express negative restriction in some important cases."[10]

As Gary Lawson observes, the meaning of the Bill of Rights is to be found primarily in the text, structure, and history of the original Constitution, rather than in any specific wording of the individual amendments.[11] The amendments draw upon the same background norms found in the original Constitution, with the primary norm being the doctrine of limited government. For this reason, as Lawson concludes, the Bill of Rights in large measure simply reformulates the restrictions on federal power built into the original Constitution, rather than creating new ones.[12] Thus, the Bill of Rights revolves around the same theme that pervades the original Constitution—namely, limited government.

According to Mark Graber, the provisions in the Bill of Rights "were originally understood merely as examples of the individual liberties that the Constitution would protect when governing institutions were functioning as the Framers anticipated."[13] But this does not mean that the Bill of Rights served no function. Lawson argues that the bill focused attention on instances of federal overreaching that might otherwise have escaped notice.[14] For instance, there could be circumstances in which it would be far simpler or more convenient to invoke the First Amendment as a ground for invalidating a law, rather than to rely on the scheme of enumerated powers. Or, as Madison put it, a Bill of Rights was added "for greater caution" to ensure a limited government.[15]

Madison also envisioned that the Bill of Rights would serve an educational purpose, helping to "rouse the attention of the whole community" toward the value of liberty and the dangers of government abuses.[16] Supporters of the Bill of Rights felt that it would set out more specific standards that would enable the people to judge whether the central government had violated the limits of its power.[17]

When he introduced his proposal for a bill of rights in the First Congress in June of 1789, Madison explained that the purpose of the bill was "to limit and qualify the powers of government."[18] Indeed, the first eight amendments are all purely power-limiting clauses, deemed necessary so as to negate the implication of certain additional powers from such open-ended clauses of the Constitution as the necessary and proper clause.[19] The Anti-Federalists argued that this clause would grant unlimited authority to Congress, and for this reason pushed for additional power-limiting provisions such as those in the Ninth and Tenth Amendments.[20] Whereas the limits of the original Constitution were implicit in the concept of enumerated powers, the Bill of Rights contained explicit limitations on government,[21] carving out particular areas from the reach of government power that might otherwise be exercised under the necessary and proper clause.[22] The Anti-Federalists, though agreeing that the conveyance of limited powers to the federal government may indeed serve to secure individual liberty, nonetheless claimed that the Constitution's actual granted powers were not clearly enough defined to supply a strong enough boundary against overreaching and abuse.[23]

All the language and debates about the Bill of Rights at the time of ratification involved limitations on government power. The Bill of Rights would set "limits" and build "barriers" against governmental expansion or abuse of its powers.[24] These barriers would set the boundaries of permissible government action; it was understood that if the government did cross these boundaries, it would not only cause harm to the individuals affected, but would also undermine the very foundation of government itself. According to the theory at the time, the limitations contained in the Bill of Rights would stop the government's exercise of enumerated powers from extending into unwanted areas.[25] Thus, the power-negating limits of the Bill of Rights would act as a double security for limited government, placing limits even on the enumerated powers set out in the Constitution.[26] As Michael Dorf argues, the "Constitution's architecture reveals a two-fold strategy for limiting government—first, by delegating only certain powers, and second, by checking valid exercises of those powers" through the Bill of Rights.[27] Under this view, the

Bill of Rights does not seek to fulfill certain individual values, but simply provides an additional constitutional mandate for limited government. For instance, as Dorf maintains, "it may be possible to defend the privacy right in terms that focus more clearly on impermissible government action rather than on impermissible burdens on individuals."[28] Indeed, perhaps the strongest rationale for a constitutional right of privacy is based not on notions of individual rights but on the limits of government power. A comparable argument can be made regarding the specific areas of individual freedom listed in the Bill of Rights.[29]

The motivation for drafting and ratifying the Bill of Rights was not out of a singular focus on protecting natural rights or individual autonomy. As one historian has concluded, "[T]he Bill of Rights was more the chance product of political expediency on all sides than a principled commitment to personal liberties."[30] James Madison, who was the primary author of the Bill of Rights, had vehemently opposed such a bill during the ratification of the original Constitution.[31] Madison's eventual support for the Bill of Rights stemmed from his promise to the Anti-Federalists to include such a bill in return for their votes to ratify the Constitution.[32] And of course, the primary objection of the Anti-Federalists to the original Constitution was that it insufficiently limited the federal government. They saw that federal powers, even though enumerated, were monumental—e.g., the power to tax, spend, wage war, regulate commerce, and enact laws necessary and proper for the exercise of any of those enumerated powers. With respect to their campaign of limiting government, the Anti-Federalists realized that the absence of a bill of rights in the original Constitution was an issue that attracted the most popular support.

The fears of concentrated power in a central government distant from the citizenry and not accountable enough to the citizenry, as Rakove argues, were deeply rooted within American political culture.[33] Moreover, the fears of unlimited and arbitrary power were directed not just to the executive branch, but to the judiciary as well.[34] Indeed, because oppressive action had often come from British courts, the Anti-Federalists mistrusted judicial authority as much as they did executive power, and were therefore uncertain as to whether they wanted to empower federal judges to act as the guardians of individual rights.[35] Eighteenth-century Americans did not trust the federal judiciary to remedy the wrongs of the federal government. For these reasons, instead of relying on the federal judiciary to prevent the Congress or executive from trampling on individual liberty, the framers of the Bill of Rights thought it was best to simply focus on limiting the power of the federal government to act beyond its proper boundaries.

This is why the jury was so valued by the Anti-Federalists—because it was a vital protection of local and customary rights against the arbitrary acts of a central power.[36] At the time of the ratification of the Constitution, it was widely believed that the jury provided the best means of opposing abusive government action, as exemplified by the Peter Zenger case, which showed that the way to protect freedoms of speech and press was not through a specific individual-rights provision in a written constitution, but through a process or structure of combating oppressive government action in whatever form it took. As Rakove argues, the two rights that seemed especially important to late-eighteenth-century Americans were the right to representation and the right to trial by jury.[37] These two rights would in effect protect all the other rights of the people, since these two rights would enable the people to limit and control their government.

In their campaign for the Bill of Rights, the Anti-Federalists wanted not only to prevent the government from exerting its power in certain areas concerning individual liberty, but also to reserve to the states all powers not granted to the federal government.[38] The Anti-Federalists were not as concerned about the power of their state legislatures as they were about Congress, because they saw state legislatures as being more accountable to the people and hence less likely to violate liberties.[39] But the push for a bill of rights was not the result of a simple desire to protect certain individual rights; it was part of a much broader demand that the Constitution receive more structural protections against unduly expansive federal government power.[40] As one scholar observes,

> It would be a mistake to characterize the Bill of Rights as a guarantee of the rights of the people in general; instead it was a limited protection against depredation by the national government. It supplemented the enumerated powers limitation by further requiring that even if the national government were engaged in an activity authorized by Articles I, II or III of the Constitution, it could only do so within the boundaries set up by the Bill of Rights. What is typically forgotten (or deliberately obscured) in the popular telling of the story of the Bill of Rights is that the states retained the power to do precisely those things (establishing a state religion, punishing unpopular speech, denying the right to trial by jury, etc.) that were forbidden to the national government.[41]

Under this limited-government model, the rights set out in the Bill of Rights were those seen to be particularly necessary to limit the power of government and preserve the people's right to control the power of government and keep it in a limited position. This point was made by Hardin Burnley in a letter to James Madison: "By protecting the rights of the people and of the states, an improper extension of power will be prevented and safety made equally certain."[42]

The debates over the Bill of Rights reveal that there was very little disagreement over the listing of freedoms guaranteed in the first eight amendments.[43] The framers and ratifiers did not engage in extensive discussion about the nature or parameters of the rights mentioned in the Bill of Rights. For instance, with the First Amendment, there was no discussion about the role of a free press in a democracy or whether certain measures to control, regulate, or protect the press would be enforceable, or what the limits are of free speech, or what the definition of speech actually is, or whether certain harmful speech would be protected by the First Amendment. There was, as Robert Goldwin points out, "no discussion of any of the issues that have become so important in First Amendment and Fourteenth Amendment constitutional law."[44]

The debate over the Bill of Rights involved what the amendments' impact would be on the distribution of powers within a federalism type of political structure, not the nature and parameters of the rights themselves.[45] If the focus had been on defining the nature of the rights, there would have been much more intense debate and discussion over the definition of those rights. But the Anti-Federalists did not trust legal or constitutional statements about individual rights; rather, they trusted that liberty would be protected through limited government.[46]

Reflective of the goal to impose more effective checks on government power, the Tenth Amendment specifically recognizes the limited nature of federal power. Although the Tenth Amendment does not grant power to any people or government, it does acknowledge a preexisting power that has been retained and not delegated to the federal government. It indicates, for instance, that the delegated powers under the commerce clause are indeed limited. In demanding a provision like the Tenth Amendment, Patrick Henry expressed the widespread desire for a general reservation-of-power clause that would guard against federal overreach.[47] For Anti-Federalists such as Henry, the Constitution lacked explicit limitations on federal power, as well as provisions reserving to the people and the states all powers not delegated to the national government.[48]

The limited-government nature of the Bill of Rights can be seen in the opposition to the Alien and Sedition Acts. The opponents of these laws interpreted the First Amendment as resting on premises of federalism more than on concepts of personal liberty and natural rights.[49] Focusing not on personal rights but on the allocation of power between federal and state governments, James Madison criticized the laws on the grounds that Congress had exercised a power not delegated by the Constitution.[50] Madison did not argue that the Sedition Act violated a fundamental right or individual autonomy; instead, his argument was based on the fact that the government had been limited from acting in this area.[51] Thus, in the case of the Alien and Sedition Acts, the First Amendment acted as a backstop where the enumerated powers scheme failed to operate as a barrier to unwarranted federal activity.[52]

The Bill of Rights is more than just a way to generally limit the power of the federal government; the rights protected within the Bill of Rights are those that can be most effective in controlling and limiting government. Not only did the Bill of Rights create limitations to government, but it specifically identified areas of freedom that, when exercised, can continue to limit government. For instance, the Anti-Federalists often contended that freedom of speech and press are invaluable bulwarks against tyranny, and that exercise of those rights is necessary to control and limit government.[53] Freedoms of speech and press were seen as the essence of free government, in which people can be free to govern themselves and consequently to limit government by political means.[54]

Reconciling Liberty and Democracy

The perceived tension between the goals of personal liberty and political freedom can best be relieved by a limited-government model, since this model both achieves personal liberty and allows for full political freedom in the areas in which government is authorized to act. According to Ralph Ketcham, James Madison, in seeking to reconcile these two goals, drafted the Bill of Rights in a way that "none of the proposed rights would be such as to deprive the government of its necessary strength or stability."[55] On the other hand, the maintenance of limited government would ensure that the liberty ideals of the Bill of Rights could never be extinguished.

For the framers, the only real way to prevent government from violating the liberty of its citizens was to give those citizens the capacity to limit government.[56] Again, the focus was on the structure and workings of government, not on the status or fulfillment of particular individual rights. The framers and ratifiers had much more faith in the structural provisions of the Constitution, in terms of the protection of liberty, than they did in any list of various individual rights, which would inevitably be incomplete. As Ketcham explains, there was a constant linkage in the debates over ratification between individual liberty and the nature and structure of government.

In late-eighteenth-century America, the notions of rights and liberty were very much connected with the notion of the rule of law. As John Phillip Reid points out, the rule of law made those rights possible.[57] But the rule of law was also very much tied in with the notion of limited government. To eighteenth-century Americans, the rule of law had provided a powerful constraint on the power of the king and Parliament to infringe on liberty.[58] It was only through a limited government that the rule of law could exist, and it was only through the rule of law that individual liberty could be protected.

The limited-government model also explains John Locke's compact theory relating to the formation of government. Under this theory, persons surrendered the natural rights they possessed in a state of nature so as to join a civil society and form a government, which in turn would ensure their security against outside forces. The individual-rights explanation of the compact theory tries to identify which rights people surrendered and which rights they retained—and regarding the rights they retained, the individual-rights model seeks to define the degree of protection of those rights. The limited-governmental model, however, does not focus on individual rights but on the nature of the government formed. This is a simpler and clearer approach to the compact theory, since it focuses on the extent of the power possessed by government. The focus is on the government formed— the affirmative act of social consent—rather than on the degree of individual rights to be exercised according to the discretion of those individuals—the non-act of individual retention.

The historical record shows that the debate over the Bill of Rights was not really a debate over the extent of protection of individual rights. Instead, it was a debate over the power of the federal government and how it could be limited. The framers obviously wanted to protect individual rights, but the focus was not on the exact nature of those rights or the degree to which they should be protected, or on preserving to individuals the freedom to do whatever they wanted; instead, the debate was over how much power should be allocated to the federal government.

To eighteenth-century Americans, it was an impossible task to list all the rights they wished to protect, as well as to describe the nature of those rights and the degree to which they needed to be protected. The more direct and simple focus was on the limited power of government and the structural barriers between what government could and could not do. When drafting the Bill of Rights, Madison warned against any absolute statements of rights because he knew there would be certain emergencies that would require those rights to be overridden.[59] Consequently, what was important to Madison was that government generally be limited, not that individuals always enjoy a certain defined level of "rights." Madison did not think that the Bill of Rights was going to precisely define a particular view of individual autonomy that would be applied by the courts to trump government action that was exercised within the limited and legitimate sphere of government.

Viewing the Bill of Rights as a limited-government provision achieves a balance between the sometimes seemingly contradictory goals of democratic government and individual rights. Under the limited-government model, individual rights do not occupy a separate and independent realm from democratic government that in turn can provide a separate and independent basis to invalidate democratic laws. Rather, the provisions in the Bill of Rights exist and operate on the same level as democratic government, properly limiting it to its authorized function. Indeed, just as people possess individual rights, they also possess the right to be ruled by democratically enacted law.[60]

The framers knew that a society that emphasized personal rights was inherently factious and conflict creating.[61] Consequently, the framing generation was particularly wary of creating a democracy characterized by extreme individualism. This is why the framers did not see the Bill of Rights as primarily a guarantor of individual autonomy; instead, they thought of it in the larger context of government power. And it was only through the limited-government model that the framers could think of individual rights in this larger context and in a way that did not create an adversarial culture. This has become the problem with the modern preoccupation with individual rights, creating an adversarial relationship between individuals and the democratic process. But to see individual rights as the primary constitutional focus is to undermine the most basic purpose of the Constitution, which is to provide for the general welfare and to create a common republican system of government that is limited in power, with sufficient checks and balances to control that government.

Ketcham uses the constitutions of communist governments to illustrate the futility of relying on statements of individual rights to protect liberty. According to Ketcham, the Soviet constitution of 1936 and the Chinese constitution of 1954 contained statements of individual rights, including freedom of expression.[62] These statements are classic examples of what Madison called "parchment barriers" because they have no effect when pitted against the actions of an all-powerful state, which can do what it pleases, regardless of constitutional statements about individual rights. As Madison realized, freedom depends not on statements of rights contained in a constitution, but on a government that is prevented from infringing on individual liberty in the first place.

In drafting the Bill of Rights, Madison took great care to make sure that its provisions were consistent with the original Constitution and altered nothing in it.[63] Consequently, the Bill of Rights should be seen as supporting and reinforcing the main theme of the original Constitution—namely, the provision of limited government. For if the Bill of Rights was intended to primarily protect or guarantee individual autonomy, one might expect that there would have been a grant of power made to Congress to achieve such a protection. But instead, the Bill of Rights is only a denial of power to government, preventing the government from acting in certain ways or areas.

By making the Bill of Rights consistent with the overall constitutional scheme, Madison wanted to make it part and parcel of a larger pattern of government, with attention focused primarily on a limited structure of government rather than on particular statements of individual rights.[64] Under this view, all the provisions of the Constitution should be seen as parts of a coherent, single whole. When seen as a whole, the Constitution is primarily a document of "powers, structures and procedures, not of values."[65]

Envisioning the Constitution as a coherent whole rather than a collection of assorted clauses, Akhil Amar sees the Bill of Rights as "largely republican and collective, sounding mainly in political rights," downplaying the role of individual rights.[66] Although the Bill of Rights does protect certain individual rights, that function is "not the sole, or even the dominant, motif."[67] With respect to the Ninth Amendment, for instance, Amar argues that the rights referenced in that amendment mean rights of the people collectively, rather than individual rights.[68] And collective rights can include a right of a democratic people to constitutionally limit the power of government.

The Ninth Amendment Model

The limited-government theme is often overlooked in the analysis of individual rights.[69] But this theme is particularly evident in the Ninth and Tenth Amendments, both of which aim directly to limit centralized government power.[70] James Madison, for instance, saw the Ninth Amendment as serving to limit overly broad interpretations of federal power, and to preserve state autonomy.[71] In a speech to the House of Representatives, Madison stated that the Ninth Amendment expressed a rule of strict construction of federal power—a rule that protected the people's right to regulate local matters free from federal interference.[72]

The danger of including a bill of rights in the Constitution was that it might lead to an inference that the federal government was a government of general legislative powers, as were the states, able to do whatever was not forbidden it by the bill. This was the purpose of the Ninth Amendment: to ensure that a bill of rights would not lead to this inference about the federal government. As Kurt Lash explains, while the purpose of the Tenth Amendment was to declare that the federal government possessed only limited, enumerated powers, the purpose of the Ninth Amendment was to prevent the interpretation of those enumerated powers in a way that resulted in their undue expansion. According to Lash, the Ninth Amendment "was conceived and received as a federalist provision preserving the people's retained right to local self-government."[73] This federalist model of the Ninth Amendment looks at retained rights in a much broader way than simply through an individual natural rights lens; instead, the model applies the Ninth Amendment anytime federal power is unjustifiably extended, regardless of whether that extension affects individual rights or collective rights, such as the right to local self-government.[74]

Both Amar and Lash interpret the Bill of Rights collectively rather than individually, meaning that they see the Ninth Amendment as aimed at preserving the collective right of the people to local self-government, rather than primarily as a provision for judicial enforcement of unenumerated individual natural rights. This collectivist interpretation of the Bill of Rights is similar to the limited-government model. In either case, the rights protected relate to something more than simply individual autonomy. Indeed, if the Bill of Rights were concerned primarily with individual freedom and autonomy, one would think that Madison would have done more to protect against what he perceived as a principal threat to individual rights—majoritarian actions at the state level.[75]

Lash argues that the Ninth Amendment was meant to preserve all retained rights, whether individual or collective, from undue federal interference, reserving control of them to local majority rule. Under this view, the Ninth Amendment requires courts to limit the interpretation of enumerated federal power in order to preserve the people's retained right to local self-government. According to Lash's review of the early case law and scholarly literature, the Ninth Amendment was consistently seen as a federalist provision establishing a rule of strict construction of federal power and protecting the autonomy and power of the states; it was not interpreted as an individual-rights provision.[76] Under Lash's theory, Madison drafted the Ninth Amendment to address state concerns that the federal government would interpret its enumerated powers in a way that would overly expand its own powers and diminish the rights and powers of the states.[77] Similarly, as Thomas McAffee argues, the Ninth Amendment was intended not to protect unenumerated natural rights, but to make sure that the insertion of a federal bill of rights into the U.S.

Constitution would not undermine the limited-government scheme already in that document.

However, the federalist or limited-government model of the Ninth Amendment, protecting reserved state powers, was abandoned by the courts, according to Lash. During the nineteenth century and up to the New Deal, the courts had used the Ninth Amendment to protect state powers and self-government in the states from federal infringement.[78] But in the New Deal era, so as to uphold the greatly increasing powers of the federal government—e.g., its commerce clause powers—the courts dismissed the Ninth Amendment's government-limiting rule of construction.[79] This dismissal also occurred with the Tenth Amendment in 1941, although it was revived during the Rehnquist Court's "federalism revolution" in the 1990s.

The residual-rights interpretation of McAffee, the collectivist interpretation of Amar, and the federalism model of Lash can all be reconciled and subsumed under the limited-government model. What all three models have in common is that they aim to limit the power of the federal government. Under all the models, the Ninth Amendment acts as a limitation on government power, not as a clause seeking to preserve or fulfill individual autonomy.[80] According to McAffee, the Bill of Rights should not be seen "as a manifesto of any moral principle" or as an open-ended invitation for judges to select their own preferred social values for constitutional protection, but rather as a "set of eighteenth century precepts" about limited government.[81]

Amar argues that the essence of the Bill of Rights is more structural, concerned more with political rights and public liberty than with individual rights.[82] Likewise, he theorizes that the Ninth Amendment is not about individual rights, but is aimed at limiting the power of the federal government and protecting the collective right of the people to local self-government from interference by the federal government.

To Amar, the grand idea of the Bill of Rights is the collective right to self-government. Under the theory put forth in this book, the grand idea is one of limiting the power of the federal government. Just as Amar minimizes the role of individual rights within the Bill of Rights, the limited-government model places primary emphasis on the allocation of power to the federal government rather than on the definition and nature of particular individual rights. Similar to the limited-government model, for instance, are Amar's claims that the jury trial is more fundamentally a question of government structure than an individual right, and that juries are an important check on the overreaching power of government.[83]

In a theory somewhat akin to Amar's, Lash sees the Ninth Amendment as an active federalist provision calling upon courts to limit the interpretation of enumerated federal power in order to preserve the people's retained right to local self-government.[84] Under this federalist interpretation of the Ninth Amendment, its protections are triggered any time federal power is unjustifiably extended, regardless of whether the extension affects an individual or non-individual right, such as the collective right to local self-government. Thus, the federalist model of the Ninth Amendment embraces a much broader category of rights than that proposed by the libertarian model, which focuses only on the protection of unenumerated individual rights.[85]

The libertarian or individual natural rights model of the Ninth Amendment is promoted by Randy Barnett. This model asserts that the Ninth Amendment provides an enforcement vehicle whereby judges can protect all natural rights retained by individuals at the creation of the federal government, even though those rights are not enumerated in the Constitution. As with any model based on individual natural rights, however, the vexing problem is one of determining on a case-by-case basis which rights were "retained" and what the definitions or parameters of those rights are.

Recently, in the wake of *Griswold v. Connecticut,* some courts and commentators have started adopting this libertarian model, looking on the Ninth Amendment as a protection of individual rights.[86] However, Lash observes that for more than a hundred years after adoption, the Ninth Amendment was understood and applied as a rule of construction preserving the autonomy of the states.[87] During that time, the Ninth Amendment was commonly paired up with the Tenth Amendment to limit federal power so as to preserve the right to local self-government.[88] According to Lash, the Ninth Amendment is not a source of rights, but simply forbids interpreting constitutional provisions in a way that gives unduly broad power to the federal government.[89]

The only way to achieve a comprehensive protection of all undefined rights and liberty is through seeing the Ninth Amendment as a limited-government provision—limiting government so as to protect all forms of liberty. Lash claims that the Ninth Amendment protects the right of local self-government, which is one of the retained rights of the people, whereas this book argues that the Ninth Amendment protects the right of the people to a limited federal government. But in a way, these are one and the same. According to Lash, when ratifying the Constitution, the people of the individual states retained their right to control local matters. However, this is very close to saying that the right they built into the Constitution was the right simply to limit the power of the federal government, so as to then preserve their freedom to govern themselves on all matters of state and local interest. Indeed, the right of local majorities to self-govern is possible only if the federal government is limited. In this way, the Ninth and Tenth Amendments work in coordination to limit federal power. The Tenth Amendment limits the federal government to only enumerated powers, whereas the Ninth Amendment limits the interpretation of enumerated powers.[90]

A unifying theme among the different theories or interpretations of the Ninth Amendment is the theme of limited government. Such a theme is also reflected in the view that the Ninth operates as a limited rule of construction, preventing the constructive expansion of federal power through the argument that the explicit mention of some rights in the Bill of Rights meant that government had the power to deny or disparage rights not explicitly mentioned.[91] Under this view, the Ninth was intended to negate any inference that, because certain rights were listed in the Bill of Rights, all other, unenumerated rights had been surrendered to government control. This view relies on the text of the Ninth, as well as on the drafting and ratification history, in which much of the debate centered on "powers denied to the federal government rather than rights granted to individuals."[92] The purpose and evolution of the Ninth Amendment were explained in correspondence with James Madison:

> Since the rights declared in the first ten of the proposed amendments were not all that a free people would require the exercise of; and that as there was no criterion by which it could be determined whither any other particular right was retained or not, it would be more safe, & more consistent with the spirit of the 1st & 17th amendments proposed by Virginia, that this reservation against constructive power, should operate rather as a provision against extending the powers of Congress by their own authority, than as a protection to rights reducible to no definitive certainty.[93]

Thus, among the various theories of the Ninth Amendment, the one consistent aspect is the framers' desire through the Bill of Rights to impose additional limiting restrictions on the power of the federal government.

4

Balancing Judicial Restraint and Democratic Rule

A Definable Judicial Role

A pervasive concern during the adoption of the Constitution was that the federal judiciary would expand its own powers beyond its constitutionally limited confines, thus subverting the separation of powers.[1] Opponents worried that federal courts, exercising unbridled equitable powers, would decide cases as "their opinions, their caprice, or their politics might dictate."[2]

Many of the framers feared judicial encroachment into the legislative sphere more than they feared any other breach of the separation of powers. Alexander Hamilton argued that "there is no liberty if the power of judging be not separated from the legislative and executive powers."[3] Believing judges to have aristocratic tendencies and to be too far removed from the people, James Madison saw the need of keeping the elite governmental powers—the judiciary—from exercising any legislative power.[4]

One of the problems with an individual-autonomy view of the Bill of Rights is that individual autonomy is difficult to define, and the Bill of Rights in fact does not define with any real specificity the nature of the individual rights or freedoms protected. However, because of this lack of definition, any judicial attempt to enforce individual-autonomy norms will itself be undefined and therefore unlimited, which in turn can give judges freedom to make rather than simply apply the law. Such a jurisprudence would obviously contradict the desire of the framers for limited government.

For a text or doctrine to serve as the foundation of law, it must be lawlike—it must contain a sufficient specificity that will allow courts to apply it.[5] According to Keith Whittington, if constitutional provisions are seen as undefined and open ended, they will allow judges to exercise much discretion in their application, and this discretion contradicts rule-of-law notions. Therefore, constitutional provisions should be interpreted in a manner that will give specificity to them and sufficient direction to the courts. Constitutional provisions should not be interpreted in such a manner that allows justices to inject their own personal views into the application of those provisions. The rule of law can only be applied if judges are bound to decide cases based upon a defined law, rather than on their own personal views.

The problem with unlimited judicial power, aside from its negative effect on the rule of law and its contradiction of the constitutional principle of limited government, is that when judges make a wrong decision, it is very difficult to reverse that decision. If a democratic legislature makes a wrong or bad decision, there is greater flexibility to change the decision through a political movement aimed at influencing the legislature. However, the people do not have similar powers to change or modify decisions of the courts.

It is an undefined individual-autonomy view of the First Amendment that has allowed judges and scholars to interpret it in a way that gives the judiciary almost unlimited power. Even though the free speech clause is phrased as a negative liberty, for instance, Frederick Schauer argues that it protects "a right to investigate the truth freely."[6] But such a right is nowhere specified within the First Amendment and is the result of an expansive interpretation of that amendment. Similarly, Owen Fiss argues that even when private action has the effect of distorting or stunting the needs of the electorate for public debate, government has a duty to correct this problem and make the marketplace of ideas work properly.[7] But of course, this confers great power on both the government and the courts to decide when the democratic dialogue is not working properly and then how to "fix" the problem.

According to Fiss and Cass Sunstein, the First Amendment gives government the power to apply the free speech clause in a way that will create the kind of public debate necessary for a properly functioning deliberative democracy. But this approach contradicts the framers' desire for a limited government. The actual functioning of individual and social speech patterns becomes the focus, rather than the degree and application of government power. However, the First Amendment was ratified as an attempt to limit government power in certain areas; it was not ratified as an additional grant of power to the government to act with undefined and unlimited power in certain areas.

Under the Fiss and Sunstein views, the First Amendment would actually empower the government to aggressively intervene into the marketplace of ideas so as to ensure that the "proper" information is being expressed. Even when public discourse is being affected by private action, Fiss and Sunstein would still have the courts use the First Amendment to give government the power to "clear up" any deficiencies in public discourse. The free speech clause would then become an open-ended tool that could be used by the courts to fashion democratic government and the marketplace of ideas in any way that judges deem fit. The First Amendment in this sense becomes a tool for unlimited government, rather than a provision for limited government. For if the government can act so as to achieve the kind of public speech it considers appropriate, it basically has unlimited power.

The Supreme Court's decision in *Roper v. Simmons* illustrates the problems of employing an individual-autonomy view of the Bill of Rights, since such a view is not bounded by any constitutional parameters or definitions.[8] In *Roper*, the Court had to decide whether the Eighth Amendment, as incorporated into the Fourteenth Amendment, forbids executing a juvenile offender for the commission of a capital crime. Even though noting that it must look to the Constitution's text, history, tradition, and precedent, the Court stated that "evolving standards of decency that mark the progress of a maturing society" should inform its decisions about which punishments are cruel and unusual and thus constitutionally proscribed. After then defining these evolving standards of decency, the Court held that the Fourteenth Amendment prohibits states from executing juveniles for the commission of capital crimes.

In *Roper*, the Court also used international law to interpret the Eighth Amendment. As Justice Sandra Day O'Connor stated, "This nation's evolving understanding of human dignity certainly is neither wholly isolated from nor inherently at odds with the values prevailing in other countries."[9] Thus, not only did the Court on its own initiative define "evolving standards of decency," but it also looked to outside international law to discover the evolving standards of decency in this country. This decision reflected the fact that there are few, if any, constitutional parameters or boundaries directing the courts on how to interpret provisions of the Bill of Rights, as long as those provisions are seen as reflecting the individual-autonomy view.

A limited-government model of the Bill of Rights focuses on limiting the power of government to act in certain ways, which in turn allows society to have more flexibility in how it expresses and incorporates the kind of social and moral values that are connected with or reflected by the Bill of Rights. But under an individual-autonomy approach, the U.S. Supreme Court dictates to the whole country how each different provision in the Bill of Rights will be applied so as to preserve or facilitate the Court's definition of individual autonomy.[10] Rather than trying to fulfill ambiguous and undefined norms relating to individual autonomy, the limited-government model of the Bill of Rights holds that the more defined and specific principle of limited government should be the first focus of the courts in enforcing the Bill of Rights.

An individual-autonomy view of the Bill of Rights has also led to an inherent tension being built into judicial application of the Bill of Rights, involving a continually adversarial relationship between the individual and society. The limited-government model, on the other hand, does not incorporate such an inherently adversarial model. The focus under the limited-government model is primarily on one subject: government. It looks only at whether government should be limited in a particular situation or area; it does not at the same time try to outline the ways in which individual autonomy should be preserved or promoted. Indeed, the concept of limited government does not envision the individual as being in constant conflict with the government. Instead, it simply sees that the government has authority only to act in certain areas—but when it does act legitimately, the government and the individual are seen in harmony. The only issue is whether and how much government should be limited in certain functions. Nor does it direct the courts to take the view that the individual in a state of nature is more preferred than the individual in the context of community.

One of the reasons the Bill of Rights has come to be interpreted as involving a continual clash between the individual and the community is that, since the Warren Court era, the Constitution has been seen as concerned primarily with the protection of individual rights, even more so than with the very structure of government itself and the power of a democratic people to make law. However, the framers were not concerned primarily with the protection of individuals in a state of nature; indeed, they had seen the problems created by the Articles of Confederation, which gave too little power to a democratic community to act for the common welfare. The primary focus of the Constitution was the formation and functioning of government; it was not the creation of conditions in which the public would be governed by courts applying undefined and open-ended provisions relating to individual autonomy. The Bill of Rights was a way to limit the power of government; it was not meant as a way to disable government and to constantly set the individual apart from government. The framers wanted the democratic public to be ruled by itself, not by the decisions of courts.[11]

With a natural-rights or individual-autonomy view of the Bill of Rights, it is impossible for courts to legitimately identify the limits of those rights or freedoms. Since one person's exercise of his rights cannot be allowed to deprive another person of her rights, a court must determine the parameters not only of the first person's right but of any other individual rights with which the exercise of that right may conflict.[12] Even aside from trying to determine the boundaries of conflicting rights, the courts have a hard enough time trying to determine the nature of a right by itself. For instance, if the First Amendment is seen as protecting the value of self-realization through the free expression of the thoughts and feelings of individuals, it is very difficult for a court to determine when and how self-expression in fact realizes an individual's subjective self.

As Steven Heyman observes, privacy is a fundamental right, and as such it can be understood as the right to maintain the integrity of one's inner life by preserving the boundary that separates one from other persons.[13] But if privacy is a fundamental right, the question for courts then is how to reconcile the clash between privacy and free speech, which is also a fundamental right, especially when defamation or offensive speech disturbs the privacy of another.

All these questions arise if the First Amendment is seen as primarily serving to protect individual autonomy, which includes the right of self-realization. This view of the Bill of Rights puts too much emphasis on the subjective feelings and reactions of people, as well as permitting the courts boundless discretion in determining the nature and parameter of the provisions of the Bill of Rights. If the purpose of the First Amendment free speech clause is to "make men free to develop their faculties," as stated by Justice Louis Brandeis in *Whitney v. California,*[14] then the application of the First Amendment will depend on judges' determinations of how individuals should be left free to develop their faculties. This is too subjective of an approach for courts to take and still abide by the rule of law.

Distortions Resulting from an
Individual-Autonomy Jurisprudence

The existing Bill of Rights jurisprudence has led to some distorting and perhaps unintended results. An example can be found in the content-neutral doctrine that has developed in the courts' free speech jurisprudence. Courts have allowed "restrictions on the time, place, or manner of protected speech,"[15] as long as those regulations are deemed to be content neutral and leave open alternative means for communicating the regulated expressions.[16] For instance, in *Heffron v. International Society for Krishna Consciousness, Inc.,* the Court upheld a statute that forbade members of a religious sect from distributing their religious material in face-to-face encounters with State Fair attendees, ruling that the First Amendment "does not guarantee the right to communicate one's views . . . in any manner that may be desired."[17] In *Madsen v. Women's Health Center, Inc.,* the Court sustained an injunction preventing protestors from entering a thirty-six-foot buffer zone around abortion clinics.[18] And in *Members of the City Council of the City of Los Angeles v. Taxpayers for Vincent,* the Court upheld an ordinance that completely prohibited the posting of signs (even political posters) on public property.[19] The Court has even upheld zoning restrictions aimed specifically at adult entertainment businesses, finding that the "secondary effects" of these businesses are valid objects of government regulation.[20]

Geographic restrictions on where speech may occur are given only an "intermediate" level of scrutiny by the courts.[21] However, even though developed during an era when perhaps the most disruptive and threatening of speech occurred in physical venues such as parks and streets, the time-manner-place doctrine has never envisioned a connection between the content of speech and a particular physical venue–e.g., that the content of speech outside an IRS office would most likely be protest of government tax policies.[22] This failure to recognize the connection between the content of the speech and the location at which it is expressed allows courts to sustain supposedly content-neutral laws that in fact single out and severely burden a particular content of speech, even political speech.

At the 2004 Democratic National Convention, protestors were confined to a free speech cage made of chain-link fencing and coiled razor wire.[23] During the 1999 World Trade Organization meetings in Seattle, all protests within a twenty-five-block "restricted zone" were banned.[24] A nearly one-block "bubble" zone shielded New York City Mayor Michael Bloomberg from union protestors at the 2004

Republican National Convention.[25] Outside abortion clinics, speech–free zones in which protestors are prohibited have been enacted and upheld.[26] For instance, in *Hill v. Colorado,* the Court upheld a statute creating a "floating buffer zone" prohibiting anyone from coming within eight feet of another person outside of an abortion clinic for the purpose of passing out a leaflet or engaging in oral protest or counseling.[27] Even though recognizing that the speech of the abortion protestors was protected by the First Amendment and that the public sidewalks covered by the statute were "quintessential" public forums for free speech, the Court nonetheless categorized the statute as content neutral. The dissent in *Hill,* however, argued that the speech burdens imposed on the protestors were significant.[28] Yet despite the burdens, and even though the speech at issue was clearly political speech, the Court still allowed a supposedly content-neutral time-manner-place regulation to virtually suppress that speech.

All these regulations impacting traditional political speech fall under the category of time-manner-place restrictions. Since on their face these regulations focus only on the place of the speech, they are seen to be content neutral. However, one of the most powerful and traditional forms of political protest occurs in connection with unique and focused physical locations—e.g., outside government buildings and political conventions.[29] Thus, supposedly content-neutral time-manner-place restrictions end up having a selective effect not only on political speech, but on the speech of political protest. For instance, in *Coalition to Protest the Democratic Nat'l Convention v. City of Boston,* the court upheld the City's use of a "designated demonstration zone" in which to contain protestors, even though the court admitted that this fenced-in demonstration zone resembled "an internment camp."[30] Justifying this decision was the court's finding that the "demonstration zone" resulted from a content-neutral regulation governing the mere location of speech.[31]

Such regulations have also been justified by the argument that protestors could resort to mass-media coverage as an alternative to the physical act of protesting at a political convention.[32] Of course, even if the protestors did opt for the mass-media route, there would be no guarantee as to how the media would portray or edit their message. Nor would there be any guarantee that their intended audience—the convention delegates—would be watching television at the exact time the protestors' message was aired. Nor would there be any guarantee that the opportunity to shout and chant for fifteen seconds to a television camera would be sufficiently appealing to attract a sizable crowd of protestors.[33]

A First Amendment jurisprudence grounded on individual autonomy has thus allowed restrictions on what the Court has recognized to be the type of speech with which the First Amendment is primarily concerned—political speech. This is the kind of speech the framers and ratifiers were most intent on protecting, and it is the kind of speech that would receive highest protections from the limited-government model.

The Substantive Due Process Analogy

An individual-autonomy view of the Bill of Rights requires courts, in enforcing the provisions of the Bill of Rights, to define the elements and parameters of individual autonomy. The problems and pitfalls of such endeavors can be seen in the Supreme Court's substantive due process jurisprudence. This jurisprudence, focused as it is on individual dignity and autonomy concerns, is particularly highlighted by the constitutional right-to-privacy cases.

The Court's recognition of a constitutional right of privacy began in *Griswold v. Connecticut,* where the Court struck down a Connecticut law prohibiting the use of contraceptives, even by married couples.[34] The Court ruled that the statute, as applied to married couples, violated "a zone of privacy" created by the "penumbras" that gave "life and substance" to the specific guarantees in the Bill of Rights.[35] In outlining this zone of privacy, the Court stated that even though some rights are not specifically mentioned in the Constitution, they are nonetheless "peripheral" to various freedoms in the Bill of Rights.[36]

The Court in *Carey v. Population Services International* later stated that "the reasoning of *Griswold* could not be confined to the protection of rights of married adults."[37] In overturning a statute that banned the distribution of contraceptives to minors as part of a state policy against teen pregnancy, *Carey* extended the right of privacy to minors engaging in consensual sexual behavior. The Court saw the right of privacy, as protected by the due process clause of the Fourteenth Amendment, to include "the interest in independence in making certain kinds of important decisions."[38]

In *Roe v. Wade,* the Court held that the right of privacy recognized in the contraception cases was "broad enough to cover the abortion decision."[39] Later, in reaffirming *Roe,* Justice Anthony Kennedy elaborated on the right to privacy: "These matters, involving the most intimate and personal choices a person may make in a lifetime, choices central to personal dignity and autonomy, are central to the liberty protected by the Fourteenth Amendment. At the heart of liberty is the right to define one's own concept of existence, of meaning, of the universe, and of the mystery of human life."[40] This "right to define one's concept of the universe" and of the "mystery of human life," obviously a right applicable to a host of intimate choices, was an offshoot of the "emanations from penumbras" that had first led the Court to recognize a right to privacy.[41] The Court's privacy rulings presume that judges have the ability and duty to determine those personal choices that define human life and sustain personal dignity. These rulings presume that courts can adequately draw the fine lines between individual privacy, democratic values, and social policies. The constitutional right of privacy further presumes that a centralized judiciary can better determine the parameters of individual autonomy than can any democratically elected legislature. And in doing so, the Court has uniformly defined what constitutes the vital ingredients of personal dignity and autonomy for all Americans, even though the Court has applied the constitutional privacy right almost exclusively to sexual activity freedoms.

The Court defines privacy as involving those individual choices "central to personal dignity and autonomy" that help "define one's own concept of meaning."[42] And the type of choices that qualify as those vital to human development, according to the Court, are the choice to engage in sexual conduct and the choice to have an abortion. Even though human privacy is being assaulted every day by technologies allowing unlimited opportunities to collect and disseminate intimate personal information, the Court has not extended its privacy doctrine to those conditions or concerns.

The irony of the constitutional right of privacy is that it exists in a society where nearly every aspect of personal privacy other than sexual conduct is being eroded. Even more ironic, especially when one considers the constitutional efforts the judiciary has made to create a right of privacy, the Supreme Court has greatly aided the invasion of identity and informational privacy by ruling that the media may publish or broadcast the contents of intercepted communications known to have been unlawfully intercepted, just as long as the media did not participate in the unlawful interception.[43]

Because of the way privacy has evolved as a court-created right, there is an arbitrariness to the current constitutional doctrines. Why, for instance, did the Court pick sexual activity as the area covered by privacy rights? What if there are many people who define themselves not through their sexual activities but through some other activity?[44] Who is to say that the only real or ultimate measure of privacy is in sexual relations? Is sexual privacy so much more important to human autonomy and dignity than informational privacy?

Within the judicial arena, privacy has come to reflect an unrealistic and unworkable notion of individual autonomy. The Court's privacy doctrine, for instance, promotes "the illusion that individuals are sovereign jurisdictions, entitled to and able to exercise the most significant personal liberties without concern for others."[45] This illusion views the individual as separate from society, not dependent on society for his or her physical comfort, emotional satisfaction, or personal security and liberty. It sees individuals as completely self-defining, and imagines their ideal existence as a "state of nature." But this is not how the Constitution sees individuals who are members of a democratic society. The Constitution is primarily concerned with the workings of the democratic community, not with trying to return individuals to some imaginary "state of nature," with no relationships or obligations to society.[46] When society is formed, individuals give up the liberty they have "enjoyed" in the state of nature, exchanging it for a more limited set of liberties and rights under civil society.[47]

Since *Griswold,* the due process clause of the Fourteenth Amendment has served as the Court's "chosen vessel" for the protection of unenumerated rights.[48] Under a substantive due process approach, the Court recognizes a right as fundamental when, for instance, it can be shown that the right is grounded in tradition—but tradition can be a highly subjective concept.[49] John Hart Ely points out that "people have come to understand that tradition can be invoked in support of almost any cause."[50] Consequently, the substantive due process approach has been criticized as allowing judges to impose their own personal views to the detriment of the democratic process. According to Chief Justice William Rehnquist, judges can use substantive due process to effectively rob the legislatures of the ability to consider important issues of self-governance.[51]

In articulating privacy rights or liberty interests under its substantive due process jurisprudence, the Court has used several approaches. One approach has been to protect those liberties that are "deeply rooted in this nation's history and tradition."[52] In addition to historical tradition, the Court has also used a kind of political-moral reasoning process to determine whether a particular interest deserves protection as a constitutional right.[53] In *Casey*, for instance, the Court used a process of "reasoned judgment" to define the liberty interests of a woman seeking an abortion.[54] This "reasoned judgment" is not based on tradition, but on the Court's own definition of individual liberty.[55] However, according to critics, such a reasoned-judgment process results in a relatively unrestrained type of judicial review "that permits the Supreme Court to protect new rights and to invalidate governmental policies even if those policies have longstanding and continuing support in American law and society."[56] Using this moral-judgment approach, "the Court is free to invalidate legislation, and thus to repudiate the policymaking of elected officials, based on the court's own political-moral judgment, its own determination that the legislation improperly interferes with individual liberty."[57]

A third approach in the Court's substantive due process jurisprudence involves an enforcement of "evolving national values." This approach was used in *Lawrence v. Texas*, when the Court cited recent developments in the legal treatment of consensual sodomy and found "an emerging awareness that liberty gives substantial protection to adult persons in deciding how to conduct their private lives in matters pertaining to sex."[58] To the Court, these developments reflected an evolving national value that supported a liberty interest in intimate sexual relations. Holding that a state statute criminalizing same-sex sodomy violated the Fourteenth Amendment's due process clause, the Court stated, "The protected right of homosexual adults to engage in intimate consensual conduct . . . has been accepted as an integral part of human freedom in many other countries . . . [and] there has been no showing that in this country the government interest in circumscribing personal choice is somehow more legitimate or urgent."[59] However, the problem with this "evolving national values" approach is that it provides no clear or consistent constitutional standards.

In *Washington v. Glucksberg*, which declined to hold physician-assisted suicide a fundamental right, the Court cautioned against expanding the scope of substantive due process.[60] This was an echo of Justice John Marshall Harlan II, who in a pre-*Griswold* case involving state restrictions on contraceptives rejected the kind of expansive jurisprudence that would produce a constitutional right of privacy.[61] Heeding Justice Harlan's advice, the Court in *Glucksberg* upheld Washington's ban on assisted suicide, despite Justice Antonin Scalia's observation in an earlier case about the difficulties in differentiating between a right to refuse medical treatment and a right to physician-assisted suicide.[62]

The *Glucksberg* Court distinguished its ruling from that in the abortion-rights case of *Planned Parenthood v. Casey* by stating that a fundamental right involved only "those personal activities and decisions that this Court has identified as so deeply rooted in our history and traditions, or so fundamental to our concept of constitutionally ordered liberty, that they are protected by the Fourteenth Amendment."[63] The Court also admitted that just because "many of the rights and liberties protected by the Due Process Clause sound in personal autonomy does not warrant the sweeping conclusion that any and all important, intimate, and personal decisions are so protected."[64] But the underlying question remains: How is assisted suicide not as fundamental of a right as assisted abortion? Why is sodomy protected, but not prostitution? Why does the right of privacy not extend to polygamy or the use of recreational drugs?

Although in *Glucksberg* the Court found no substantive due process right, the Court in *Cruzan v. Director, Mo. Dept. of Health* stated that the "choice between life and death is a deeply personal decision" in which the "Due Process Clause protects an interest in life as well as an interest in refusing life-sustaining medical treatment."[65] Moreover, a comparison of *Glucksberg* with *Casey* and *Lawrence* suggests that substantive due process permits and perhaps requires an ever-changing approach to constitutional law, in which each generation reads its own opinions and lifestyle into the Constitution.

Even though the Court previously in *Bowers v. Hardwick* had ruled against a fundamental right of homosexuals to engage in sodomy, based upon a lack of history or tradition in protecting such a practice, the *Lawrence* Court found just the opposite type of history and tradition, which in turn led to the ruling that sodomy statutes violate the Constitution.[66] After examining whether American history and tradition had in effect created such a fundamental right, the *Bowers* Court concluded that prohibitions against sodomy "have ancient roots" and that sodomy had been criminalized by many states "since the colonial era."[67] Seventeen years later, however, the Court reversed itself in *Lawrence*. As Justice Kennedy wrote, history and traditions "show an emerging awareness that liberty gives substantial protection to adult persons in deciding how to conduct their private lives in matters pertaining to sex."[68]

In his *Lawrence* dissent, Justice Scalia argued that "an emerging awareness does not establish a fundamental right."[69] Scalia also noted that, contrary to the majority's ruling that the Texas anti-sodomy law had no rational basis, countless "judicial decisions and legislative enactments have relied on the ancient proposition that a governing majority's belief that certain sexual behavior is immoral and unacceptable constitutes a rational basis for regulation."[70]

Aside from the *Bowers* reversal, substantive due process has historically proved to be unreliable. The first era of substantive due process took place from the latter part of the nineteenth century to the 1930s. During this era, defined by the Court's decision in *Lochner v. New York*,[71] property and economic rights were protected under a substantive due process approach.[72] *Lochner* rested on the Court's assertion that liberty of contract was a fundamental right protected by the due process clause of the Fourteenth Amendment.[73] This conclusion flowed from an earlier decision in *Allgeyer v. Louisiana,* in which the due process clause was interpreted as protecting "the right of the citizen to be free in the enjoyment of all his faculties; to be free to use them in all lawful ways; to live and work where he will; to earn his livelihood by any lawful calling; to pursue any livelihood or avocation."[74] Likewise, to the *Lochner* Court, liberty of contract was seen as vital to a free life.[75]

During the *Lochner* era, the Court struck down nearly two hundred state laws for violating the liberty of contract inherent in the due process clause.[76] But the constitutional revolution of the New Deal brought an end to this era.[77] Under pressure from President Roosevelt's court-packing plan, the Court ceased using substantive due process to strike down New Deal economic legislation.[78] When *Lochner* was overruled in 1937, the Court criticized the use of substantive due process to define liberty of contract as a fundamental right:

> What is this freedom? The Constitution does not speak of freedom of contract. . . . There is not absolute freedom to do as one wills or to contract as one chooses. The guaranty of liberty does not withdraw from legislative supervision that wide department of activity which consists in the making of contracts. . . . Liberty implies the absence of arbitrary restraint, not immunity from reasonable regulations and prohibitions imposed in the interests of the community.[79]

Lochner was not only abandoned, it was ridiculed as a very bad decision by an activist Court.[80] The *Lochner* decision was criticized because it was seen as a way in which the justices could transform their own ideological beliefs—e.g., laissez-faire economic policy—into constitutional doctrine, even though liberty of contract is never specifically mentioned in the Constitution. *Lochner* particularly conflicted with the Progressive movement's desire to use government power to address an array of social problems. But even if *Lochner* was wrong in its use of the Fourteenth Amendment to protect unenumerated natural rights, it was right in its fears of the kind of wide-ranging state power advocated by Progressives.

However, despite all this criticism of substantive due process as a means to protect the liberty of contract during the pre/-New Deal period, it has nonetheless been embraced as a source of protection for another judicially created fundamental right—the right of privacy. With the demise of *Lochner,* substantive due process was abandoned until the Court decided *Griswold v. Connecticut* in 1965. As articulated in *Planned Parenthood v. Casey,* in terms that could have come straight from *Lochner,* the Court ruled that substantive due process protects those subjects and choices "central to personal dignity and autonomy."[81] And yet, the *Casey* Court admitted that *Lochner* had been wrongly decided and had rested on "fundamentally false factual assumptions" about human needs.[82]

The fate of *Lochner* and the demise of economic substantive due process cast significant doubt on the constitutional basis of the right of privacy. If economic rights, seen as fundamental during the early twentieth century, could be suddenly downgraded because of the changing political environment of the New Deal, then why would not privacy rights, now seen as fundamental, suffer the same fate if political sensibilities changed?[83] Indeed, the Court has become so indifferent to property rights that in 2005 in *Kelo v. City of New London* it ruled that the government could take by eminent domain a number of homes from their working-class owners and then convey the property to private corporations for the purpose of economic development.[84]

As the Court has been developing a right to privacy, it has downplayed property rights, which for a century and a half were a primary focus of constitutional law. In fact, only after the Court ceased treating property rights as fundamental rights, requiring a substantive due process analysis, did it begin to adopt such an analysis for cases involving noneconomic individual rights.[85] But the unanswered question resulting from this legacy is still whether property rights are less important to individual fulfillment and dignity than are sexual privacy rights.

5

Applying the Bill of Rights as Government-Limiting Provisions

The Bill of Rights came into being because of a mistrust that the general structural provisions of the Constitution would sufficiently limit the power of the new central government. Consequently, the Bill of Rights specified particular areas in which government could not exert power. To interpret particular provisions of the Bill of Rights is to determine the nature of rights necessary to limit the power of government, in a way so as to preserve an area of social or individual life that in turn can be free to control and limit government. Thus, the focus is not on what the individual needs in order to feel or to exercise a certain sense of autonomy, but rather on the state and on what ways it should be limited and on how to keep it limited. This is a more objective and defined focus. This is similar to the distinctions between negative and positive liberties: whereas the boundaries of negative liberties (i.e., the determination of whether a person's actions are being physically obstructed by the state) are at least somewhat clear, the boundaries of positive liberties (i.e., how free a person actually is) are much more vague and uncertain.

When an issue of government interference with a right contained in the Bill of Rights arises, one question that must be addressed is whether the exercise of that particular right is needed to keep an effective limit or control on government. If government restriction of the right will eliminate an effective source of individual or social control over government, then that government restriction is unconstitutional. The burden here is on the government to prove that the exercise of the right is not necessary to keep government limited.

In the area of speech, for instance, obscenity and certain types of defamation have never been given constitutional protections. This is because those kinds of speech are not necessary to control or limit the power of government.[1] Furthermore, courts have often allowed restrictions on speech when those restrictions are necessary to protect the rights of others and yet not necessary to limit government. In *Gompers v. Buck's Stove and Range Co.*, for instance, the Supreme Court upheld an injunction against the president of the American Federation of Labor, preventing him from organizing a boycott of the plaintiff's business, stating that such a boycott could cause irreparable damage to the business and violate the property rights of that business.[2] But it is important to note that the speech in this case was directed not against the government but against private employers.[3] Therefore, the speech was not necessary to limit or control the power of government. The limited-government model can also explain the Court's decision in *Associated Press v. United States,* where the Court upheld the application of antitrust laws to the press, stating that such laws actually further the values underlying the First Amendment.[4] But the freedom of the press from antitrust laws—or, conversely, the freedom of the press to become a monopoly—is not a freedom that is reflective of limited government or necessary to limit government.

The Second and Third Amendments likewise serve to limit the power of the central government. In his *Second Treatise of Government,* John Locke argued that the people's right to control or eliminate an abusive government requires a popular appeal to arms.[5] Consequently, the Second Amendment was aimed at the fear that Congress could use its power to disarm the state militias.[6] The framers were highly suspicious about a standing army kept by the central government, and to alleviate this suspicion they strove to maintain the state militias.[7] The Third Amendment similarly aims at limiting the power of an overbearing federal army. Essentially, the Third Amendment forbids Congress to conscript civilians as involuntary innkeepers and roommates of soldiers in peacetime.[8] As Akhil Amar argues, the Third Amendment "stands as an important reaffirmation of separation of powers, and limited executive authority."[9]

In *District of Columbia v. Heller* in 2008, the Supreme Court held that the Second Amendment right to keep and bear arms was an individual right.[10] In *Heller,* the Court ruled that the Second Amendment protects an individual right to possess a firearm in the home for self-defense, unconnected with militia service. Prior to this decision, most circuits had rejected the individual-rights interpretation of the Second Amendment, adopting instead a collectivist or state-right interpretation.[11] The lower federal courts had read the amendment to protect only a militia-based right.[12] Shortly after the decision was handed down by the Supreme Court, Fourth Circuit Judge J. Harvie Wilkinson criticized *Heller* as a result of judicial activism akin to that of *Roe v. Wade*'s creation of a right to an abortion.[13] Similarly, Judge Bork stated in 1989 that the Second Amendment "guarantees the right of states to form militia, not for individuals to bear arms."[14]

In *From Parchment to Power,* Robert Goldwin argues that "there is no reason to believe that the authors of the Second Amendment thought it had anything to do with private ownership of arms for the personal uses of guns, such as hunting or defense of the home."[15] Ralph Ketcham likewise argues that "the private, merely personal bearing of arms would seem not to be the point" of the Second Amendment.[16] Similarly, Amar argues that the Second Amendment focuses on federalism concerns and structural protections of limited government (e.g., preventing federal government from prohibiting state militias).[17]

Yet even though the *Heller* Court ruled the Second Amendment to be an individual right, it still can be argued that this right is better understood through the limited-government model than the personal-autonomy model. For instance, the Court acknowledged that the individual right was not an unlimited one. The Court in fact listed a number of "longstanding prohibitions" on firearms that are not undermined by the *Heller* ruling: prohibitions such as bans on possession of guns by ex-felons and the mentally ill, restrictions on commercial sales of firearms, and bans on guns in such places as schools and government buildings. Essentially, according to the Court, most gun-control laws currently in existence are not unconstitutional under *Heller*.

Because of all the ways in which the individual right to own and bear arms can be regulated, the *Heller* ruling cannot be seen as primarily striving to serve the autonomy interests of individual gun owners. Instead, a better interpretation is that *Heller* seeks to limit the government from being able to effectively eliminate a person's right or ability to defend herself in her own home. Thus, the Second Amendment stands as a barrier to the government's power to achieve complete disarmament of its citizens.

Goldwin also notes that when the House of Representatives debated the proposed Bill of Rights, it covered in one day the Second and Third Amendments, plus all or significant parts of what are now the Fourth, Fifth, Sixth, Seventh, Eighth, and Ninth Amendments. This suggests that what the House thought it was doing was not incorporating all the different facets or parameters of individual autonomy that were going to be protected, but instead providing for a much more unifying or universal principle—that of limiting government. Moreover, the individual amendments contain relatively few provisions and are sparse in detail. The Sixth Amendment, for instance, contains a generally stated right to counsel, right to jury trial, and right to confront opposition witnesses. And as the Court has often held, these provisions, as do the other provisions in the Bill of Rights, reflect a distrust of governmental power.[18]

Viewing the Bill of Rights from an individual-autonomy point of view could lead to some far-reaching judicial applications of those rights, which in turn can greatly increase the power and discretion of the judiciary. For instance, the argument was made in *San Antonio Independent School District v. Rodriguez*, where parents were seeking increased or equalized funding for education, that the First Amendment should be interpreted to provide a positive right to the educational services that would make citizen speech more effective.[19] The Court rejected such a positive or affirmative application of the First Amendment, ruling instead in favor of the more traditional conception of the First Amendment as a negative one. To rule in favor of parties challenging the "adequacy" of state-provided education would entail separation-of-powers concerns, since courts would have to impose remedies that would override legislative judgments, including even judicially directed budgetary allocations. Similarly, in *Hudgens v. NLRB*, the Court held that the First Amendment does not generally restrict nongovernmental abridgers of speech or impose obligations of noninterference on the owners of private forums for speech.[20] To hold otherwise would give individuals the ability to use the First Amendment to require that the government affirmatively take action to facilitate speech opportunities. Instead, the First Amendment is a negative provision, denying power to the government.

As a limited-government provision, the First Amendment protects the independence of certain expressive institutions that serve as a check on government. Such First Amendment institutions as religious organizations, the press, and the university are protected by the First Amendment, in part because they act as nonstate institutions that can provide powerful checks on and supervision of government. The First Amendment helps to create institutional sovereignty in these kinds of institutions, which allows them to operate in ways that can either guide, check, or limit the activities of the state. In a sense, these institutions serve as a counterweight to the state, ensuring that it never dominates or monopolizes society.

The jury provisions in the Fourth and Seventh Amendments also serve to empower the public against an overreaching and abusive central government.[21] As Amar argues, the dominant strategy of the Fifth, Sixth, Seventh, and Eighth Amendments was to keep agents "of the central government under control" by using the populist and local institution of the jury.[22] Just as a state militia could provide a check on a standing army of the central government, a jury having independent investigative powers could similarly check abuses by federal prosecutors and judges. According to Amar, "[T]he jury summed up—indeed embodied—the ideals of populism, federalism, and civic virtue that were the essence of the original Bill of Rights."[23] Thus, the jury right was not so much an individual right as a structural provision aimed at limiting government.[24]

The very text of the Seventh Amendment negates the application to it of an individual-autonomy model. The amendment preserves the jury-trial right for certain "suits at common law." This means that a jury-trial right exists where one existed under English common law in 1791.[25] Thus, the Seventh Amendment is not an individual-autonomy clause, since it does not give individuals a jury trial in all cases. Instead, it serves to limit the government's ability to expand its power by contracting the jury-trial right from where it stood in 1791, when the Seventh Amendment was adopted.

As Alexis de Tocqueville observed, the jury "places the real direction of society in the hands of the governed . . . and not in that of the government."[26] In this way, the "jury trial was not simply and always an individual right, but also an institution of localism and popular sovereignty."[27] As Amar points out, the jury-trial right was seen as the most treasured right in eighteenth-century America. This was because it had served as colonial America's only way of checking the aggressions of the British government. According to Thomas Jefferson, trial by jury was "the only anchor, ever yet imagined by man, by which a government can be held to the principles of its constitution."[28]

Although the individual-autonomy model of the Bill of Rights holds that the protection of privacy is the underlying and primary purpose of the Fourth Amendment, the Supreme Court has in fact applied it primarily as a government-limiting principle.[29] The primary goal of the Fourth Amendment "is the same as that of the entire Constitution—to define and to limit governmental power."[30] The fear of unfettered governmental power, rather than the desire to preserve individual privacy, was the motivating impulse of the framers.[31] With the Fourth Amendment, the framers "were more concerned about limiting government's power to invade any aspect of life without sufficient cause than with defining what aspects of life should be off limits to government."[32]

Even though conventional wisdom often interprets the Fourth Amendment as concerned with individual autonomy or individual privacy, scholars and jurists alike have discounted or contradicted that interpretation.[33] They argue that, contrary to the modern conception of the Fourth Amendment as being focused on privacy, the framers were primarily concerned with general liberty and limitations on government.[34] Indeed, the more historically consistent interpretations of the Fourth Amendment focus not on personal privacy or autonomy, but on a more narrow limitation on government abuses and arbitrary action. For instance, scholars contend that the framers did not intend the Fourth Amendment to govern criminal arrest and search standards; instead, the purpose of the Fourth Amendment was to prohibit the use of "too-loose" general warrants for revenue searches of houses for untaxed goods.[35]

The framers' opposition to such general warrants stemmed in large part from the arguments James Otis had made during the 1761 *Writs of Assistance* case, where he argued against the legality of the general writ of assistance, an extreme form of a general warrant that provided customs officers with standing authority to make discretionary searches of houses.[36] Otis had attacked these writs as "against the fundamental principles of law."[37] Even though Otis lost the case, his arguments gained much popularity in America and led to public hostility toward the exercise of such unbounded government power.

The historical record reveals that limited-government concerns were the primary motivation for the Fourth Amendment, with individual privacy or autonomy considerations much less prominent. Moreover, the record shows that there were two different limited-government concerns that underlay the Fourth Amendment: the desire to limit legislative power to authorize general warrants and the desire to limit the executive power of customs or excise-tax collectors to enforce those general warrants. As Thomas Davies argues, the framers of the Fourth Amendment were "primarily concerned with prohibiting legislative authorization of general warrants for searches of houses to enforce customs or excise tax collections, but seldom expressed any concern with general arrest warrants."[38] According to Davies, the controversy over the use of general writs of assistance for revenue searches of houses was the far more important catalyst for the Fourth Amendment. Additionally, as creatures of legislation rather than of common law, such revenue-search warrants were not necessarily controlled by the dictates of common law or traditional concepts of due process.[39]

The American opposition to general warrants heightened in reaction to the Townshend Duties Act of 1767, when Parliament reauthorized the use of general writs of assistance for customs searches in America.[40] Later, during the constitutional period, the fears giving rise to the Fourth Amendment were directed not just at the abuses caused by the general writs, but at the fear that Congress would give unlimited power to federal-excise-tax collectors.[41] Excise searches—based as they were on excise taxes, which could potentially be levied on a wide variety of domestic commodities—were already widely unpopular in America and, unlike customs-tax searches, which mostly threatened only merchants in port cities, excise-tax searches could extend to any house located anywhere.[42] For this reason, the Fourth Amendment arose not only with respect to the opposition to general warrants, but also in connection with the American objection to excise-tax collections. According to James Madison, the Fourth Amendment was necessary to ensure that Congress could not authorize general warrants for revenue searches under the necessary and proper clause.[43] Madison, as were the other framers, was primarily concerned with regulating revenue-search warrants rather than criminal warrants.[44] The concern with customs or excise searches stemmed from the fact that such taxes were to be the primary sources of revenue for the new federal government.[45]

General searches were the principal concern of the framers of the Fourth Amendment, rather than the kinds of ordinary criminal arrests and searches that are the frequent subject of modern Fourth Amendment case law.[46] Whereas little mention of ordinary criminal arrests and searches was made in the debates on the Bill of Rights, there was much discussion about federal tax collectors searching private homes with impunity.[47] Speeches by people like Patrick Henry focused on controlling the power and activities of tax collectors.[48] George Mason expressed the concern that excise taxes would "carry the excise man to every farmer's house who distills a little brandy, where he may search and ransack as he pleases."[49] Other critics saw writs of assistance as a "detestable instrument of arbitrary power" that "invited capricious house searches by insolent officers of the new central government."[50] These were the kinds of searches and government actions the framers had in mind, not the arrests and searches of individuals suspected of ordinary criminal activity. Furthermore, the framers would have wanted ordinary criminals to be caught and punished, and would not have confused the need to prevent arbitrary uses of government power with the need to shield criminals from the reach of the law.[51] As long as the federal government could be prevented from conducting general searches and seizures, the framers would have been satisfied that they had taken care of the most serious problem of aggressive government searches and seizures.[52] The Fourth Amendment framers envisioned that searches and seizures could be accomplished, as long as they were done according to due process of law.[53]

Another interpretation of the Fourth Amendment that likewise supports the limited-government model is the reasonableness view. In numerous cases, the

Court has emphasized that the primary principle of the Fourth Amendment is reasonableness.[54] In *Ohio v. Robinette*, the Court asserted, "We have long held that the touchstone of the Fourth Amendment is reasonableness."[55] Under this reasonableness standard, government intrusions violate the Fourth Amendment if they are not reasonable under the circumstances.[56] And according to the limited-government model, only unreasonable interferences are seen as beyond the scope of government power and hence unconstitutional.

The reasonableness test for the Fourth Amendment focuses more on the actions of government—i.e., the reasonableness of the search—than on individual-autonomy values. For instance, in *Illinois v. Rodriguez*, the Court focused on whether the police had a reasonable belief in a person's authority to consent to a search of a home.[57] Thus, the focus is more on the actions of government than on the actual violations of individual autonomy that may or may not have occurred with the search. In taking such a focus, courts incorporate a more policy-oriented view concerning the actions of police and the need for crime control.[58] Furthermore, in the course of applying the reasonableness test, courts often end up balancing any intrusion on individual autonomy against law-enforcement needs.[59] This concern with the power and activities of government was evident in *Kentucky v. King*, where the Court stated that warrantless searches of homes can be justified by exigent circumstances, except when the police create the exigency "unreasonably."[60] As one commentator has noted, the Fourth Amendment reasonableness test puts more emphasis on the state's crime-control activities than on individual-autonomy interests.[61]

This reasonableness element focuses attention on the government action rather than on notions of personal privacy or autonomy. The reasonableness principle limits the government from acting arbitrarily or unreasonably; it does not seek to preserve personal autonomy under every circumstance. For instance, there are circumstances in which entry into a house can be legitimate even if it is done without a warrant—for instance, if law-enforcement officers are in hot pursuit. Moreover, the Court has increasingly employed a balancing test as a measure of reasonableness.[62] This balancing test has been used to justify all kinds of government searches and intrusions, including searches of prison inmates and detainees, entries onto property to investigate fires, inventory searches of individuals taken into police custody, searches of employee areas of governmental workplaces, searches of public-school students, and drug testing of persons in an array of settings.[63] In addition, suspicionless checkpoints like roadblocks have long been allowed under the Fourth Amendment, despite their intrusion into personal privacy.[64] Moreover, there are a vast number of individuals subjected to airport and other such screenings every year, without any constitutional problem.[65] Other allowable searches or seizures that do not satisfy the warrant requirement involve instances in which law-enforcement officers act with good faith.[66] Another allowable exception to the Fourth Amendment's warrant requirements involves a search or seizure done pursuant to exigent circumstances, even those that intrude on individual privacy.

The Court has crafted an entire body of Fourth Amendment jurisprudence dealing with imminent threats and emergencies. The warrant requirement, for instance, is generally waived when "the exigencies of the situation make the needs of law enforcement so compelling that the warrantless search is objectively reasonable under the Fourth Amendment."[67] The Court has found that "the need to protect or preserve life or avoid serious injury is justification for what would be otherwise illegal absent an exigency or an emergency," thus lifting the warrant requirement.[68]

With respect to the exclusionary rule, the good-faith exception was formally recognized by the Court in *United States v. Leon*.[69] This good-faith exception permits the admission of evidence notwithstanding violations of the Fourth Amendment, if the law-enforcement official relied in good faith on a facially valid warrant. Obviously, the good faith of a police officer has nothing to do with the personal-autonomy interests of the person whose Fourth Amendment rights are being violated. Therefore, this good-faith exception is another clear indication that the Bill of Rights should be interpreted under the limited-government model.

Interpreting the amendments in the Bill of Rights as provisions by which to limit governmental power allows for a more dynamic and flexible process of balancing individual rights against the needs of society.[70] As provisions seeking to limit governmental power, the Bill of Rights does not elevate individual rights to an untouchable place, as a trump card against all other social interests. The Bill of Rights serves to keep government in its prescribed position, ensuring a democratic society's ability to monitor, criticize, and direct its government. Viewing the Bill of Rights this way allows a balance to be struck between liberty and governmental authority, whereby each individual surrenders enough control over his or her rights so as to permit government to have enough power (but no more) to accomplish its legitimate goals.[71]

This focus of the Bill of Rights on determining the boundaries of government power rather than ensuring personal autonomy is illustrated by how the Supreme Court applies the Bill of Rights in cases involving the threat of imminent harm. In these cases, the focus is not on personal autonomy, since the rulings go directly against autonomy interests. Instead, the Court ends up not enforcing the provisions of the Bill of Rights, finding that in such cases the government should not be subject to limitations on its power and that it does possess the authority to address without restraint the imminent harm at issue.

In an array of circumstances, the Supreme Court has recognized that in times of imminent danger or harm, the provisions in the Bill of Rights should not act as limits on government power. In *Brandenburg v. Ohio*, for instance, the Court found that the First Amendment does not restrict the government from punishing speech that is "directed to inciting or producing imminent lawless action and is likely to incite or produce such action."[72] In *Chaplinsky v. New Hampshire*, the Court affirmed the government's power to regulate "fighting words"—those words that by their very utterance inflict injury or tend to incite an immediate breach of the peace.[73] According to the Court, any restraint on personal autonomy through the regulation of fighting words is "clearly outweighed by the social interest in order and morality."[74]

In Fifth Amendment cases, the Supreme Court has likewise recognized an imminent-harm exception to the application of that amendment. The Court recognized a public-safety exception to the *Miranda* rule in *New York v. Quarles,* where Benjamin Quarles had fled the police, armed with a .38-caliber revolver. When the police captured him in a supermarket and asked where his gun was located, he told the officer where he had thrown it.[75] The officer then seized the weapon before reading Quarles the *Miranda* warning. However, finding that "overriding considerations of public safety justify the officer's failure to provide Miranda warnings," the Court did not suppress the seized firearm, recognizing law enforcement's immediate necessity to protect the lives of the other patrons and employees in the supermarket.[76]

There has been a continuing debate over whether the Bill of Rights should be incorporated by the Fourteenth Amendment to apply to the states.[77] This debate about whether the Fourteenth Amendment incorporates the Bill of Rights stems from a much larger debate about the meaning of the Fourteenth Amendment. According to one commentator, gaining an original understanding of the Constitution of 1787 "is a snap compared to making sense of" the Fourteenth Amendment.[78] Indeed, the Fourteenth Amendment has been the subject of more litigation than all the other provisions of the Constitution.[79]

As the *Slaughterhouse* Court stated, the framers of the Fourteenth Amendment did not intend to alter the settled understandings of national-state relations.[80] This contrasts with the claim that the Fourteenth Amendment was intended to dramatically expand national powers in a way that would greatly diminish state powers. But the Fourteenth Amendment can also be viewed as simply an attempt to limit the powers of state government, just as the original Bill of Rights had limited the powers of the federal government. Under this view, the Fourteenth Amendment provides a way for the national government to ensure that the state governments are in fact limited by the Bill of Rights. As Bruce Ackerman argues, Reconstruction did not alter the scope of national power generally when constitutionally protected rights were not at issue; but with respect to the Bill of Rights' being applied to the states, the national government was after the Civil War going to be a force for limited state government, just as the state governments had previously been a force for limited federal government.[81] It was not that the nation had undertaken to recognize a new set of nationally enforced individual-autonomy rights during Reconstruction; rather, the Fourteenth Amendment was a reaction to the evils of slavery and was adopted to make sure that the states would be subject to the same limited-government provisions that bound the federal government.

The fundamental question posed by the incorporation debate is whether the Fourteenth Amendment drastically altered the meaning of the Bill of Rights. In other words, did the Bill of Rights cease being a limited-government provision and become a more affirmative protection of individual autonomy? Of course, a preliminary question is whether the Fourteenth Amendment in fact did extend the Bill of Rights to the states. Often ignored in the debate over this question is the fact that courts almost uniformly rejected applying the Bill of Rights to the states during the decades following the Fourteenth Amendment's ratification.[82] Generally, not until the mid-twentieth century did the Supreme Court begin to decide that the Fourteenth Amendment due process clause had incorporated any of the provisions of the Bill of Rights against the states.[83] However, even if one accepts the incorporation argument, as the Supreme Court generally has, one can still recognize that the Fourteenth Amendment was largely inspired by the struggle against slavery, during which it was realized that the states could pose a threat to individual liberty, just as the federal government was seen to pose such a threat in the late eighteenth century.[84] But those who argue that the Fourteenth Amendment brought about a radical transformation of state and federal relationships, by converting the Bill of Rights into a weapon the national government could use against the states, ignore that such a result would contradict the Ninth and Tenth Amendments. The Ninth Amendment, according to Kurt Lash, preserves the right of local autonomy, and the Fourteenth Amendment could not change this without some specific amendment overturning the Ninth Amendment. Consequently, there must be some explanation for the Fourteenth Amendment that still preserves the integrity of the Ninth and Tenth Amendments, as well as the freedom of state and local autonomy.[85]

The Ninth Amendment may have been altered somewhat by the Fourteenth Amendment, insofar as the states did not have as much freedom as they once had, but it is difficult to believe that the Ninth Amendment was altered as much as is argued by those who say that the Fourteenth Amendment gave vast powers to the federal government to control the states. Such a scenario would go way beyond limiting the power of the states; it would dramatically undermine the limited-federal-government scheme so painstakingly set out in the Constitution, and it would unduly intrude upon the people's retained right to local self-government.[86]

Regardless of all its specific effects, the Fourteenth Amendment still has to be reconciled with the Ninth Amendment. The limited-government model achieves such a reconciliation, insofar as it holds that the Fourteenth Amendment only attempted to limit state governments in the same way that federal governments were limited by the original Constitution. The limited-government model reflects such a reading of the Fourteenth Amendment—one that is consistent both with the original scheme of the Constitution as well as with the original meaning of the Bill of Rights.

Under the limited-government model, the Bill of Rights prevents the government from acting in certain areas. In so doing, it preserves certain rights to the people that will allow them to democratically control the actions of government. The Fourteenth Amendment simply elaborated upon this scheme, by imposing government-limiting provisions on state governments as well as the federal government.[87] Indeed, this extension of limited-government provisions to state governments was intended to prevent the kind of Southern-state oppression that had instigated the Civil War.

The greatest challenge facing the Thirty-ninth Congress, which passed the Fourteenth Amendment, involved how to "secure the peace" after the Civil War and prevent a future war.[88] The Fourteenth Amendment was prompted by postwar violence in the South aimed at overthrowing the results of the war, as well as by the enactment of the black codes, which indicated to the drafters and ratifiers of the Fourteenth Amendment that Southern-state governments could not be trusted to refrain from using their power to oppress African Americans.[89] Consequently, federal enforcement of the limited-government provisions of the Bill of Rights was necessary so as to prevent their infringement by the states.[90]

As Richard Aynes has pointed out, the ultimate goal of the Thirty-ninth Congress was to keep a civil war from happening again.[91] And one of the causes of the Civil War was seen to be the denial by the Southern states of the right of free speech to those who disagreed with slavery.[92] Thus, limiting the power of the states to deny such freedoms would be a way to prevent a future war from occurring. Republicans believed that had they been able to campaign and proclaim their message in the South prior to the war, without being censored, there never would have been a Civil War.[93] There was protection against federal obstruction of free speech before the war, but the ratifiers of the Fourteenth Amendment wanted the same speech protections that applied to the federal government to be applied to the states.[94]

In the wake of the Civil War, the Republicans saw free speech as a vital means of controlling government. As Michael Kent Curtis argues, Republicans believed that free speech would prevent a government from expanding its power so much as to be able to perpetuate an unjust system like slavery. Free speech was necessary to keep government under control and to prevent its oppressive expansion of power.

An aspect of the Fourteenth Amendment that causes problems in determining its original intent is that it was presented as a complete package, on a take-it-or-leave-it basis.[95] The ratifiers could not pick and choose among the various clauses contained within the Fourteenth Amendment. This means, according to Aynes, that some of the consequences anticipated by the framers of the Fourteenth Amendment may not have been intended or desired by the ratifiers.

After having been outraged at the *Dred Scott* decision, the framers of the Fourteenth Amendment were not entirely trusting of the judiciary's ability and willingness to interpret constitutional text or protect individual liberty. This is one of the reasons that in the Fourteenth Amendment, Congress was given the power to enforce the provisions of that amendment.[96]

Some scholars argue that the Fourteenth Amendment not only altered the fundamental structural principles of the relationship between the states and the national government, but also that it changed the original structural alignment of national power.[97] Section 5 of the Fourteenth Amendment, it is argued, gives Congress the power to enforce the Fourteenth Amendment and hence revolutionizes the role of Congress with respect to individual liberties.[98] However, in the wake of the Fourteenth Amendment's ratification, the Supreme Court did not so interpret that amendment. In the *Civil Rights Cases,* the Court struck down congressional attempts to regulate civil rights.[99] Thus, less than two decades after passage of the Fourteenth Amendment, the Court was still attentive to limitations on federal government power. Obviously, the Supreme Court did not feel that the Fourteenth Amendment fundamentally altered that aspect of the original Constitution, nor had it altered fundamental federalism principles.

It can be argued instead that the Fourteenth Amendment was aimed at limiting the power of the states, not at expanding the power of the federal government. Such a result was reached in the *Slaughterhouse* cases, in which the Court found that the Fourteenth Amendment was narrowly aimed at protecting the rights of the newly freed slaves, not with radically expanding the power of the federal government. Similarly, in *United States v. Cruikshank,* the Court was still concerned about preserving federalism and the integrity of state power in the federal system.[100] Thus, Section 5 of the Fourteenth Amendment was seen as a way to limit the power of states to infringe on freedoms protected by the Bill of Rights, not as a means of dramatically expanding the power of Congress to regulate the states.

In modern times, the Fourteenth Amendment has taken on quite different meanings and interpretations from those originally intended. It has been used as a basis for dramatic expansions of government power to fight just about any type of alleged discrimination. But the Fourteenth Amendment was originally focused on and motivated by the racial discrimination in the post/-Civil War South. It was not meant as a radical transformation of America's federalism scheme.[101]

In recognition of the more limited reach of the Fourteenth Amendment, the Supreme Court has recently begun narrowing the scope of federal powers conferred by Section 5. In *City of Boerne v. Flores,* the Court set new limitations on congressional power.[102] Using this narrower standard, the Court on several subsequent occasions has ruled that Congress exceeded its Section 5 powers in passing various civil rights laws.[103] As the Court in *City of Boerne* ruled, Congress's power to enforce the provisions of the Fourteenth Amendment is a remedial power, not a power to "decree the substance of the Fourteenth Amendment's restrictions on the states" or "to determine what constitutes a constitutional violation."[104] This latter power belongs exclusively with the Court, and applying Section 5 so as to give Congress the power to interpret the Constitution "would require an enormous extension" of that provision.[105]

In *City of Boerne,* the Court seemed to heed the advice of Justice John Marshall Harlan II in his dissent in *Katzenbach v. Morgan,* where he argued that to allow Congress to transcend judicial interpretations of the Constitution would be to give it unwarranted and undefined power.[106] Consistent with Harlan's warnings, the *City of Boerne* Court concluded that the Religious Freedom and Restoration Act was far "out of proportion to a supposed remedial or preventative object," and that Congress had passed a law with "sweeping coverage" that imposed "substantial costs" on the states.[107] Consequently, by limiting Congress to a remedial role, the Court in *City of Boerne* "foreclose[d] any substantive participation by Congress in the development of constitutional norms."[108] And by requiring Congress "to craft remedies that are congruent and proportional to specifically determine constitutional violations, *City of Boerne* limits the range of Congress' discretion."[109]

The Fourteenth Amendment is better seen as a reaction against the theory of states' rights that was asserted by Southern leaders such as John Calhoun, not as a rejection of the basic principles of federalism. As such, Section 5 of the Fourteenth Amendment does not give Congress the ability to affirmatively legislate in areas prohibited by the Bill of Rights; instead, it leaves to Congress, rather than exclusively to the courts, the duty of enforcing limitations on state government.

Since the framers of the Fourteenth Amendment did not trust the courts to protect liberty, it was by default left up to the Congress to provide such protection. But this is not the same as suddenly transforming the doctrine of federalism or radically expanding federal power. The Fourteenth Amendment did effect a change in the power of Congress, obviously giving it the power to enforce the provisions of the Fourteenth Amendment, but it did not alter the fundamental structure of constitutional government. The original understandings of the structure of constitutional government focused on the need to restrict Congress in the areas covered by the Bill of Rights, and the Court was the agency to prevent Congress from acting in such areas. However, because of the failure of the Court in cases like *Dred Scott,* the Fourteenth Amendment looked to Congress to act as the limiting force on state governments—and indeed, the Reconstruction amendments' enforcement clauses grant Congress fairly broad powers to enforce some fairly broadly worded limitations on state government power.

Originally, as expressed in the *Federalist Papers,* the framers were more concerned with restraining congressional power than with empowering it to protect individual liberties. The judiciary was given the role of enforcing doctrines of limited government on Congress. But with the Reconstruction Congress no longer trusting this judicial oversight, the Fourteenth Amendment looked more to Congress to enforce limited-government principles on the state governments. This was not a radical altering of federalism principles; it was seen as the best available means by which to enforce the Bill of Rights against the states. Whereas the Bill of Rights sought to entrust the courts with limiting the power of the federal government, the Fourteenth Amendment entrusted Congress to enforce those limited-government provisions against the states.

The narrow reading of the privileges or immunities clause of the Fourteenth Amendment in the *Slaughterhouse* cases resulted from the Court's finding that the purpose of the Amendment was to protect African Americans.[110] In seeking to overturn a Louisiana law restricting the slaughtering of meat in New Orleans to a single location, the opponents of this state-granted monopoly sought to use the Fourteenth Amendment to overturn the laws of the Reconstruction legislature. But the Court rejected these arguments and stated that the Fourteenth Amendment had to be interpreted in light of its primary purpose of ending racial discrimination.[111] As the *Slaughterhouse* Court recognized, if the federal government had plenary power to enact laws that could remedy state failures to protect fundamental civil rights, then federalism would come to an end.[112] According to the Court, the purpose of the Fourteenth Amendment was to end racial oppression and discrimination, not to radically alter the scheme of federalism in the Constitution.[113] Thus, the Court signaled that the principles underlying the Ninth and Tenth Amendments had not been repealed, and that the Reconstruction amendments had to be reconciled with the original Constitution.

6

The Free Speech Clause as a
Limited-Government Provision

The Protection of Rights That Limit Government

The natural-rights or individual-autonomy model is perhaps most often applied to the speech and religion freedoms stated in the First Amendment. For this reason, the First Amendment will be the focus of analysis concerning the applicability of the limited-government model. If this model cannot be applied to the First Amendment, it cannot be a workable model for the Bill of Rights in general.

Scholars and judges have looked for an organizing principle or a single theory that coherently explains which speech gets First Amendment protection and which speech does not. But no single theory explaining the First Amendment's coverage has yet been found or accepted. Neither the individual-autonomy view, the democratic-deliberation model, nor the search-for-truth theory has provided that single consistent model. None of these theories individually have been able to provide an adequate account of the boundaries and purposes of the First Amendment.

The judicial application of the First Amendment must rest on some model or understanding of why the First Amendment appears in the Constitution and what its function is. One theory is that the First Amendment directly seeks to limit the power of government, and in doing so to give a certain freedom to individuals in their speech activities, which in turn can function to maintain citizen control over government. The limited-government model tries to capture this concern. It does not put primary or exclusive emphasis on individual autonomy; but individual autonomy is definitely a side effect of limited government.

Even though the First Amendment reflects eighteenth-century notions of the natural rights of speech and religious freedoms, the role it serves in the Constitution is to work as a limit on government power and not as a constitutional guarantee of a certain vision of individual autonomy. The First Amendment begins with the words "Congress shall make no law . . . " This language affirms the rule of limited government. In this respect, the First Amendment does not express an individual right based on personal autonomy, but rather a structural provision denying power to the federal government. Indeed, it was Justice Oliver Wendell Holmes Jr.'s dissent in *Abrams v. U.S.*—a dissent that emphasized the limits rather than the scope or nature of government power—that prompted the modern development of the First Amendment.

That the First Amendment is not primarily concerned with or directed to personal autonomy is also demonstrated by all the types of speech not protected—e.g., perjury, solicitation to crime, false advertising, conspiracy speech, agreements in restraint of trade, copyright or trademark infringements, fraud, sexual harassment, nude dancing, speech subject to privacy and defamation torts, etc. Moreover, if the First Amendment primarily served the value of individual autonomy, it would not protect the speech rights of corporations. However, in *Citizens United v. Federal Election Commission,* the Supreme Court held that corporate speech (at least on political matters) is as fully protected by the First Amendment as speech by natural persons.[1] Indeed, by suggesting that great harm to First Amendment rights would occur if speech rights were "confined to individuals," Chief Justice John Roberts indicated that the First Amendment should be read as a limited-government provision.[2]

In *Broadrick v. Oklahoma,*[3] the Court upheld a statute limiting the rights of state employees to participate in partisan campaigning. Clearly such a statute infringed upon the individual-autonomy interests of state employees wishing to engage in such political activity. Under the limited-government model, however, the statute can be seen as serving to limit the power of government by prohibiting the employees of state government to engage in political acts that would further solidify or expand the power of that government.

The limited-government model suggests that the First Amendment limits government from infringing into the area of communicative speech because a democracy's ability to control and limit its government depends on a free and open political dialogue. The speech and press clauses are structural provisions insofar as they serve to safeguard the power of a democratic people against "a possibly unrepresentative and self-interested Congress."[4] The First Amendment prohibits government actions that unduly restrict open participation in the public dialogue that precedes public opinion, which in turn forms the foundation of government in a democratic state. Because the people are the ultimate sovereign in a democratic society, government may not regulate the public's speech on the grounds that such speech will lead the people to make unwise social policy decisions. Free speech plays an important role in a democratic society—that of allowing local majorities to form opinions and alliances that can control and limit the actions of government.[5] As Amar notes, the First Amendment is a federalism provision aimed at trying to achieve local control of a more distant central government.[6]

According to Ralph Ketcham in *Framed for Posterity,* James Madison intended in the First Amendment to protect the public's right to gather together and engage in the kind of debate and dialogue characteristic of self-government, not to protect strictly personal rights.[7] As Ketcham explains, the freedoms of speech and press can only be understood within the larger process of self-government.[8] The First Amendment and indeed all of the amendments in the Bill of Rights are to be seen as an essential part of the proper functioning of self-government and of the ability of society and individuals to control and limit government. Even though the First Amendment protections are valuable in their effect on private rights, they are even more important as essential contributions to the process of self-government.[9] As Robert Goldwin argues in *From Parchment to Power,* the supporters of both the Constitution and the Bill of Rights thought that individual rights were best secured by preventing a concentration of political power. Therefore, the whole purpose and intent behind the Bill of Rights was to effect the structure of government, not to specifically define substantive individual rights and delineate how government had to protect those rights.

The use of freedom of speech in limiting government is illustrated in *Cato's Letters.* For Cato, freedom of speech played an important political function in allowing the people, who were the ultimate sovereignty, the ability to supervise and check the actions of government.[10] This role of free speech in limiting government can also be seen through First Amendment case law.

In *Capital Square Review and Advisory Bd. v. Pinette,* the Court upheld the right of a private group to place a cross on public property.[11] In *Widmar v. Vincent,* the Court held that a state university policy encouraging the use of its facilities by student organizations, but prohibiting any use "for purposes of religious worship or religious teaching," violated the free speech clause.[12] The Court later held that a policy permitting community use of school facilities for "social, civic, or recreational uses," but not for "religious purposes," constituted viewpoint discrimination.[13] According to the Court, denying access to school facilities solely because the group discussed otherwise permissible subject matters from a religious viewpoint violated the free speech clause.[14] These cases demonstrate that the First Amendment limits government from denying public speech venues to discriminatorily chosen types of speech that form the bedrock of society and culture—speech that leads to and controls government.

In *Martin v. City of Struthers,* the Court struck down a local ordinance forbidding door-to-door leafleting. The Court stated that freedom to distribute information to every citizen, wherever he desires to receive it, is so clearly vital to the preservation of a free society that it must be protected. Under the limited-government model, such a ban is overbroad and threatens to completely stamp out a means of criticizing or informing government. However, in *Members of the City Council of the City of Los Angeles v. Taxpayers for Vincent,* the Court found that a municipal ordinance prohibiting the posting of signs on public property was not unconstitutional as applied to the context of political campaigns. Although recognizing that the ordinance decreased the total amount of speech, the Court did not see a First Amendment problem. The Court argued that the public interest supported the ordinance, especially the City's interests in maintaining its aesthetic appeal and preserving the safety of workers who would have to remove the signs. The focus of the ordinance was on clutter and safety—legitimate government concerns—not on squelching political speech within the community.[15] Therefore, the ordinance did not violate the First Amendment because it did not jeopardize the limited-government principle, especially since any political signs could still be posted in the vastly larger private-property sector.

The issue in *Denver Area Educational Telecommunications Consortium, Inc. v. FCC* involved the constitutionality of regulations in the Cable Act of 1992 requiring cable operators to place indecent programs on a separate channel, to block that channel, and to unblock it within thirty days of a subscriber's written request for access.[16] In holding these regulations unconstitutional, the Supreme Court was concerned with inconveniences and burdens to would-be viewers of indecent programming, including, for instance, the viewer who might want a single show as opposed to the entire channel, or the viewer who might want to choose a channel without any advance planning (the "surfer"), or the one who worries about the danger to his reputation that might result if he makes a written request to subscribe to the channel. However, none of these burdens presented insurmountable obstacles, nor did they amount to a complete ban on the subject programming. Each of these types of viewers could get access to the desired programming by simply following the established procedures. Furthermore, even though the Court recognized that the purpose of the regulations was to protect minors, that it was a compelling purpose, and that the regulations only applied to sexual material (and not to important political information), the Court still struck them down, focusing exclusively on the burdensome impact on the programming available to adults. The Court followed this principle even though, in terms of relative burdens, it may be easier for adults to access indecent material than it is for parents to avoid their children's exposure to it.

The decision in *Denver Area* reflected an individual-autonomy model of the First Amendment, as it sought to uphold the interests of the producers and consumers of indecent programming. Under the limited-government model, however, these regulations could have been upheld. There was no violation of limited government, since the subject speech had never been banned. The speech at issue had nothing to do with the scope or control of government. And there was still complete freedom of the citizenry to criticize the access regulations and to campaign for their elimination or modification.

Reflecting a limited-government approach, the D.C. Circuit, in *Action for Children's Television v. FCC*, upheld the "safe harbor" provisions of the Public Telecommunications Act of 1992 permitting indecent broadcasts only between 10 p.m. and 6 a.m.[17] The time-channeling regulations did not invoke a limited-government concern, since they involved speech not pertinent to the democratic control of government, nor did the regulations have a banning effect on the subject speech. In its ruling, the court found that those people who wished to view indecent programming would "have no difficulty in doing so through the use of subscription and pay-per-view cable channels, delayed-access viewing using VCR equipment, and the rental or purchase of readily available audio and video cassettes."[18] The court also concluded that the time-channeling rule for indecent broadcasts did not "unnecessarily interfere with the ability of adults to watch or listen to such materials both because [adults] are active after midnight and . . . have so many alternative ways of satisfying their tastes at other times."[19]

Safe harbor regulations are consistent with the ruling in *Crawford v. Lungren*, where the Ninth Circuit upheld a statute restricting the ways in which sexually oriented print material could be distributed, so as to prevent exposure of it to minors.[20] The court found no constitutional violation with a statute banning the sale of such "harmful material" from unsupervised sidewalk vending machines.[21] Again, the speech materials were not completely banned and were not related to the public's ability to limit or control government. Nor did the regulations affect an individual's or society's ability to limit government, since the subject speech was still available to adults and was not relevant to the process of political self-government.

Courts have implicitly approved a limited-government approach by upholding statutes that restrict speech in one venue while leaving open alternative channels of communication.[22] By leaving alternative channels of communication open to the subject speech, the government has not banned the speech and has not prevented the speech from limiting and controlling government. In *Hill v. Colorado*,[23] for instance, the Supreme Court upheld a "buffer zone" regulation restricting the speech rights of abortion protestors, finding that the only restricted avenue of communication was face-to-face dialogue and that the regulation left open ample alternative channels of communication. Similarly, in *Schenck v. Pro-Choice Network*, the Court noted that although speakers had to keep a distance from their intended audience, they remained "free to espouse their message" in various ways from that greater distance.[24] Through cases like *Hill* and *Schenck*, the Court seems to be saying that what is important is that the potential of communicative interchange be preserved between speakers and willing listeners. Thus, speech restrictions on certain types of speech are valid if willing listeners can still seek out and obtain the speech through an alternative channel.[25] It can be argued that the First Amendment limits the government from preventing a speaker from having access to a venue or medium of communication. But to be free, nonpolitical speech does not have to be completely uninhibited in all venues or forums.

The availability of alternative channels of communication is a vital element for the sustainability of time-manner-place regulations that serve a significant governmental interest.[26] Such regulations are needed for government to manage public order, and yet they do not jeopardize the limited-government principle because they leave open ample alternative channels for communication. Nonetheless, they may very well frustrate or infringe on personal autonomy, since the regulations do dictate how and when speech activities are to be conducted.

Content-neutral regulations, as long as they leave alternative channels of communication, are permissible even if those regulations have "an incidental effect on some speakers or messages."[27] But those "incidental effects" clearly restrict the personal autonomy of the individuals affected. In *Ward v. Rock Against Racism*, the Court upheld a regulation requiring performers to use a certain sound-amplifica-tion system and sound technician provided by the City.[28] In *Madsen v. Women's Health Center*, the Court upheld time-manner-place restrictions on abortion pro-testors demonstrating at abortion clinics.[29]

Court opinions upholding certain restrictions on certain new media technolo-gies can also be explained with the limited-government model. Such restrictions do not serve to expand the power of government, but simply to give more power to those who wish to be free of such speech.[30] Both the Second and Ninth Circuits, for instance, have sustained restrictions on access to dial-a-porn services, finding that these restrictions are necessary to protect the children of parents who did not wish them to hear this particular kind of speech.[31] These restrictions—e.g., requiring telephone companies to block all access to dial-a-porn services unless telephone subscribers submit written requests to unblock them—were enacted in response to an earlier Supreme Court decision striking down a complete ban on dial-a-porn services.[32] Thus, an important factor leading the Second and Ninth Circuits to rule as they did was the fact that the restrictions did not amount to a complete ban on the indecent speech, but merely shifted the burdens of accessing such speech.

In *Bland v. Fessler*, the court upheld a restriction on telemarketers' use of auto-matic dialing and announcing devices (ADADs).[33] It ruled that ADADs were much more disruptive than door-to-door solicitors and "more of a nuisance and a greater invasion of privacy than telemarketing with live operators."[34] The court then held that the regulation at issue did not amount to an absolute ban on speech, since the use of ADADs was permitted so long as the called party consented to the message (although it is difficult to imagine that many people would ever so consent). The court also found that a do-not-call list was not a less restrictive means of accom-plishing the government's objective, since such a list would place the burden on the public to stop disruptive ADAD calls from arriving at their homes. Nor did the court accept the argument that people should be left to themselves to combat ADADs, by turning off their ringers or screening their calls or simply hanging up on the prerecorded calls.[35] In other words, the court did not impose an "averting one's eyes" burden on the recipients of the calls; it did not place all the burden on the recipient to opt out.

The *Bland* decision was not in accordance with the personal-autonomy model, since it obviously infringed on the autonomy interests of telemarketers. But *Bland* can be explained by the limited-government model.

The Limited-Government Model and the Speech Activities of the Press

In *Branzburg v. Hayes*, the Supreme Court declined to grant journalists an abso-lute First Amendment privilege to refuse disclosure of confidential sources to a grand jury investigating criminal behavior.[36] The Court stated that "the preference for anonymity of those confidential informants involved in actual criminal conduct is presumably a product of their desire to escape criminal prosecution," and that such a preference "is hardly deserving of constitutional protection."[37] This refusal to give special privileges to journalists, such as immunity from divulging confidential sources, indicates that the First Amendment is not focused on the special autonomy interests of some individuals or groups—e.g., the press. Moreover, in *Branzburg*, the Court was not convinced that the press needed a special privilege to maintain confidential sources so as to be able to do its job of investigating and checking government. Thus, to the Court, such a right or privilege was not necessary to control or limit the power of government.

Contrary to the journalists' claims, Justice Byron White described as speculative any news-gathering burdens caused by requiring reporters to reveal their confidential sources to grand juries.[38] The Court depicted the relationship between reporters and their sources as "a symbiotic one which is unlikely to be greatly inhibited by the threat of subpoena."[39] Because confidential informants tend to be "members of a minority political or cultural group that relies heavily on the media to propagate its views, publicize its aims, and magnify its exposure to the public," the Court reasoned that subjecting journalists to the subpoena power of grand juries would not have "a significant constriction of the flow of news to the public."[40]

By refusing to grant to the press in *Branzburg* a special right, unavailable to the general public, the Court gave virtually no consideration to any autonomy concerns and how they might be affected by subpoenas. Even though it recognized that the press serves to keep government officials accountable to the voters, the Court found no proof that special privileges under the First Amendment were needed to fulfill this purpose of limiting the power of government. The privilege would not necessarily limit government; it would only enhance the power of the press.

Following *Branzburg*, lower courts used the opinion to support some kind of qualified privilege against compelled disclosure of anonymous sources. The qualified privilege that arose generally employs the three-part test articulated in the *Branzburg* dissent.[41] This test requires that before ordering the disclosure of confidential information, a court must find: (1) that the information sought is clearly relevant; (2) that the information cannot be obtained by alternative means; and (3) that there is a compelling need for the information.[42] This test is basically an application of the limited-government model, inquiring into whether the information is vital to the process of checking government.

Recently, however, the case-law trend has turned against the recognition of a special qualified press privilege of confidentiality.[43] This dismissal of a post-*Branzburg* qualified privilege results from a rejection of autonomy principles that had earlier led to its development. Also rejected has been the perceived connection between the press's ability to serve a governmental watchdog role and its freedom to guarantee confidentiality to sources. Even though acknowledging the public interest in a vigorous and independent press capable of stimulating a robust debate over controversial matters, courts have tended to see no chilling effect as a result of press compliance with subpoenas.[44] Because privileges exist to serve public ends—e.g., limited government—they cannot be justified unless it can be established that they are necessary to achieve that public end. But if subpoenas do not "dry up" sources, then a privilege against those subpoenas will not fulfill any First Amendment goal—e.g., the pursuit of limited government.

In the infamous case of *New York Times Co. v. Sullivan,* the Supreme Court held that defamatory speech appearing in the press about public officials enjoys First Amendment protection, unless that speech is made with knowledge of falsity or a reckless disregard for the truth.[45] By protecting speech concerning public officials, *Sullivan* allows a democratic society to engage in the kind of political speech necessary to control and limit its government. This rule functions to ensure that public debate is "robust and wide-open."[46] It also reflects a variation of the argument asserted unsuccessfully in *Branzburg:* that if the press does not have certain powers or privileges, the flow of important information to the public will dry up—and if that happens, the ability of the citizenry to control and monitor their government will dry up. But the difference between *Sullivan* and *Branzburg* is that the Court found the power or privilege at issue in *Sullivan* to be necessary for the public to control and limit its government, whereas the privilege in *Branzburg* was not.

In applying the *Sullivan* limited-government model, however, the Court has not gone to the extreme, as might be required by the autonomy model, and subjected individuals to the unlimited power of the press. Courts, for instance, have not given such unlimited power to the press so as to completely undermine a libel plaintiff's need to prove his or her case. In *Herbert v. Lando,* the Court ruled against the media's claim that in a libel action the thoughts and editorial processes of the press should be immune from examination.[47] Thus, the Court denied to the press a constitutional privilege regarding the editorial process that would effectively shield from inquiry all internal communications occurring during the editorial process. According to the Court, such a privilege would make it substantially more difficult for individuals to bring a defamation action when their reputations have been damaged by the media.[48] In so ruling, the Court dismissed media arguments that disclosure of editorial conversations would "have an intolerable chilling effect" on freedom of the press.[49]

The limited-government model can also explain the result in *Dun & Bradstreet v. Greenmoss Builders,* where the Supreme Court ruled that in cases involving false statements on matters of purely private concern (or matters of no public concern), non-public-figure plaintiffs may be awarded punitive and presumed damages without a showing of actual malice.[50] This distinction between speech relating to matters of public concern versus speech on matters of purely private concern can be justified by the limited-government model. Speech on matters of purely private concern is not the kind of speech needed to limit government; therefore, it does not warrant the same degree of protection by the First Amendment.

In this same vein, the limited-government theory reveals the reason for the distinction between *New York Times Co. v. Sullivan* and *Gertz v. Robert Welch, Inc.*[51] In the former case, the Court gave more protection to speakers when they utter defamatory statements about public officials. In the latter case, involving an action brought by a private-figure plaintiff, the Court leaned more toward compensating for defamations made about private individuals. This distinction is easy to square with the limited-government model. Under that model, individuals should be freer to criticize public officials, since by doing so they will be able to control and limit the activities of government. However, such a rationale does not exist when defamations are made against private individuals. In that case, government has a more legitimate reason to protect reputation and limit free speech.

Application of the Limited-Government Model

An array of other First Amendment cases reveal the influence and application of the limited-government model. In *Reno v. ACLU,* the Supreme Court granted full First Amendment protection to the Internet.[52] Striking down the Communications Decency Act, on the grounds that it would "confer broad powers of censorship," the Court limited the government from controlling the Internet and kept that medium as a free and open venue of communication, which in turn would provide a check on government.[53] On the other hand, in *Burson v. Freeman,* the Court upheld a restriction against campaign speech within one hundred feet of a polling place.[54] Even though the law restricted speech, and indeed a particular content of speech (although the law obviously left open nearly unlimited alternative channels of communication for the speech), the decision fulfills the goals of the First Amendment, since it serves to limit government by supporting the political process, which in turn helps a democratic society shape and control its government. The speech restrictions, since they affected such an infinitesimally small amount of speech that could be expressed in a political campaign and since they did not preclude any speech from being expressed outside the narrow geographic and temporal boundary, did not affect society's ability to limit its government.

In giving commercial speech a lower level of constitutional protection, the Supreme Court has recognized that such speech is less vital to a democratic society's ability to control and limit its government, since such speech is primarily about economic or consumer transactions occurring within the economic sphere of society.[55] In contrast to political speech, commercial speech occupies a "subordinate position . . . in the scale of First Amendment values."[56] Consequently, commercial speech is not given full constitutional protection.[57]

The argument that commercial speech should not be given full constitutional protection because it causes more harm than does fully protected political speech is made irrelevant by the limited-government model. Under this model, the question is not one of what kind of speech is "better" or "less harmful." Instead, the question is what kind of speech should be insulated from government control because that speech is necessary to the limited-government principle.

The four-part test used to determine the constitutional protection of commercial speech also reflects the limited-government model. Once the first prong is met—that the speech is not false or misleading—the three remaining prongs all relate to the nature of and justification for the government regulation. All the focus is on government power and the use of that power. The regulation must serve and directly advance a substantial governmental interest; and it must be no more extensive than necessary to serve that interest.[58]

In *Gentile v. State Bar of Nevada,* the Supreme Court held that a defense attorney could be punished for conducting a press conference during which the lawyer opines about the innocence of the client and the occurrence of police corruption in a pending case.[59] Although such speech would be protected if made by a private individual or a member of the press, this decision can be explained in terms of the limited-government model. The speech restriction is not one that unduly expands the power of government. Because it functions to maintain the integrity of the trial, it still allows the jury to have ultimate control over the matter. The lawyer may have fewer speech rights, but the protection of the jury right provides sufficient guards against government abuse. Restrictions on lawyers' speech during the pendency of a court action do not infringe on a democratic society's ability to control and limit government. Indeed, a criminal case is supposed to be free from majoritarian control. Moreover, any speech by the lawyer concerning innocence of a client or the occurrence of police corruption can be made within the courtroom, where such speech is the most relevant and has the most impact.

The limited-government aspect of the First Amendment can also be seen in the federal securities laws, which both compel certain disclosures, such as a corporation's financial condition, and restrict speech, such as unapproved proxy solicitations. Although the Supreme Court has not directly addressed the First Amendment ramifications of these regulations, it is generally believed that the free speech clause should not apply to the speech affected by such regulations.[60] Indeed, the speech subject to securities regulation can be restricted because such speech—e.g., fraudulent or misleading speech about a corporation's financial condition—is not necessary to limit the power of government. Since these types of speech relate to the functioning of the nation's capital markets and need to be part of the regulation of those markets, the government is not expanding its power in any way by regulating such speech—in fact, it is performing a legitimate and authorized government function. Regulation of securities speech provides for the effective functioning of the capital markets; it does not diminish a democratic society's ability to control and direct its government. Consequently, the First Amendment should not apply to securities regulations, because such regulations do not unduly expand the power of government such that a democratic public will be less able to control and direct that government.

There are many content-based speech restrictions in the Securities Act of 1933, the Sherman Antitrust Act, the National Labor Relations Act, the Uniform Commercial Code, and countless other areas of statutory and common law. In addition, the government routinely regulates the content of commercial and financial speech through laws against false or misleading advertising and other deceptive business practices. The First Amendment even allows the government to regulate sexually or racially harassing speech in the workplace. Under the limited-government model, such speech restrictions do not pose a problem of government unduly expanding its authority or power. To the contrary, these speech restrictions are part of government's legitimate area of power. Indeed, the most common ways of violating the proxy-solicitation rules of the Securities Act, or the Sherman Act, or the Clayton Act, or the Federal Trade Commission Act is through speech.

Another speech doctrine (involving government control over speech) relating to and supporting a legitimate governmental function is the government speech doctrine. This doctrine states that no First Amendment restraints apply to instances in which the government is speaking on its own behalf, even though that speech may have an adverse or unwelcome effect on individuals who oppose or disagree with it.[61] Thus, with the government speech doctrine, the courts give great deference to the government, ignoring the effects on individual autonomy to those who disagree with or feel harmed by the speech. There is no limited-government concern, since the state has a legitimate role in speaking on its own behalf. (If the government has the power to carry out a program, as it did in *Rust v. Sullivan* with the disbursement of Title X funds, then it also has the power to dictate and shape the speech integral to that program, and hence the power to restrict the speech of the recipients of those funds, even if those restrictions violate the personal beliefs or autonomy of the recipients.) Likewise, there is no limited-government concern with the public employee speech doctrine, which allows the government to regulate the speech activities of its employees acting in the course of their job duties.[62] Again, even though such regulations may obviously violate the individual-autonomy interests of public employees, those regulations are connected with the legitimate power of the government to act as employer and to conduct its proper business.

A limited-government interpretation of the free speech clause is also supported by the Supreme Court's decisions upholding speech-related conditions on government spending programs, even though those conditions obviously interfere with or restrain the personal-autonomy interests of individuals associated with the programs. In *National Endowment for the Arts v. Finely,* for instance, the Court upheld a law enacted because of public outrage over various controversial artists funded by the NEA and requiring the NEA to consider the "general standards of decency" of the American public when awarding grants.[63] And in *U.S. v. American Library Ass'n,* the Court approved a congressional requirement that any library receiving federal funding to provide Internet service had to install filtering software that would protect minors from accessing obscenity or child pornography.[64] Again, despite the adverse effect on the personal-autonomy interests of those patrons wishing unhindered access to the filtered material, the Court upheld the government's ability to "define the limits of a program" it has funded and to insist that "public funds be spent for the purposes for which they were authorized."[65]

The applicability of a limited-government model of the free speech clause can be seen through a comparison of the Supreme Court's opposing approaches in *Dennis v. U.S.* (1951), which upheld Smith Act convictions of U.S. Communist Party leaders for advocating communist revolution, and *Brandenburg v. Ohio* (1969), which invalidated convictions under Ohio's criminal syndicalism statute. Even though *Brandenburg* appeared to craft a new test, conferring First Amendment protection to all speech short of advocacy of law violation directed to inciting imminent lawless action and likely to produce that action, the Court nonetheless described this standard similarly to the one in *Dennis*. But perhaps what explains the opposite results in the two cases is the fact that the justices in *Dennis* had concluded that communist advocacy did indeed threaten the survival of constitutional democracy in the United States, whereas in *Brandenburg* the justices did not see that the speech and activities of a member of the Ku Klux Klan could ever have such an effect. The focus of the Court was not on the personal-autonomy interests or natural rights of the Communists or Ku Klux Klan members, but on the functioning and survival of democratic government. The focus was on the boundaries of what acts a limited government could take to protect itself.

The focus on government and political stability was also apparent in *Timmons v. Twin Cities Area New Party*, where the Court upheld Minnesota's ban of fusion candidacies, through which minor parties could themselves nominate a major party candidate whose name would then appear on the ballot lines of both the major and minor parties. According to the Court, the states' "strong interest in the stability of their political systems" overrode any First Amendment challenge by minor parties.[66] The concern was not with the autonomy interests of candidates or minor parties, but with the rightful bounds of government power exerted to maintain its own stability and integrity.

Government power and the use of that power lie at the heart of the Supreme Court's tiered approach for dealing with most speech-clause issues. The strict-scrutiny approach, used with content-based regulations, requires a compelling state interest; the intermediate-scrutiny test, on the other hand, requires a substantial or important state interest. But under either approach, the focus is on the government, not on the nature or fulfillment of individual autonomy.

The applicability of the limited-government model can also be seen in decisions like *NBC v. United States* and *Red Lion Broadcasting Co. v. FCC*, where the Court gave to the broadcast industry a lesser degree of First Amendment protection, thus allowing a greater range of structural and content regulations to be imposed on it. In *Red Lion Broadcasting Co. v. FCC*, the Court upheld the Fairness Doctrine against a First Amendment challenge.[67] In *CBS Inc. v. Federal Communications Commission*, the Court rejected a First Amendment challenge to Congress's mandate that broadcasters sell airtime to political candidates.[68] And in *NBC v. United*

States, the Court upheld the FCC's chain broadcasting regulations, which barred certain relationships between broadcast licensees and networks as contrary to the public interest.[69] In these decisions, the Court was concerned with limiting the monopolistic power of broadcasters; the Court did not see the regulations as overly expanding the power of government, but as limiting the power of inherent monopolistic industries.

In *Arkansas Educational Television Commission v. Forbes,*[70] the Court sustained a public broadcaster's decision to exclude an independent candidate for Congress from a televised debate. This holding went against the individual-autonomy interests of the candidate, who brought a First Amendment challenge to his exclusion. Instead, it focused on the ability of a debate sponsor to organize a meaningful and effective debate, which in turn better allows the public to make informed political decisions, which in turn serve to control and direct the government.

The tort of disclosure of private information, which penalizes the public dissemination of non-newsworthy personal information that most people would consider highly private, is another example of the limited-government model, insofar as it allows some speech regulation when that regulation poses no danger of the expansion of government power. In *Diaz v. Oakland Tribune,* for instance, the plaintiff sued the defendant for publishing the fact that she was a transsexual. The Court of Appeals allowed the lawsuit to go forward, finding that the plaintiff's transsexuality was not newsworthy. Again, this restriction on the speech rights of the newspaper was not aimed at expanding government power, but at vindicating the privacy rights of a private individual.

Likewise, in *Briscoe v. Readers Digest Association,* the defendant was held liable for revealing that Briscoe had eleven years earlier been convicted of armed robbery. The Court held that the revelation of Briscoe's identity eleven years after his crime served no public purpose and that there was no longer any legitimate public interest in the story—hence, the speech at issue held no limited-government function. Similarly, in *Cohen v. Cowles Media,* the speech rights of editors were restricted not for the goal of expanding government but for the goal of enforcing the contract rights of a private individual who had given his story to a reporter in return for a promise of confidentiality.

Political Speech and the Limited-Government Model

The limited-government model suggests that political speech should be given the highest First Amendment protections. This is because free political speech is needed to maintain democratic control of government. As long as a democratic society has the freedom to engage in open and uninhibited political speech, that society is able to direct, control, and alter the course of its government. But if any laws infringe on political speech, those laws essentially enlarge the power of government by making it less amenable to change by a democratic society. As Justice

William Douglas explained in *Terminiello v. City of Chicago,* "[I]t is only through free debate and free exchange of ideas that government remains responsive to the will of the people."[71]

Under the limited-government model, the First Amendment gives its primary and highest protection to that speech that is vital in sustaining self-government. According to this theory, the role of free speech in the process of self-government provides the only compelling justification for the constitutional protection of speech. Alexander Meiklejohn was an early advocate of this self-governance value of free speech.[72] Although Meiklejohn advocated an absolute protection of free speech, he limited that protection to political speech—e.g., speech necessary for the conduct of self-government.[73] Meiklejohn defined political speech as "speech which bears, directly or indirectly, upon issues with which voters have to deal."[74] Essentially, Meiklejohn took a Madisonian view of the First Amendment, seeing its protections as existing primarily to serve democratic processes.[75] Meiklejohn argued that since "self-governance is the *whole point*" of the American constitutional scheme, then "*freedom of speech* must be defined in 'relation to self-governance.'"[76] Meiklejohn sought not to protect the marketplace of ideas, but to protect only a certain kind of speech—that kind of speech that is relevant to democratic processes.

A number of legal scholars have adopted at least a form of Meiklejohn's political speech theory.[77] According to Lillian BeVier, for instance, "[T]he sole legitimate First Amendment principle protects only speech that participates in the process of representative democracy."[78] Moreover, on numerous occasions, the Supreme Court has opined on the role of political speech within the First Amendment. In *Burson v. Freeman,* the Court stated that the First Amendment serves primarily "to protect the free discussion of governmental affairs."[79] According to the Court in *FCC v. League of Women Voters,* political speech occupies the "highest rung" of constitutional concerns and is the "most protected" by the First Amendment."[80] The Court in *Buckley v. Valeo* stated that "the First Amendment affords the broadest protection to such political expression."[81] In *Mills v. Alabama,* the Court wrote that "a major purpose of the First Amendment was to protect the free discussion of governmental affairs."[82] And yet, even though "the Supreme Court has repeatedly emphasized the importance of political speech," it has never ruled that to qualify for high levels of constitutional protection the speech at issue must relate to self-government.[83]

The First Amendment's focus on political speech fits into the limited-government model of the Bill of Rights. Political speech receives highest protection under the First Amendment because such speech directly relates to the conduct of democratic self-government, and it is within the process of self-government that democratic society can control and limit the power of its government. Laws impacting or restricting political speech can hobble the individual's or the public's ability to control or limit government. For instance, a law imposing a special tax on the paper and ink used by certain newspapers may very well restrict the flow of political speech by penalizing newspapers that criticize the government.[84] On the other hand, speech on matters of merely private concern is not the kind of speech needed to limit government; therefore, it does not receive as high a protection from the First Amendment.

An example of nonpolitical speech appears in *United States v. Playboy Entertainment Group,* where the Supreme Court overturned regulations in the Telecommunications Act of 1996, requiring cable channels "primarily dedicated to sexually-oriented programming," like the Playboy Channel, to limit their programming transmission to the late-night hours of 10:00 p.m. to 6:00 a.m., when children are unlikely to be among the viewing audience.[85] Prior to this law, sexually explicit cable operators had used signal scrambling as a means of limiting programming access to their subscribing customers. But this scrambling had proven ineffective, often leading to signal bleed, which allowed nonpaying viewers, including children, to hear and see the sexually explicit programming.[86] Although recognizing the public interest in shielding children from such programming, the Court nonetheless struck down the law on the grounds that it was too burdensome on adult viewers.[87]

In reaching its decision, the *Playboy* Court more or less assumed that a less restrictive alternative was available to parents who wished to keep their children from watching indecent programming. This alternative required that the objecting parent request her cable operator to block any channel she did not wish to receive. For this alternative to work, however, the cable operator would have to provide "adequate notice" to their subscribers that certain channels would broadcast sexually oriented programming, that signal bleed may occur, that children may then see portions of the programming, and that parents should contact the cable operator to request a channel-blocking device.[88] This notice, apparently, would be provided as an insert in the monthly cable bills.

In dissent, Justice Stephen Breyer argued that the law simply placed a manageable burden on sexually explicit cable programming, not a ban.[89] According to Breyer, "[A]dults may continue to watch adult channels, though less conveniently, by watching at night, recording programs with a VCR, or by subscribing to digital cable with better blocking systems."[90] He argued that the law applied only to programming involving "virtually 100% sexually-explicit material." And finally, Breyer noted that due to signal bleed almost 29 million children each year were exposed to sexually explicit cable programming.

According to Breyer, where tens of millions of children have no parents at home after school, and where children may spend afternoons and evenings watching television outside of the home with friends, the time-channeling law offered "independent protection for a large number of families."[91] Given the compelling interest of child protection at issue, Breyer concluded that the majority's proposed alternative was not at all an effective one. In support of this conclusion, he cited evidence reflecting all the problems people had experienced in trying to get their cable operators to block certain channels. Moreover, Breyer pointed out, the programming involved in *Playboy* was not the kind of speech on which the First Amendment should confer its highest protections.

In *Playboy*, the requirement that cable purveyors of sexually explicit material confine their programming to nighttime hours, when young children would least likely be watching television, had no real impact on the public's structural ability to limit government. Unlike the newsprint and ink tax case, which affected the ways in which individuals could engage in political speech, *Playboy* dealt only with scheduling issues surrounding when certain commercial cable vendors of sexually explicit material could transmit their programming. Thus, under the limited-government model, *Playboy* could have been decided differently.

The argument that political speech lies at the heart of the First Amendment is based on both original intent and constitutional logic. Not only was political debate vital to the American crusade for independence, but in the late eighteenth century, political speech was the primary kind of speech existing in the public domain. The vast majority of newspaper and pamphlet content was devoted to political subjects. Thus, it can be argued that when the framers decided to protect the public expression of speech, they obviously intended to protect the kind of speech that had traditionally been publicly expressed. Even aside from this original intent, however, constitutional logic dictates that the indispensable role of political speech in sustaining self-government provides the only compelling rationale for the free speech clause.

Despite its prominence in modern free speech theory, individual self-actualization or autonomy cannot provide a sound basis for the First Amendment, especially since this rationale can apply to nonspeech activities as much as it can to speech. For instance, individual autonomy and self-fulfillment can just as easily result from winning a game or succeeding at a hobby or even enjoying a meal. Self-fulfillment and self-realization are not uniquely characterized by speech; they can be accomplished "through virtually all voluntary conduct, including one's choice of profession, dress, and consumer goods."[92] Furthermore, there is absolutely no evidence that the framers of the First Amendment were at all concerned with self-realization. Nor is it clear that self-realization is even something to be constitutionally desired. To some people, the achievement of self-realization may come through ways that are damaging to society or other individuals. Indeed, self-realization may mean "nothing more than a glorification of self-gratification or social irresponsibility."[93]

The fact that there are many areas of speech that are not protected by the First Amendment tends to support the theory that the First Amendment is not aimed at preserving individual autonomy. If it were, then defamation, fighting words, advocacy of illegal conduct, and obscene speech would be protected. Further supporting the argument that political speech was the only type of speech believed to warrant high constitutional protection is the fact that following ratification of the First Amendment there were no attempts to challenge or question such speech restrictions as those contained in theatrical licensing acts. Theater productions or entertainment speech were not seen to be protected speech. There was no serious discussion in the eighteenth or nineteenth century suggesting that theater and popular entertainment were worthy of the same type of protection as political speech.[94]

In *Citizens United*, Justice Anthony Kennedy noted that "at the founding, speech was open, comprehensive, and vital to society's definition of itself; there were no limits on the sources of speech and knowledge."[95] But this statement is true only if it is confined to political speech, since at the time of adoption of the First Amendment "blasphemy was illegal in every state, and prohibitions against other forms of undesirable speech, such as pornography or other lewd material, was entirely unprotected."[96]

Opponents of the "political speech" interpretation of the First Amendment argue that it gives insufficient protection to various kinds of nonpolitical, "low-value" speech. And yet, whenever these opponents argue against any restrictions on, for instance, graphically violent video entertainment programming or sexually explicit television entertainment programming, they cite as their justification the need to protect controversial and unpopular political speech. They rarely argue that violent and sexually explicit entertainment should be protected for its own sake. Therefore, why not codify this position into First Amendment doctrine? Why not specifically state that all controversial and unpopular political speech is indeed fully protected by the First Amendment, but that all nonpolitical speech is subject to a lower standard of scrutiny?

The failure of the Supreme Court to make any distinctions in the type of speech protected by the First Amendment was evident in the case of *United States v. Stevens*. In *Stevens*, the Court overturned the defendant's conviction for violating a statute prohibiting depictions of animal cruelty, where the defendant was accused of selling videos of animals fighting. Even though the Court recognized that there are some types of speech of such slight social value, such as obscenity and fighting words, that they do not qualify for First Amendment protection, the Court also recognized that there was no existing test that could be applied as a general matter to determine whether certain speech was protected or not protected. The Court was unwilling to expand certain historically unprotected categories of speech or to consider including depictions of animal cruelty in any of the existing categories. However, the limited-government model would create a framework for the Court to determine whether speech regulations were constitutional without determining the exact nature or social value of each type of speech, or whether it fit into an existing category of unprotected speech.

Given the rapidly increasing volume and diversity of modern media entertainment speech, distinctions between high-value political speech and low-value nonpolitical speech are becoming vital. Without singling out political speech from the vast sea of entertainment speech, the danger is that the public and the courts will lose sight of the unique and special needs of the former, as illustrated in the way time-manner-place regulations have been allowed to impact political speech more than nonpolitical media entertainment speech.

Unquestionably, the task of defining political speech is a daunting one. But as difficult a task as it is, the job of clarifying the parameters and characteristics of the kind of speech protected by the First Amendment is a job that needs to be done, especially as the amount of "speech" in our media society increases exponentially.[97] The mere difficulty of the task is no reason to abandon it.[98] Furthermore, the temptation is to define it too broadly, so as to leave room for any and all contingencies, but this temptation must be avoided.

Political speech is that speech having a reasoned, cognitive connection to some identifiable political issue that has the potential of entering the legislative arena.[99] It is speech capable of being logically debated, and speech expressed in a form that can lead to some level of rational debate.[100] It must be an expression of ideas, speech whose purpose is to contribute to a public debate, not to be bought and sold as a mere entertainment commodity having little or no connection to the democratic dialogue and bought primarily for its special effects or its maker's celebrity persona.[101]

Political speech must be communicated "for its expressive content" and for injecting an idea into the marketplace of ideas.[102] Pornography, on the other hand, is not communicated for the purpose of injecting an argument into the marketplace of ideas; it is merely "a tool for sexually arousing people."[103] Moreover, pornography is private rather than public in nature; its purpose "is not to contribute to political, social, and cultural debate, but to stimulate or fulfill the sexual desires of individuals."[104]

Judge Robert Bork once went so far as to argue that the First Amendment should be limited to protecting only explicitly political speech.[105] He wrote that freedom of speech for literature, for instance, would depend not on constitutional mandates but upon the "enlightenment of society and its elected representatives."[106] This is not as harsh a view as it might first seem. For instance, even if a book were banned because it had no First Amendment protection, there would be full constitutional protection for any protest that arose over that decision. In other words, while the book itself might not constitute political speech covered by the First Amendment, any protest over a book-banning law would certainly be protected speech.[107] The advantage of the Bork approach is that it gives communities the flexibility to deal with troublesome media like violent video games, whereas the everything-is-protected approach of existing First Amendment jurisprudence has helped dull society's duty to make judgments about the state of civilized discourse in the public arena.[108]

In The Constitutionalist, George Anastaplo also argues that the First Amendment applies only to political speech, or speech having to do with the duties and concerns of self-governing citizens.[109] According to Anastaplo, the First Amendment was based upon the principle that the American citizen should be free to criticize his government whenever he believes that the government has acted improperly.[110] Not only does the First Amendment protect the right of citizens to criticize their government whenever it steps beyond its limited powers, but according to Anastaplo the First Amendment also stands as a barrier to an overbroad application of the necessary and proper clause.[111]

The identity crisis of the First Amendment today is not the result of any constitutional deficiency or inadequacy of vision on the part of the framers; instead, the crisis is a result of all the cultural concerns that have been attached to the free speech clause.[112] The self-realization movement has demanded freedom for whatever expressive conduct individuals wish to display—and the crusade for the breakdown of traditional sexual restraints or behavioral standards has injected into the public domain a type of speech that, prior to the 1960s, had never been there before. It is movements such as these that have helped erode the long-standing distinction between protected political speech and other types of "private" or non-political speech.

The limited-government rationale for free speech is the only rationale that is specifically provided for in the Constitution, since the entire Constitution is focused on the limited-government doctrine. The Constitution is not concerned with individual autonomy. This is a value that has been derived outside of the Constitution.

Other Free Speech Theories

Courts and scholars have articulated a number of theories regarding the First Amendment and justifying freedom of speech. All of these theories argue that free speech serves some larger goal beyond simply that of individuals' having no restrictions on their speech activities or expressions. The Supreme Court has often oscillated between two or more of these theories, and this inconsistency among theories has often led to confusions and inconsistencies in the Court's First Amendment jurisprudence. The limited-government model would replace all these different theories regarding the various values of free speech with one incorporating the value of limited government.

One theory underlying the First Amendment speech protections involves the search for truth. Zechariah Chafee Jr., in his 1920 book *Freedom of Speech*, wrote that free speech is needed because it facilitates a search for truth through the marketplace of ideas. By separating the meaning of free speech from any reliance on individual autonomy, Chafee attached it to a larger social interest—namely, the achievement of social truth through a marketplace of ideas. Justice Oliver Wendell Holmes Jr. adopted this theory in his dissent in *Abrams v. U.S.*, suggesting that the free trade in ideas, rather than any fulfillment of individual freedom, constitutes the ultimate goal of the First Amendment.[113] Thus, both Chafee and Holmes wanted to rest the protection of free speech on something broader than mere individual autonomy.

According to the marketplace-of-ideas metaphor, free speech needs to be protected because only through free speech can society discover the kind of truth it needs to govern itself. However, as history has shown, the marketplace of ideas does not always produce the truth. In fact, the strongest opinions in the marketplace of ideas often can be the most false or destructive. Moreover, the attainment of truth is usually not empirically verifiable, so the actual workings and success of the marketplace of ideas model is uncertain. The marketplace theory does not care about the content of speech, because it assumes that a process of robust debate will lead to the discovery of truth. However, because of the realities of the modern media, the process does not always work like this. There are many areas of market failure. Hence, the marketplace of ideas may provide a weak justification for the First Amendment.

A somewhat similar justification for free speech is the democratic participation value. According to this value or theory, free speech is needed in a democracy because it creates opportunities for citizens to participate in the democratic process. Justice Louis Brandeis's concurring opinion in the 1927 case of *Whitney v. California* is often seen as the articulation of the self-governance rationale theory of the First Amendment.[114] Justice Brandeis argued that free speech fosters public discussion and promotes self-governance in a democratic society. The goal of free speech protections under this theory is that of facilitating and maximizing participation in the public dialogue, which in turn facilitates participation in the political process. Reflecting this view of free speech as an essential component of democratic participation, the Supreme Court in *Schneider v. Irvington* characterized freedom of speech as one of those activities or liberties vital to the maintenance of democratic institutions. But even though a diversity of speakers and viewpoints may be valuable to a democracy, such diversity is not mandated by the Constitution; nor are there any guidelines set out in the Constitution regarding the achievement of this diversity of speakers. And even though diversity of viewpoints and political participation are values and result from free speech, the constitutional recognition and protection of diversity and democratic participation are more directly found in constitutional provisions other than the First Amendment.

Chafee, Holmes, and Brandeis all argued that free speech should be protected not as a matter of an individual natural right, but rather because it is instrumentally valuable in the democratic process and the discovery of truth. Indeed, all theories and justification of free speech, except for the individual-autonomy justification, see the protection of speech as instrumentally valuable to serve certain political purposes of importance in a democratic society. In other words, free speech is protected because of some larger common good, aside from whatever role it plays in fulfilling individual autonomy. In *Bartnicki v. Vopper,* where the Supreme Court struck down a statute that prohibited the intentional or knowing disclosure of the contents of illegally intercepted electronic communications, as applied to a radio station's broadcasts of threats made by a teacher's union leader, the Court concluded that privacy concerns of the individual should give way when balanced against the interest in publishing matters of public importance. Under this logic, the First Amendment downplays individual-autonomy interests when larger matters of self-government are involved. Thus, the First Amendment is not about individual natural rights or fundamental rights, but about the larger conduct of democratic government. What the First Amendment focuses on is preventing unlimited government, and providing the means of limiting government authority and activity.

Over the past three or four decades, the individual-autonomy model has provided an important mode of analysis in First Amendment cases.[115] As Justice Anthony Kennedy has declared, "At the heart of the First Amendment lies the principle that each person should decide for himself or herself the ideas and beliefs deserving of expression, consideration, and adherence."[116] But this individual-autonomy theory can be hard to define. For instance, does free speech focus on the autonomy of the speaker or of the listener? Depending on where the autonomy is focused, we can get different rules for free speech. Moreover, the autonomy of the listener may conflict with the autonomy of the speaker, since the listener may not want to receive or hear information that the speaker wishes to convey. In addition, since the individual-autonomy theory relates to the subjective feelings of an individual concerning his or her autonomy, it is impossible to determine which speech maximizes individual growth and fulfillment. In his *Commentaries on the Constitution of the United States,* Joseph Story characterized the claim that the First Amendment was intended to secure to every citizen an absolute right to speak whatever he might please without any responsibility as a supposition too wild to be indulged by any rational man.

The individual-autonomy theory argues that free speech is valuable because it serves the goals of self-realization and self-fulfillment, but the theory fails to explain why speech activities are particularly conducive to self-realization or self-fulfillment. Moreover, as Martin Redish argues, a constitutional commitment to the development of individual powers and abilities, or to the individual's control of his or her own destiny through making life-affecting decisions, is inconsistent with the entire concept of unprotected speech, such as obscenity and fighting words.[117]

Thomas Emerson is often associated with the self-fulfillment rationale for protecting speech. In *The System of Freedom of Expression,* Emerson declared that "the proper end of man is the realization of his character and potentialities as a human being."[118] To Emerson, free speech was one way to realize those potentialities. Unlike Chafee, who argued that the social interests in the search for truth were a more important rationale than the individual interests in expression for the protection of free speech, Emerson argued that freedom of expression is an essential means of attaining individual self-fulfillment.

A problem with the individual-autonomy model of the First Amendment is one of deciding how to balance various individual fundamental rights. For instance, we may see free speech as a natural, fundamental right; but how do we apply a free speech doctrine when the speech rights of one individual conflict with the fundamental privacy rights and reputation of another individual? Another problem occurs when the speech rights of one person—e.g., a labor picketer—conflict with the fundamental property right of another person—an employer. Generally, the Supreme Court has reconciled this dilemma by upholding the use of injunctions against boycotts and other types of speech harmful to property owners. In *Gompers v. Buck's Stove and Range Co.,*[119] for instance, the Supreme Court sustained an injunction against Samuel Gompers, the president of the American Federation of

Labor, preventing him from organizing a boycott of the plaintiff's business and from publishing its name on a list of employers labeled with the descriptions "Unfair" and "We Don't Patronize." This injunction was upheld on the basis of a finding that the boycott would cause irreparable damage to the property interests of the business being boycotted. As this and subsequent cases have shown, courts have frequently invoked property rights as a basis for defeating free speech defenses. In other words, an individual right of free speech cannot necessarily defeat an individual right in property. Of course, the speech at issue in these cases is not seen as speech directly related to the pursuit or maintenance of limited government. But under an individual-autonomy model of the First Amendment, speech rights would have to be upheld regardless of their effect on property rights.

Under a limited-government approach, the courts will tend not to grant First Amendment rights to one private party against another. If a First Amendment right is not aimed at limiting government power, it will not be granted under the limited-government model. This is the result reached in *Hurley v. Irish-American Gay, Lesbian and Bisexual Group of Boston,* where the Supreme Court ruled that the First Amendment did not require and in fact did not allow the state to mandate private parade organizers to include a group of gay Irish in the parade. Thus, the Court does not grant affirmative First Amendment rights in disputes between private parties, no matter how much benefit those affirmative rights would have on the personal-autonomy interests of the individuals seeking them. Moreover, the power of the state, through its antidiscrimination laws, cannot be allowed to restrict the First Amendment speech and associational rights of other individuals or groups, which in turn would restrict the ability of social groups to exist and function in society.

Unlike the individual-autonomy model, the limited-government model rests the protection of speech on a theory or justification that transcends the individual— namely, the preservation of limited government. (Of course, one very important value of limited government is that it promotes and protects individual liberty.) In *Kovacs v. Cooper,* for instance, the Court sustained a Trenton, New Jersey, ordinance prohibiting the use of soundtracks emitting "loud and raucous noises."[120] The Court based its decision on the need to protect the privacy and tranquility of its citizens. The ordinance was not an unnecessary or illegitimate expansion of government power, but an attempt to protect private citizens in the enjoyment of their homes. In *Bethel School District No. 408 v. Fraser,* the Court upheld a three-day suspension of a high school student who used indecent speech when delivering a speech before a school assembly.[121] The Court sided in favor of society's interest in teaching the boundaries of socially appropriate behavior.[122] Since the government has legitimate power and authority to operate a school system and to educate future democratic citizens, this decision coincides with the limited-government model. In other words, the speech right argued in the case is not needed so as to maintain a limited government; to the contrary, the government's activity was consistent with a vital function in its legitimate scope of authority.

The secondary-effects doctrine also seeks to recognize a legitimate area of governmental authority. Under this doctrine, the government seeks to address the secondary, or nonspeech, effects of speech, or those effects that are "unrelated to the suppression of free expression."[123] In *City of Renton v. Playtime Theatres*, the Supreme Court upheld a zoning ordinance regulating the location of adult theaters. In doing so, the Court treated the ordinance as content neutral, since its purpose was to regulate the secondary effects of those types of theaters—the prevention of crime, the support of the city's retail trade, the maintenance of property values, and the protection of the quality of surrounding neighborhoods.[124] Clearly, the government has the legitimate authority to address all of those concerns.

The secondary-effects doctrine recognizes that the government does not have power to target ideas, but it does have power to regulate certain social effects caused by certain types of businesses, such as adult movie theaters. This secondary-effects doctrine is best explained by the limited-government model, because such secondary-effects regulations nonetheless do infringe on the individual autonomy of those persons who wish to own or patronize such theaters.

Likewise, the symbolic-speech doctrine also fits in with the limited-government model. This doctrine was articulated by the Supreme Court in *United States v. O'Brien*, where the Court upheld the conviction of a man prosecuted for burning his draft card in protest of the Vietnam War.[125] Under the symbolic-speech doctrine, the Court must consider three elements: (1) whether the government has an important or substantial interest in its actions or regulation; (2) whether that interest is unrelated to the restriction of free expression; and (3) whether the resulting restriction on speech is no greater than necessary to achieve the governmental interest.[126] Again, the focus is on the legitimate governmental interest, rather than on the violation of or infringement on individual autonomy—because obviously O'Brien would have felt that his autonomy was being violated by his prosecution for burning his draft card in protest of the war.

The limited-government model focuses first and primarily on the boundaries of authority possessed by the government. The focus is on whether government has an area of legitimate authority, and whether it is acting within that area. This concern and focus, as discussed above, is frequently incorporated in the First Amendment decisions of the Supreme Court. For instance, in *Thornburgh v. Abbott*, the Supreme Court upheld a regulatory regime of various restrictions on publications that federal prisoners may receive.[127] This regulatory regime allowed the warden to censor publications that were thought to undermine the "security, good order, or discipline of the prison."[128] The focus of the *Thornburgh* Court was on the legitimate interest of the government in running a prison, not on the effect on individual autonomy of prisoners who wanted to receive publications deemed inappropriate by the warden.

In the area of privacy torts, regulation of certain speech has been allowed because the regulation is done in behalf of individual privacy, not in behalf of expanding government power. If speech were a right of individual autonomy, it could not be restricted at all. But because it can be restricted in the privacy area, speech (in a constitutional sense) must be a means to some goal other than individual autonomy. In *Zacchini v. Scripps-Howard Broadcasting Co.,* a freelance reporter televised the complete fifteen-second "human cannonball" act of Hugo Zacchini. Zacchini then brought an action for damages, asserting a violation of his publicity rights. The Ohio Supreme Court held that Zacchini's publicity rights were preempted by the First Amendment, but the United States Supreme Court reversed, holding that freedom of speech was not paramount to Zacchini's publicity interests in his act.[129] In doing so, the Court upheld the state's interest in protecting the proprietary interests of the individual to reap the rewards of his endeavors.

Another aspect of the limited-government model can be seen in *Florida Star v. B.J.F.,* where a newspaper published the name of a person who had been raped by an unknown assailant.[130] The reporter had obtained the name from a sheriff's report from which the official had inadvertently failed to delete the victim's name. Furthermore, the reporter knew from a sign in the pressroom that the names of rape victims were not matters of public record and that Florida law prohibited publication of the names of sexual assault victims. After harassment suffered because of publication of her name, the victim brought a civil action against the *Star* for violating the Florida statute and won. On appeal, the Supreme Court overturned the jury verdict for the plaintiff. As the Court stated, the case presented a conflict between the right of the press to publish truthful information and the state interest in protecting the privacy and safety of rape victims.

Yet even though the Court ruled that the government cannot punish the press for publishing truthful information lawfully obtained, the Court did not suggest that government is restrained at all from not producing information to the press. In this respect, *Florida Star* was consistent with the limited-government model, as the focus of the decision was not on speech, since the amount of speech could well be diminished by the government's withholding that information from the press. Seen from this perspective, *Florida Star* is all about limiting government power over the publishing activities of the press.

7

The Religion Clause and
Limited Government

The Free Exercise Clause

The religion clauses of the First Amendment are a limitation on the power of government to infringe on society's religious exercise and institutions. The religion clauses recognize that government must be limited in the area of religion, since religion, as seen by religious believers, involves a higher sovereignty. The clauses are not based on a commitment to individual autonomy and are not intended to fulfill individual autonomy regarding one's private religious beliefs or practices.

A primary reason for the religion clauses of the First Amendment is that the area of religion and spiritual belief was long seen as an area over which government should have no control, since religion involved something transcendent and beyond the state.[1] The founding generation believed religion is unique because it entails duties owed to God and to a higher sovereignty.[2] For James Madison and many others in the founding generation, religious obligations were superior to civil obligations, and defining the proper relation between religion and civil government meant drawing a jurisdictional boundary between two potentially competing authorities.[3] Religion was thus seen as an ultimate limit on the power of the state, and this limitation was expressed in the First Amendment.

However, under many modern views, religion is no longer seen as a higher duty, but merely a matter of personal autonomy. Consequently, religion cases often focus not on state action but on the needs of individual autonomy. Under the limited-government view, however, the focus is on the state and its duty to refrain from defining or regulating the relationship between individuals, society, and religion; whereas under the individual-autonomy view, the focus is more on the subjective value of religion to the individual. Yet the more simple and coherent way of deciding religion-clause cases is to concentrate on the actions of the state and to enforce the principle of limited government in this area.

James Madison believed that freedom of religion arose from a multiplicity of sects, which was the best and only security for religious liberty in any society.[4] This belief reflects the notion that the courts should not be enforcing some substantive view of liberty, but should be enforcing the structural conditions necessary for liberty. A limited-government approach can help create those structural conditions in which a multiplicity of sects can thrive. This of course meshes with Madison's larger theory that in a republic the dispersal of power among many factions and interests (and away from government monopolization) is the most fundamental safeguard against oppression and the infringement of liberty.

But at least in the area of religion, there is another aspect to the limited-government model. Not only should the First Amendment be interpreted as a provision aimed at enforcing limited government, but its enforcement should be done in a way that further strengthens the structural conditions needed to preserve limited government. For instance, religion is often considered an institution in society that can help check government. Because of its nature as a source of values superior to and preceding the state, religion can operate as a check on government abuses of power.[5] As Justice William Brennan Jr. recognized in *Walz v. Tax Commission*,[6] religious organizations should be protected from infringement by the government because those organizations "contribute to the diversity of association, viewpoint and enterprise essential to a vigorous, pluralistic society." Private social associations, and particularly religious associations, have always provided a valuable check and counterpoint to the state, and especially to an oppressive government. (Indeed, the American Revolution, the Civil War, and the civil rights movement were all inspired by religious organizations and beliefs.)

Up until the mid-twentieth century, First Amendment law granted freedom to religious believers only up to the point where their practices threatened public order. However, in the 1940s, the Supreme Court began significantly expanding the rights of religious believers, exempting them even from laws considered generally beneficial to society.[7] This transformation in the Court's First Amendment jurisprudence indicated that the Court was looking at the First Amendment through an individual-autonomy view. But more recently, the Court in its free exercise decisions has followed a limited-government model of the First Amendment.

The limited-government approach in free exercise cases largely began with *Employment Division v. Smith*, where the Court upheld an Oregon statute outlawing the use of peyote, even though this law affected the right of American Indians to use that substance in their religious ceremonies.[8] In *Smith*, two American Indians who had ingested peyote as part of a religious observance at their church, the Native American Church, were fired from their jobs as counselors at a private drug rehabilitation center, since peyote was illegal under Oregon law; subsequently they were denied unemployment benefits, as they had been fired for work-related misconduct.[9] The Court adopted a narrower construction of the free exercise clause and denied the availability of free exercise exemptions from neutral, generally applicable laws.[10]

In applying the limited-government model, *Smith* bans government from singling out the weak or minority religions, whereas majority or dominant religions can obviously survive on their political strength. Thus, the Court in *Smith* did not try to protect religious exercise as some kind of fundamental individual right. Instead, the decision focused upon limiting government from acting in certain discriminatory ways.[11]

In moving away from the individual-autonomy model, the *Smith* rule states that government does not violate the right to free exercise unless it targets some particular religious practice. To target a religious practice is to expand government power beyond its rightful bounds. At the same time, it is permissible for legislatures to grant free exercise exemptions from generally applicable neutral laws, since those exemptions (those immunities *from* regulation) do not reflect an expansion of government power. Using the limited-government approach, *Smith* indicates that rights do not exist solely for the individual, but as a means of limiting government. The *Smith* rule forbids government from singling out the weak religions, but it presumes that the strong ones can survive without the need of constitutional protection.

The individual-autonomy view, however, sees the free exercise clause as "best understood as an affirmative guarantee of the right to participate in religious practices and conduct without impermissible government interference, even when such conduct conflicts with a neutral generally applicable law."[12] This view, as expressed by Justice Sandra Day O'Connor in her *Flores* dissent, looks not to the state but to the actual religious beliefs and conduct of the individual. It says that the state must do more than simply refrain from targeting religious practices; it must affirmatively accommodate believers by going so far as to grant conscientious exemptions from burdensome laws, even those with purely secular motives. But Gerard Bradley argues that no constitutional tradition of free exercise exemptions ever existed prior to 1963 and the *Sherbert* decision.[13] Indeed, *Sherbert* resulted from a 1960s embrace of individual autonomy, which was an unprecedented mutation of the American constitutional tradition. According to Bradley, the *Smith* case "rightly jettisoned the conduct exemption because it is manifestly contrary to the plain meaning of the Free Exercise Clause."[14] Also underlying *Smith* was concern over the legitimacy of the judiciary's subjective, value-based approach of *Sherbert* and *Yoder*.[15]

The *Smith* rule and its rejection of a personal-autonomy model of the free exercise clause coincides with the position taken by the Supreme Court in its first free exercise case, in 1879. In *Reynolds v. U.S.*, where the Court upheld congressional prohibition of Mormon polygamy, the Court rejected the natural-rights interpretation of the free exercise clause offered by the defenders of Mormon polygamy. Instead, as one scholar has noted, the Court's decision rested not on any recognition of individual-autonomy interests but on the government's legitimate role in extending the "civilized" principles of Reconstruction into the West through an antipolygamy campaign, similar to its earlier antislavery crusade.[16] And as the lesson of the Civil War had shown, government had to be powerful when combating forces seen to be threatening to the civilized Union.[17]

The Relationship between the Two Clauses

The exercise clause prohibits government action that singles out and imposes discriminatory burdens on members of minority religious sects. It prohibits the state from either prescribing or proscribing any religious practices. The establishment clause, on the other hand, works at the institutional level, rather than at the individual level. It protects the institutional autonomy of religious organizations from intrusions by the state.[18] In so doing, the establishment clause serves as a kind of subset of the exercise clause: it seeks to reduce the potential for one type of friction between the state and the religious practices of society.[19]

The establishment clause has an institutional focus, protecting the autonomy of religious institutions.[20] The establishment clause, according to Richard Garnett, affirms the independence of religious institutions from government control, putting such institutions beyond the reach of government authority.[21] It does not reflect a mistrust of religion, nor does it serve to insulate a secular society from the influence and presence of religion, as various justices and commentators have advocated.[22] Rather, it protects against the government's improperly involving itself in the functions, powers, or identity of a religious organization.[23] The establishment clause aims to keep religious institutions as free as possible to pursue their chosen missions.[24] This interpretation is much narrower than the separationist theory espoused in cases adhering to a "wall of separation" approach, which uses the clause to essentially mandate a radical transformation of American society in which religion is strictly separated from civil society and to redefine society along strictly secular lines.[25]

The establishment clause is not some grand constitutional command that is intended to separate religion from the nation's civic life.[26] It is not a protector of secular society, nor does it act to shield people from the controversial and challenging views of religion.[27] The establishment clause, contrary to the suggestion in *Everson v. Board of Education,* was not intended to counteract history and create some grandiose wall of separation between civil society and religion. The establishment clause "is not a limitation on churches or religion; it is a limitation on the role of government with respect to churches and religious life in general."[28] To interpret the establishment clause, for instance, as restraining the democratic freedom of religion and religious associations is to interpret the clause contrary to its nature as a structural provision within the constitutional scheme of limited government.

Taken together, the two religion clauses can be seen as preventing two separate threats to religious freedom: on one hand, government action that discriminates against the religious beliefs or exercise of individuals or minority sects; and on the other, government action that interferes in the institutions freely chosen and shaped by the various religious denominations.[29] As Michael McConnell explains, "The Establishment Clause guarantees that the federal . . . government will not give . . . preference to any religion . . . , and the Free Exercise Clause guarantees that it will not [restrict or] interfere . . . with beliefs and practices" of any individual.[30]

The majority of Americans living during the late eighteenth century believed that religion was essential for the preservation of civil society because it instilled necessary morals and virtue in the people, while providing for a stable social order.[31] By providing a separate social institutional structure and an overarching ideological framework, religion also served as an important means by which society could judge and control government. But to preserve the freedom and vibrancy of religion, the framers did not want Congress to be able to mandate a government-imposed uniformity in religion throughout the United States.[32]

The framers believed that public opinion should control government, and that religion was an important institution for the formation and dissemination of public opinion.[33] Religious organizations, as was the press, were a vital means for the formation of social character and opinion. Not only should government not control such a means, but both religion and the press were important for subsequently controlling and limiting government. Under the First Amendment, opinion formation and dissemination was to be left to private, decentralized institutions, among which religion was to be one of the most prominent.[34]

Given that the establishment clause was meant to prevent the federal government from establishing a national state religion, such as existed in England, it serves as yet another constitutional mandate for limited government—it limits the federal government from acting to establish a particular religion.[35] It restrains the federal government from imposing a single, uniform religious code on a religiously diverse nation.[36] Freedom and democracy, to the framers, required a national government of limited powers, particularly regarding the freedom of religious institutions.

A number of scholars have demonstrated the federalism considerations underlying the establishment clause.[37] According to Daniel Conkle, the clause was intended by the framers to effect "a policy of federalism on questions of church and state."[38] As originally conceived, the establishment clause would prohibit the federal government from interfering with the states' freedom to legislate on matters of religion.[39] Indeed, the issue of federalism was central to the debate surrounding the drafting of the First Amendment.[40] Bradley argues that the establishment clause served to prevent federal interference into state practices regarding religion, and that the establishment clause was primarily a jurisdictional device intended to remove religion from federal jurisdiction.[41] According to Steven Smith, the "religion clauses were understood as a federalist measure, not as the enactment of any substantive principle of religious freedom."[42] Akhil Amar also argues that the establishment clause was a pure federalism provision, mandating that the issue be decided state by state and that the federal government not have any power to act in this area.[43] As Amar explains, the possibility of national control over such a powerful social institution as religion, which shaped the behavior and cultivated the habits of the citizenry, struck fear in the hearts of Anti-Federalists. However, "local control over such intermediate organizations seemed far less threatening, less distant, less aristocratic, less monopolistic." National control over religion would have been horribly oppressive to many of the framing generation, but local control over religion "would allow dissenters in any place to vote with their feet and find a community with the right religious tone."[44]

The effect of such a federalist provision is to facilitate a greater freedom and experimentation by the states in terms of their relationships with religion and religious organizations, especially in the areas of education and other social-welfare programs that might involve religious organizations. As James Madison asserted regarding the lack of federal authority over religious matters, "[T]here is not a shadow of right in the federal government to intermeddle with religion."[45] James Iredell, later to become a justice of the Supreme Court, argued that Congress had no authority to interfere in religious matters or relationships whatsoever; instead, each state was left free to deal with the subject in its own way.[46]

In the first 150 years of the Constitution's existence, very few religion-clause cases were decided.[47] This is because it was generally agreed that the framers did not intend to apply the clause to the states.[48] However, in the past half century, ever since the Court incorporated the religion clauses into the Fourteenth Amendment, there has been a flood of First Amendment litigation.[49] Furthermore, with the incorporation of the establishment clause in *Everson v. Board of Education,* the Supreme Court shifted its First Amendment jurisprudence in an increasingly nationalized direction, denying the states much room for independent action.[50]

Not only did the drafters not intend to apply the establishment clause to states and localities, but the historical evidence "strongly suggests that the Fourteenth Amendment, as originally understood, did not incorporate the Establishment Clause for application to state government action."[51] Without such incorporation, states and localities would have more freedom to interact with religion than they currently have. Indeed, some critics even argue that the incorporation of the establishment clause through the Fourteenth Amendment, and hence its applicability to the states, should be reversed.[52] Such a strategy would "certainly give the states far more latitude to acknowledge, accommodate, and promote religion than current doctrine allows."[53]

This is the view Justice Clarence Thomas has adopted, leading him to argue that the establishment clause never should have been applied to the states by way of incorporation through the Fourteenth Amendment.[54] According to Justice Thomas, "[T]he Establishment Clause is a federalism provision which . . . resists incorporation."[55] As he explained in his concurring opinion in *Elk River School District v. Newdow,* the "text and history of the Establishment Clause strongly suggests that it is a federalism provision intended to prevent Congress from interfering with [the] state[s]."[56] In this same vein, Justice Potter Stewart had earlier recognized that "the establishment clause was primarily an attempt to insure that

Congress not only would be powerless to establish a national church but would also be unable to interfere with existing state establishments."[57]

The Establishment Clause

The First Amendment denies Congress the power to make laws about "an establishment" of religion. By denying such power to Congress and the federal government, the establishment clause placed a structural and jurisdictional limitation on the national government, leaving any "matters respecting an establishment in the hands of the people and their religious societies."[58] Thus, the essential meaning of the clause can only be found in the intention to limit federal government jurisdiction.[59]

Even though the establishment clause was intended as a structural limitation on the power of government, courts have instead applied the clause as an individual-autonomy provision, aimed at securing the autonomy of those opposed to religion. In particular, the Supreme Court's endorsement test reflects this individual-autonomy view.

The United States Supreme Court has used the establishment clause to strike down many local accommodations of religious exercise, including all kinds of public displays of religious symbols.[60] Creating a minority "dissenter's right" out of the establishment clause, the Court has given a constitutional trump card to individuals who claim their rights have been violated by a prayer delivered by a rabbi at a high school graduation,[61] a crèche displayed on public grounds,[62] a prayer recited by a student prior to the start of a high school football game,[63] and most recently by a plaque of the Ten Commandments hanging in a courtroom.[64] This minority dissenter's right has been uniformly applied throughout the whole nation to block the religious expressions of the larger community, regardless of the religious traditions or sensibilities of the local communities in which the religious displays or expressions take place. Through enforcement of this judicially created right, the decisions of the Supreme Court have "reduced the role of religion in public life, and the scope of religious freedom in private life, to less than that intended by the framers and ratifiers of the First Amendment's religion clauses."[65]

In a case that reflects a dissenter's-rights view of the establishment clause, *Skoros v. City of New York,* the United States Court of Appeals for the Second Circuit upheld a New York City public school policy on holiday season displays that forbade Christmas crèches, but allowed the Chanukah menorah and the star and crescent of Islam.[66] The government defended this policy on the ground that the Jewish and Islamic symbols had "secular" meanings for most students—e.g., Christians, since two-thirds of the students were from Christian families—but that the Christian nativity scene had only religious significance.[67] Thus, according to the court, the establishment clause extends only to majority religions, and functions primarily as a protection for minority religions that, in turn, possess privileges of religious expression that the majority religions do not enjoy.

The use of a dissenter's-rights application of the establishment clause also occurred in *Santa Fe Independent School Dist. v. Doe.*[68] At issue in *Santa Fe* was a Texas school district's practice of having a student, who was annually elected to the office of student council chaplain, deliver a prayer over the public address system before each varsity football game.[69] The United States Supreme Court held that this practice was a violation of the establishment clause.[70] The Court found that the prayer was coercive, insofar as objecting witnesses who were in the minority were put into the position of either attending a personally offensive religious ritual or foregoing a traditional gathering of the school community.[71]

Previously, in *Lee v. Weisman,* the Court likewise held that a religious activity is unconstitutionally coercive if the government directs it in a way that forces objectors to participate.[72] At issue in *Lee* was a prayer offered by a school-invited rabbi at a graduation ceremony.[73] The Court held that because graduation exercises are virtually obligatory, objectors to the prayer were unconstitutionally coerced into participating.[74] Acutely sensitive to the feelings of minority objectors, the Court implied that "non-governmental social pressure occurring in a government-provided forum could constitute coercion forbidden by the establishment clause."[75] Thus, because of feelings of exclusion or discomfort, a minority dissenter can stop a public prayer inserted into a high school graduation ceremony, even when that dissenter had no obligation to participate in the prayer, and even when the only pressure felt by the dissenter was the result of some social discomfort for not participating.[76] Yet in rendering its decision, the Court used this discomfort, felt by a very small minority, to transform a three-minute prayer recitation by a Jewish rabbi in an overwhelmingly Christian community into a state establishment of religion.[77]

The Court's use of the endorsement test reveals the ways in which it has created and applied a minority dissenter's right. In *Lynch v. Donnelly*[78] in 1984, the Court began using the endorsement test to decide establishment clause issues, particularly involving the constitutionality of religious symbols and expression on public property.[79] Under this test, the Court considers the government to be unconstitutionally endorsing religion whenever it conveys the message that a religion or particular religious belief is favored by the state.[80] In *County of Allegheny v. ACLU,*[81] the Court decided that the display of a crèche violated the establishment clause, but that the display of a menorah next to a Christmas tree did not.[82] The crèche was considered an endorsement of the Christian faith, but the tree and menorah were acceptable, insofar as together they did not give the impression that the state was endorsing any one religion.[83] The Court held that a crèche located on the steps of a county courthouse was prominent enough to constitute an endorsement.[84] On the other hand, the religious message conveyed by a publicly displayed menorah was sufficiently diluted by the presence of a Christmas tree to keep it from becoming a state endorsement.[85]

The endorsement test is grounded on the premise that the establishment clause prohibits the government from conveying ideas that divide the community into outsiders (the minority) and insiders (the majority).[86] In *Lynch v.*

Donnelly, Justice O'Connor explained, "[e]ndorsement sends a message to non-adherents that they are outsiders, not full members of the political community, and an accompanying message to adherents that they are insiders, favored members of the political community."[87] But under this interpretation, the endorsement test becomes a vehicle for ensuring a kind of emotional contentment or autonomy of individuals.

Strict separationists argue that the endorsement test should even prohibit private religious speech that ostracizes nonadherents.[88] They claim that private religious speech on government property can marginalize religious dissenters; for example, a private religious group might so dominate a public forum that a dissenter might feel that he or she is not welcome as a full-fledged member of the political community.[89] In such a scenario, the establishment clause would be used to protect anyone who might suffer a sense of alienation because of his or her nonbelief.[90] If necessary, strict separationists argue, the establishment clause should impose special regulations (similar to time-manner-place restrictions) aimed at ameliorating any isolating effects of religious speech in public forums.[91] According to proponents of a broadly empowered establishment clause, this sense of exclusion is what the First Amendment is all about—and the only way to combat the isolation that minority groups feel may be to ban all religious messages from public property.[92] But the First Amendment is all about limited government, not social engineering or preventing individual feelings of exclusion. Moreover, if government actions ever rise to the point of truly excluding minority religious beliefs from the public square, then the free exercise clause should come into play. Other suggestions include interpreting the establishment clause to include a kind of *Brown v. Board of Education* element, imposing a sort of social affirmative-action policy aimed at achieving equality between believers and nonbelievers.[93]

The endorsement test examines government conduct from both an objective and a subjective viewpoint, recognizing that the message sent may be different from the message received.[94] Focusing on the latter, the *Allegheny* Court concluded that, as to the crèche, "[n]o viewer could reasonably think that it occupied this location without the support and approval of the government."[95] The tree and menorah, on the other hand, did not present a "sufficiently likely" probability that observers would perceive a government endorsement of a particular religion.[96] This subjectivity, regarding a court's conclusions as to what perceptions viewers might have of some religious display or speech, is a serious problem with the endorsement test, because it calls for judges to make assumptions about the impressions that unknown people may have received from certain religious speech or symbols.[97] One judge has written that the endorsement test requires "scrutiny more commonly associated with interior decorators than with the judiciary."[98] In *County of Allegheny,* Justice Anthony Kennedy noted that this meant the Court had to examine "whether the city has included Santas, talking wishing wells, reindeer, or other secular symbols" to draw attention away from the religious symbol in the display.[99] Kennedy, a critic of the endorsement test, declared it to be "flawed in its fundamentals and unworkable in practice."[100] According to Kennedy, using the endorsement test equated to a "jurisprudence of minutia."[101] In *Allegheny,* he argued that neither the crèche nor the menorah posed a "realistic risk" of creating an establishment of religion.[102] Furthermore, with regard to the banning of the crèche, Kennedy asserted that the majority's decision reflected "an unjustified hostility toward religion" and a "callous indifference toward religious faith that our cases and traditions do not require."[103]

Under the endorsement test, the individual dissenter's rights have almost no concrete boundaries. In other words, there is nothing so minute that it cannot rise to the level of an official government endorsement of religion. For instance, a court held that the singing of the Lord's Prayer by a high school choir violated the establishment clause.[104] According to the court, just the rehearsal of the prayer during choir practice was enough to constitute a violation.[105]

Perception is obviously key to the endorsement test. Public school teachers, for instance, can be prohibited from engaging in religious speech while on the job; because no matter how vociferously they disavow government sanction of their views, the courts presume that the students will perceive a link, thereby causing an establishment clause violation. In *Roberts v. Madigan,* a teacher at a public elementary school was barred from keeping a Bible on his desk during the school day, reading his Bible in front of the students during a daily fifteen-minute silent reading period, or keeping two Christian religious books on his classroom shelves.[106] And in *Bishop v. Aronov,* an exercise physiology professor at a public university was sanctioned for making a series of religious remarks to his class and for organizing an after-class meeting on religious topics, even though the professor avoided attributing his personal religious views to the university.[107]

These cases also illustrate another potential problem with the endorsement test. Not only does it subjectively measure perception, it also requires extensive judicial oversight of private religious speech conducted on public property, even when the government is not officially sponsoring or sanctioning that speech, lest the perception mistakenly occur that the government is so sponsoring it.[108] Thus, the endorsement test diverts the courts from the essential focus of the establishment clause—state interference in the institutional autonomy of religious organizations—and turns it instead to all the possible individual perceptions of various religious expressions being made on public property.

The applicability of the limited-government model is particularly illustrated in *Larkin v. Grendel's Den, Inc.,* which involved a zoning statute that sought to protect houses of worship from the various problems of being located close to taverns and bars. Under the statute, when a proprietor applying for a liquor license selected a site within five hundred feet of a house of worship, the affected religious organization was notified and permitted to veto the license's issuance. The Supreme Court ruled that this statute violated the establishment clause, holding that the sovereign power of the government could not be delegated to a religious organization. Moreover, the manner of an organization's exercise of its veto power was arbitrary, for there were no standards to which the organization was to conform. This violated the limited-government principle by unduly expanding the power of government. Just as government cannot interfere with the internal governance of a church, the government cannot delegate to religious organizations government powers and thereby expand the power and reach of the government.

On the other hand, a case in which the limited-government model would have supported an opposite result is *Texas Monthly v. Bullock,* where the Court held that a sales-tax exemption for periodicals published or distributed by religious denominations violated the establishment clause, because similar exemptions were not given to nonreligious publications.[109] There was no allegation that Texas discriminated among different religious sects, only that a benefit was given to religion in general that was not otherwise available to nonreligious organizations. There was also no allegation that this benefit had any adverse effect on anyone's free exercise rights. The only issues before the Court were whether the state could make an accommodation to religion that was not required under the free exercise clause, whether religious organizations in general could be given benefits not accorded to nonreligious organizations, or whether the establishment clause required mandatory indifference to the impact of government action (e.g., sales taxes) on religious activity or institutions.[110] However, the Court ignored these issues and focused its analysis simply on whether the benefits flowed exclusively to religious groups, assuming that the establishment clause forbids the government from favoring religion in general.[111]

Because *Texas Monthly* dealt with a governmental benefit aimed at further expanding the free exercise rights of religious denominations that published and distributed periodicals, it presented the question of whether those expanded exercise rights rose to the level of a state establishment of religion. The Court, however, did not directly address this issue. Instead, it saw the sales-tax exemption as unconstitutional because it benefited only religion and gave an accommodation not required by free exercise. But contrary to what *Texas Monthly* might suggest, nonmandatory accommodations of religion occur quite frequently. Municipalities, for instance, frequently adopt ordinances that protect churches.[112] In these ordinances, certain types of establishments, such as theaters, fire stations, and bars are often excluded within a certain distance from religious houses of worship.[113] The presumption is that religious exercise is a valuable activity to protect, and minimizing the types of businesses that might be "demoralizing or annoying" to churchgoers is one such way of doing so.[114]

The Court's decision in *Texas Monthly* is not supported under the limited-government model, since the sales-tax exemption for religious publications is not an undue enlargement or expansion of government power. Rather, it simply enlarges the ability of religious organizations to carry on their work. Moreover, the exemption increases the capacity of religion to act as a check on government and a counterpoint to its policies and messages.

The Historical View of Religion as a
Constraint on Government

To Americans of the constitutional period, religion was an indispensable ingredient to self-government.[115] Political writers and theorists emphasized the need for a virtuous citizenry to sustain the democratic process.[116] John Adams believed there was "no government armed with power capable of contending with human passions unbridled by morality and religion."[117] He wrote that "religion and virtue are the only foundations not only of republicanism and of all free government, but of social felicity under all governments and in all the combinations of human society."[118]

The constitutional framers "saw clearly that religion would be a great aid in maintaining civil government on a high plane," and hence would be "a great moral asset to the nation."[119] According to George Washington, religion is inseparable from good government, and "no true patriot" would attempt to weaken the political influence of religion and morality.[120] And in his farewell address to the nation at the end of his presidency, Washington warned that "reason and experience both forbid us to expect that national morality can prevail in exclusion of religious principle."[121]

Late-eighteenth-century Americans generally agreed that the only solid ground for the kind of morality needed to build a virtuous citizenry was religious observance.[122] In early America, churches were the primary institutions for the formation of democratic character and the transmission of community values.[123] According to the constitutional framing generation, a "belief in religion would preserve the peace and good order of society by improving men's morals and restraining their vices."[124]

The Bill of Rights was ratified in an age of close and ongoing interaction between government and religion.[125] Congress appointed and funded chaplains who offered daily prayers, presidents proclaimed days of prayer and fasting, and the government paid for missionaries to the Indians.[126] In the Northwest Ordinance, Congress even set aside land to endow schools that would teach religion and morality.[127]

Religious beliefs found frequent expression in the acts and proceedings of early American legislative bodies. Five references to God appear in the Declaration of Independence. Early in its first session, the Continental Congress resolved to open its daily sessions with a prayer,[128] and in 1782 it supported "the pious and laudable undertaking" of printing an American edition of the Scriptures.[129] When the First Congress, which had created the Bill of Rights, reenacted the Northwest Ordinance in 1789, it declared that religion and morality were "necessary to good government."[130] Congress also consistently permitted invocations and other religious practices to be performed in public facilities.[131] And on September 26, 1789, the day after Congress adopted the final language of the First Amendment, the House and Senate, feeling a spirit of jubilation over passage of the Bill of Rights, both adopted a resolution asking the president to "recommend to the people of the United States a day of public thanksgiving and prayer, to be observed, by acknowledging, with grateful hearts, the many signal favors of the Almighty God."[132]

In the years following ratification of the First Amendment, presidents George Washington and John Adams continued to issue broad proclamations for days of national prayer.[133] James Madison likewise recognized that the government could designate days of solemn observance or prayer.[134] During his presidential administration, Madison issued at least four proclamations recommending days of national prayer and thanksgiving.[135] He also oversaw federal funding of congressional and military chaplains, as well as missionaries charged with "teaching the great duties of religion and morality to the Indians."[136]

According to perhaps the most eminent nineteenth-century constitutional scholar, the framers did not intend to expunge religious influence from society.[137] The primary objective of the First Amendment was not to insulate society from religion, but to advance the interests of religion, which in turn would influence the conduct of social and civic affairs.[138] With the free exercise clause, the framers wanted to create an environment in which the strong moral voice of religious congregations would be free to judge the actions of the federal government and where the clergy could speak out boldly, without restraint or fear of retribution, on matters of public morality and the nation's spiritual condition.[139] Indeed, a vocal clergy had often taken the lead in the colonial resistance to British oppression.[140]

Therefore, it makes no sense to apply the establishment clause in a way that limits religion. Instead, the more logical interpretation is to view the two clauses as protecting against two different threats to that freedom: on one hand, government action that restricts the religious practices of individuals or minority sects, and on the other, government action that interferes in the institutions freely chosen and shaped by the various religious denominations.[141]

The exercise clause focuses on the individual; it protects members of minority religious sects from any kind of religious censorship or restrictions discriminatorily imposed by the majority.[142] It guarantees that the state can neither prescribe nor proscribe any religious practices. The establishment clause, on the other hand, works at the institutional level.[143] It guards against state interference in the institutional autonomy of religious organizations.[144] The intent behind the enactment of the establishment clause was to limit government from imposing ecclesiastical coercion on religious institutions.[145] The establishment clause is concerned with majoritarian self-rule aspects—preserving the freedom of people to choose and operate their religious organizations, free of any minority-imposed, state-established religion. But to the framers, "government noninvolvement in the province of the church did not mean total government separation from general religious ideas and affirmations relevant to civic life."[146] In a society in which over 90 percent of the citizens claim to be religious, "[t]o say that government should not be responsive to religion is to say that government should not be responsive to the opinion of the people."[147]

As the history of the First Amendment and the eighteenth-century relationship between law and religion reveals, the religion clauses sought to promote limited government in two ways. First, they prevented government from having the power to adversely intrude into an important area of individual and social life. And second, they sought to protect the integrity and vibrancy of religious belief and practice in America, since religion had proved to be an important social means of controlling and directing government, and hence keeping it limited to its legitimate areas of authority.

8

How the First Amendment
Protects Individual Rights

An Equal Protection View
of the First Amendment

If a limited-government interpretation of the Bill of Rights is to be adopted, do the various individual rights set out in the bill have any meaning beyond that of serving as structural provisions for a limited government? Do the rights and freedoms set out in the Bill of Rights have any protection in and of themselves, or is the only thing about which the Bill of Rights is concerned the maintenance of limited government?

Aside from acting as a further provision for the maintenance of limited government, the Bill of Rights serves to protect the freedoms listed in it through the incorporation of equal protection norms. This approach is consistent with the limited-government model and best harmonizes the rights listed in the Bill of Rights with the workings of the democratic process outlined in the original Constitution. In a democracy, society governs itself according to its best judgment; but the glaring problem with any democracy is how to handle minorities and minority rights. An equal protection approach best serves this concern, while at the same time allowing democratic society to govern itself—the proviso being that whatever the majority does to the minority it must do to itself.

Many current First Amendment doctrines already incorporate an equal protection approach, but a more explicit equal protection approach could eliminate much of the complexity and confusions in First Amendment doctrines, thus greatly simplifying the Court's jurisprudence in this area. The key element in a methodology for applying an equal protection approach is the identification of the proper baseline or comparison point for determining equality of treatment. But the judicial determination of appropriate baselines is a more definable and boundaried endeavor than many of the approaches currently used by the Court in its First Amendment jurisprudence.

By viewing the Bill of Rights as a provision aimed at first ensuring that government possesses only limited powers, and second mandating that the various listed freedoms be protected through an equal protection approach, courts would be relieved of having to identify the parameters and underlying values and purposes of various individual rights and freedoms. Defining the parameters of individual rights, as well as which parameters are necessary to achieve a particular degree of individual autonomy, often puts courts into a quasi-lawmaking role. Such a role exposes the judiciary to intense criticism, since it assigns functions that have no clear boundaries and that often transgress on the workings of the democratic process. But by seeking to protect individual freedoms through an equal protection approach, courts can better avoid interjecting their own substantive values into constitutional doctrines. Thus, their role can be both more narrow and more defined, which in turn will help preserve judicial integrity and authority.

James Madison articulated a classic concern of equal protection in *Federalist No. 10*. He worried about the potential in a democracy for "the most numerous party, or, in other words, the most powerful faction" to "trample on" the rights of minority groups.[1] For Madison, the goal was to create "a government which will protect all parties, the weaker as well as the more powerful."[2] But this has also traditionally been seen as a goal of the Bill of Rights, which then by definition must incorporate notions of equal protection. Thus, in connection with the concerns of *Federalist No. 10* and the protection of minority rights, equal protection should be a primary focus of courts in a democratic society. And it is through the Bill of Rights that the Constitution first sought to protect liberty through equal protection norms. Later, this equal protection concern incorporated within the Bill of Rights was extended by way of the Fourteenth Amendment.

According to Thomas McAffee, the historical evidence shows that the adopters of the Fourteenth Amendment believed they were leaving substantial power in the states to decide on the scope and content of basic rights, subject only to the requirement that their laws not embody invidious discrimination.[3] As McAffee explains, a central motivation of those who drafted and ratified the Fourteenth Amendment was to combine federal empowerment to protect the civil rights of the freed persons with a structure that did not altogether shift the basic power to regulate those rights away from the states. The equal protection clause of the Fourteenth Amendment imposed a new equality obligation upon the states, but this equality obligation is very similar to the equality component already in the Bill of Rights, in which equal protection is the means through which individual rights are protected.

The Fourteenth Amendment contains an equal protection provision that exists separately and somewhat independently of the Bill of Rights. Nonetheless, an examination of the Fourteenth Amendment's equal protection clause may help to shed light on the meaning and application of equal protection norms.

Generally speaking, equal protection norms prohibit the government from discriminating against targeted groups of people.[4] The equal protection clause mandates "that all persons similarly situated should be treated alike."[5] The Fourteenth Amendment framers intended the equal protection clause to prohibit legislation or state action that targeted a particular group for unfair treatment.[6] Specifically, the clause was aimed at the newly freed slaves in the South;[7] but more generally, it was essentially aimed at tying together the rights of the minority with those of the majority, since whatever rights were given to the majority would also have to be given to the minority.[8]

Although equal protection focuses on the characteristics of the group that is being discriminated against, while due process focuses on the characteristics of the individual right that is allegedly being infringed, both clauses employ strict scrutiny when violations of fundamental rights are involved.[9] Under the equal protection clause, strict scrutiny is used whenever a legislative classification "operates to the peculiar disadvantage of a suspect class or impermissibly interferes with the exercise of a fundamental right."[10] However, even though both equal protection and due process have been interpreted to protect fundamental rights, an equal protection approach provides for a less intrusive or arbitrary judicial review. Under this approach, courts do not need to articulate substantive individual values; they simply need to determine whether one group of individuals is being treated differently than another, similarly situated group. Thus, equal protection often provides a better way to harmonize judicial review with the legislative process. In taking an equal protection rather than substantive due process approach, courts do not create or articulate any new rights or values. Consequently, since there are no substantive standards by which equal protection claims are evaluated, resolving such claims less frequently entangles the judiciary in the kind of substantive values that legislatures are supposed to make.[11]

It is often said that strict scrutiny aims at "smoking out" illicit government motives and making sure that the government has not intentionally targeted a specific group for a particular burden.[12] However, an equal protection approach by itself can often remedy improper governmental motives. Since an improper governmental motive most likely will result in some discriminatory targeting of a particular group, an equal protection approach on its own can eliminate that discriminatory treatment, even if the specific ill motive is never uncovered.

Equal Protection as a Guardian of Individual Rights in a Democracy

The Bill of Rights lays out various areas of freedoms that the ratifying generation believed important in maintaining the health and integrity of American constitutional democracy. But the problem that has preoccupied generations of judges and scholars is how to protect those various freedoms in a manner consistent with the kind of political system that makes such freedoms possible in the first place—a system of democratic government. The solution offered here is that an equal protection approach is the best way to protect the individual freedoms specified in the Bill of Rights, while also respecting and upholding the workings of democratic governance.

According to one commentator, neutrality "is a prominent trope in both free speech and religious freedom doctrine."[13] This neutrality or equal protection approach allows courts to avoid making substantive judgments about the relative values of competing speakers and ideas.[14] Consequently, a neutrality or equal protection approach facilitates judicial restraint and keeps the courts from usurping democratic authority.

An equal protection approach acts as a structural provision of the Constitution, much like federalism or separation of powers. And as a structural norm, it can operate without having to define or apply substantive norms. But under an individual-autonomy view, free speech is seen as a substantive norm, and hence essential to personhood, which can be very hard to define.

Under an equal protection analysis, government unduly expands its authority when it targets certain groups, much more so than if it happens to burden a right or activity exercised by all of society, which in turn can use its political power to eliminate that burden. Furthermore, an equal protection analysis allows courts to focus more on the exercise of government power than on the nature of individual substantive rights. According to Michael Dorf, equal protection does not protect an interest of an individual that exists independently of the government's conduct with respect to that person.[15]

Notions of equality and neutrality, as now being applied in First Amendment jurisprudence, have had a major impact on American constitutionalism throughout the last half century. In the wake of the Supreme Court's 1954 decision in *Brown v. Board of Education,* the Court has increasingly applied equality principles, first through the equal protection clause, and later extending to such individual rights areas as the First Amendment.[16] According to Daniel Conkle, "[G]iven the ever-increasing importance of formal equality under the Equal Protection Clause and in the legal culture generally, it is hardly surprising that an analogous or parallel doctrine, formal neutrality, has risen to prominence" in the Court's First Amendment jurisprudence.[17] In the context of religious accommodation, for instance, "the Supreme Court defines the government's obligation in terms of neutrality."[18] As Justice Anthony Kennedy declared in *Rosenberger v. Rector and Visitors of the University of Virginia,* the establishment clause basically requires the government to follow "neutral criteria and even-handed policies."[19]

For the general purpose of protecting individual freedom, including those freedoms not specified in the Bill of Rights (if, that is, one believes in the constitutional protection of unenumerated rights), an equal protection approach is preferable to a substantive due process approach, which has exposed the Court to charges of "legislating from the bench."[20] As a way of demonstrating how individual freedoms can best be protected in a democracy, an equal protection approach of the kind used in this book will now be compared with the shortcomings of the Court's substantive due process approach—an approach that the Court has used to protect individual liberty.

In *Cruzan v. Director, Missouri Department of Health*, the Court used substantive due process to rule that an individual had a constitutionally protected liberty interest in refusing unwanted medical treatment.[21] However, the Court could have used an equal protection approach by finding that the law could not treat an individual wishing to refuse unwanted medical treatment differently from how it would treated an individual with respect to other medical decisions. In *Moore v. City of East Cleveland*, the Supreme Court overturned a housing ordinance that forbade persons who were not members of the same family from sharing a dwelling unit, excluding from the definition of *family* a unit comprising two first cousins and their grandmother. The Court relied on its substantive due process approach to overturn this ordinance; however, it could just as well have used an equal protection analysis, since the City had singled out very specific familial groups for beneficial treatment regarding certain living arrangements. The Court did not need to recognize some substantive right to live with family members; it just needed to apply an equal protection analysis.[22]

In *Zablocki v. Redhail*, the Court, recognizing that marriage is a fundamental right, held unconstitutional a law that required a noncustodial parent under a duty of child support to obtain judicial permission to marry.[23] However, under an equal protection approach, the Court could have reached the same decision, using the baseline for comparison as the decision to marry. And in *Troxel v. Granville*, the Court used a substantive due process approach to rule that the government could not interfere with the third-party visitation decisions of custodial biological parents, even those decisions precluding visitation by grandparents.[24] Once again, this decision could have been made using an equal protection analysis, reasoning that visitation decisions regarding grandparents could not be singled out for differential treatment from any other parental decision made by custodial parents. Similarly, in *Lawrence v. Texas*, Justice Sandra Day O'Connor would have struck down the Texas homosexual sodomy statute on the grounds that it violated the equal protection clause.[25] Although the majority in *Lawrence* viewed the case as involving a right to sexual intimacy guaranteed by the due process clause, Justice O'Connor's approach would have precluded the Court from having to articulate an independent liberty right with respect to sexual intimacy.[26] As one scholar has noted, "rather than invalidating the Texas statute on grounds of substantive due process, the court in *Lawrence v. Texas* should have invoked the equal protection clause to strike down, as irrational, the state's decision to ban homosexual sodomy but not heterosexual sodomy."[27]

Identifying the problems with the Court's substantive due process approach can be helpful in gaining insights on the meaning and application of the individual freedoms specified in the Bill of Rights. For instance, under the proposed equal protection approach, the First Amendment does not recognize specific substantive values, but rather simply denies government power to act in certain ways and in certain areas. This denial is enforced through an equal protection approach, which achieves the goal of judicial neutrality and restraint, preventing the courts from creating a value-laden view of the First Amendment, which could then lead to judicial lawmaking.

From an equal protection standpoint, the First Amendment protects a negative liberty against discriminatory treatment by the government; it does not encompass a positive liberty that can be used to achieve, for instance, a judicially created right of access. Consistent with this principle, the Supreme Court in *Lloyd Corp. v. Tanner* rejected a First Amendment claim brought by antiwar activists who sought to distribute handbills in a shopping mall.[28] Writing for the Court, Justice Lewis Powell Jr. denied that the activists had any First Amendment access right that would trump the mall owners' property right to exclude them.[29] Similarly, in *Hudgens v. NLRB*, the Court followed the rule set forth in *Lloyd Corp.* and reaffirmed the constitutional right of shopping center owners to prohibit speech access to their premises. Finally, in *Pacific Gas & Electric Co. v. Public Utilities Commission* the Court continued to deny any First Amendment right of access to expressive property, striking down a state regulatory requirement that a public utility provide space in its monthly billing envelopes to consumer advocates who opposed some of the utility's policies.[30]

An equal protection approach focuses on limiting the power of government to discriminate; it does not seek primarily to protect or fulfill individual autonomy. The focus in an equal protection approach is on government and on limiting government powers; it is not on individual autonomy. This lack of focus on individual autonomy can be seen in the Court's decision in *Minneapolis Star and Tribune Co. v. Minnesota Commissioner of Revenue*, where the Court struck down a state tax imposed only on the ink and paper used by certain newspapers.[31] Obviously, the government could far more significantly burden individual expression and autonomy by simply imposing a high general tax on all businesses (which would be constitutional) than by imposing a lower special tax that applies only to some newspapers; but such a tax would not violate equal protection norms, and hence would probably be constitutional.

Similarly, in *R.A.V. v. City of St. Paul*, the Court held that the government could not single out certain types of fighting words to be regulated in ways that other fighting words were not regulated.[32] Thus, government cannot target certain speech for special regulation, even if that speech is generally not entitled to First Amendment protection in the first place. However, the government could heavily regulate, even to the point of censorship, all types of fighting words equally. Again, such an approach would infringe more upon individual autonomy than would a more selected approach, which was overturned in *R.A.V. v. City of St. Paul*, where equal protection norms prevailed over any kind of individual-autonomy concern. Even speech that by itself has no First Amendment protection—e.g., fighting words—nonetheless has some kind of constitutional protection under the equal protection model. What is most important about the Court's decision in *R.A.V.*

v. City of St. Paul is the rule that the government cannot engage in viewpoint discrimination, even with respect to speech that is not normally protected under the First Amendment.

As argued throughout this book, the Bill of Rights is intended primarily and directly to serve as provisions that limit government. But even though limited government is the specific and direct concern of the Bill of Rights, the protection of the individual freedoms listed in the bill is obviously an important and motivating concern. This concern was what prompted the framers to use the Bill of Rights as explicit limitations on government power. And it was through the achievement of limited government that the Bill of Rights would serve the cause of individual liberty. This cause would be further served by the equal protection approach incorporated within the Bill of Rights.

Equal Protection and the First Amendment

The Establishment Clause

An analysis of First Amendment case law reveals how equal protection notions can govern and protect individual rights.[33] As to the religion clauses of the First Amendment, the principle of equality is foremost. The establishment clause, for instance, reflects a constitutional commitment to equal treatment for all religions.[34] According to the Court, the establishment clause prohibits the government from preferring "one religion over another."[35] This prohibition against preferring one religion over another has been called "the clearest command of the Establishment Clause."[36]

In *Larson v. Valente,* the Court articulated the equality principle at the heart of the establishment clause.[37] The Court struck down a Minnesota law that exempted religious organizations from certain registration requirements imposed on groups engaged in charitable solicitations, but only if the religious entity received at least half its contributions from members or affiliated organizations. According to the Court, the law granted "denominational preferences" to certain sects but not to others.[38] The Court suggested that the registration law benefited well-established denominations that could rely on member contributions over new religious organizations that had to seek outside support. Using a neutrality approach, the Court has rejected government programs that favor students attending private religious schools over students attending public schools as an impermissible establishment of religion,[39] but has upheld programs that distribute funding evenly to students attending public and private schools.[40]

In *Board of Education of Kiryas Joel Village School District v. Grumet,* the Court struck down a New York law creating as a separate school district the village of Kiryas Joel, a community populated by members of a traditional Jewish sect, whose beliefs conflict with many of the norms and practices of contemporary American culture.[41] The goal of this law was to enable the children in the sect to receive educational services to which they were entitled under law without having to attend a school outside their home community. But the Court rejected this move, ruling that New York's creation of a separate school district for a religious community violated the establishment clause because it "singled out a particular religious sect for special treatment."[42]

In interpreting the religion clauses of the First Amendment, courts have increasingly tended toward an equal protection approach. According to Douglas Laycock, religious freedoms have changed from a substantive liberty, triggered by a burden on religious practice, to a kind of nondiscrimination right, triggered by a legal treatment that is not neutral or not generally applicable.[43] Beginning in the 1980s, the Court began relying on equal treatment norms in its establishment clause cases, drifting away from the no-aid principle.[44] Using these norms, the Court has upheld a number of programs allowing public funds to flow to religious institutions.[45] Among the programs the Court has upheld are a voucher program in which vouchers are used to pay tuition at any school, including religious schools,[46] and long-term loans of equipment to private schools, including religious schools.[47]

As early as 1968, in *Board of Education v. Allen,* the Court upheld the state provision of secular textbooks to religious schools, noting that the statute at issue was simply conferring secular benefits neutrally among all students.[48] Later, in *Tilton v. Richardson,* the Court upheld the Higher Education Facilities Act authorizing federal grants and loans for construction by colleges and universities.[49] As the federal funds would be used to finance construction of buildings on the campuses of religiously affiliated universities, as well as secular universities, the Court found that the statute strove to equalize the governmental benefits available to all higher education students. And in *Roemer v. Board of Public Works of Maryland,* the Court upheld a state statute authorizing grants to private secular and sectarian colleges, reasoning that "religious institutions need not be quarantined from public benefits that are neutrally available to all."[50]

The Sixth Circuit applied an equal protection approach in *Wilson v. National Labor Relations Board,* which involved the constitutionality of Section 19 of the National Labor Relations Act containing an exemption from required union membership for "any employee who is a member of and adheres to established and traditional tenets or teachings of a bona fide religion, body, or sect which has historically held conscientious objections to joining or financially supporting labor organizations."[51] The court ruled that this statutory exemption discriminated among religious sects "by conferring a benefit on members of the religious organizations described in the statute."[52] For this reason, the court concluded that Section 19 violated the establishment clause.

Similarly, in *Children's Healthcare Is a Legal Duty, Inc. v. Vladeck,* plaintiffs challenged certain exemptions designed for Christian Science "sanitoria" under both the Medicare and Medicaid Acts.[53] The court ruled that these exemptions from regulations that applied to other healthcare providers eligible to receive payments under the acts facially discriminated among religions by singling out Christian Science sanitoria for preferential treatment. Finally, in *Colorado Christian University v. Weaver,* the Tenth Circuit struck down a Colorado state scholarship program in which eligible students could receive a scholarship to attend any in-state college or university other than one found to be pervasively sectarian by state officials.[54] The court ruled that this discriminatory treatment of pervasively sectarian colleges violated the establishment clause. According to the court, the Colorado scholarship program was based on the degree of religiosity of the institution and hence discriminated "among religious institutions on the basis of the pervasiveness or intensity of their belief."[55]

The Supreme Court's equality approach to the establishment clause has also been evident in cases involving free speech claims. In *Lambs Chapel v. Center Moriches Union Free School District,* the Court held that excluding religious speech from a designated forum violated the free speech clause, despite objections from the school district that the use of such school facilities would violate the establishment clause.[56] After a local church was denied permission to show a film series on school property that discussed family and child-rearing issues from a religious perspective, which would clearly have been a permitted use of the building were it not for the religious content of the series, the Court ruled that the establishment clause could not be used to single out and exclude religious groups. Earlier, in *Widmar v. Vincent,* the Court had struck down a state university regulation prohibiting the use of university facilities for religious speech purposes.[57] The Court ruled that the university had created a designated public forum when it allowed other student groups to use its buildings for speech activities; hence, the discriminatory exclusion of the religious group was overturned.[58] Not only did the Court find that the regulation violated the free speech clause, but as it would later do in *Lambs Chapel,* it also held that providing religious students the same access to university facilities that other students enjoyed for secular activities did not violate the establishment clause.[59]

In *Rosenberger v. Rector and Visitors of the University of Virginia,* the Court again addressed the exclusion of religious speech from a state-created forum.[60] In *Rosenberger,* the University of Virginia provided funding for student publications, but specifically prohibited any religious-oriented publications from eligibility for such funds. The university justified this prohibition on the grounds that direct funding of religious activities would violate the establishment clause.[61] But the Court disagreed, ruling that a denial of funding to publications with a religious perspective would constitute viewpoint discrimination in violation of the free speech clause.[62] Moreover, even though *Rosenberger* essentially involved free speech issues, the Court also rejected the university's establishment clause defense, finding that an equal funding of both religious and nonreligious student publications did not violate the establishment clause.[63] Thus, the Court adopted the same equal protection approach for establishment clause cases as it had for free speech clause cases.[64]

In a similar vein to *Rosenberger* and *Lambs Chapel* was the Court's decision in *Good News Club v. Milford Central School.*[65] In *Good News Club,* the Court held that the exclusion of a religious group from a state-created public forum (e.g., the after-hours use of public school facilities) constituted viewpoint discrimination in violation of the free speech clause; furthermore, permitting the group to use the facilities on the same terms as nonreligious groups did not violate the establishment clause.[66] In the Court's view, religious organizations and uses had to receive equal treatment with nonreligious organizations and uses. Consequently, the establishment clause cannot be used to justify viewpoint discrimination against religious organizations seeking the same kinds of public benefits enjoyed by secular groups.[67]

Compared with previous case law, neutrality appears to be an advantageous doctrine for religion. For instance, in the 1985 case of *Aguilar v. Felton,* the Supreme Court in a non-neutral decision ruled against parochial school participation in a special education program that provided remedial English and mathematics assistance to economically and educationally disadvantaged students at both public and private schools. But in a later decision employing equality principles, the Court overruled *Aguilar.*[68] In *Agostini v. Felton,* the Court stressed the importance of formal neutrality in concluding that the establishment clause did not preclude publicly funded teachers from teaching secular, remedial courses on the premises of religious schools under a federally funded program that supported teaching at nonreligious schools as well.[69] The Court suggested that establishment clause invalidation would be unlikely when "aid is allocated on the basis of neutral, secular criteria that neither favor nor disfavor religion, and is made available to both religious and secular beneficiaries on a nondiscriminating basis."[70]

The neutrality doctrine was also applied in *Zobrest v. Catalina Foothills School District,* where the Supreme Court upheld the provision of a publicly funded sign-language interpreter for a deaf student at a religious school, noting that "governmental programs that neutrally provide benefits to a broad class of citizens defined without reference to religion are not readily subject to an Establishment Clause challenge."[71] Later, in *Zelman v. Simmons-Harris,* the Court used the neutrality doctrine to uphold Cleveland's school voucher program.[72] It ruled that the vouchers promoted private choice by giving money directly to students for their use at either religious or nonreligious schools.[73] This scheme was found neutral because it left the decision of whether to apply funds toward a religious education to the private choices of parents and their children, and not to the government.[74] According to *Zelman,* so long as the programs exhibit governmental neutrality toward religion, indirect aid programs are permissible under the establishment clause, regardless of whether or not tuition money is ultimately diverted for religious purposes.[75]

The requirement of denominational equality obviously demands that all religions be treated equally. However, the requirement of equality is sometimes seen as going one step further, demanding that the government neither favor nor disfavor religion in general, as compared to nonreligion.[76] For instance, in *School District v. Schempp*, the Court stated that the First Amendment prohibited governmental action that served to advance religion.[77] Thus, the Court has often adopted a concept of religious neutrality that applies not only between different religious denominations, but also between religion and nonreligion.

This highlights a crucial issue in applying an equal protection approach—namely, that of arriving at the proper baseline to be used in determining equality of treatment. But in *Schempp*, the Court may have used the wrong baseline for its application of equality. The baseline should not be a comparison with nonreligion; instead, the baseline should only involve an inquiry into whether all religions are being treated equally. The First Amendment, concerned as it is with limiting government power to interfere with either the individual or the institutional spheres of religious observance, does not focus on drawing the same kind of limits to government intrusion into nonreligion, whatever that is.

The wrong baseline may also have been used in *Texas Monthly v. Bullock*.[78] The Court in *Texas Monthly* held that a sales-tax exemption for periodicals published or distributed by religious denominations violated the establishment clause, because similar exemptions were not given to nonreligious publications.[79] The Court's "neutrality" approach assumed that the establishment clause forbids the government from favoring religion in general over "non-religion." To Justice William Brennan Jr., the sales-tax exemption was unconstitutional because it benefited only religion and gave an accommodation not required by free exercise. However, because of the First Amendment's concern with limiting the government's power to discriminate among religious institutions, the establishment clause baseline should be all religious organizations—not every kind of organization or business or entity known to exist.[80]

Neutrality is a way of achieving limited government because it prevents government from imposing discriminatory or particularly onerous burdens on religion. After all, the First Amendment serves not only to limit government, but to protect the ability of religion to act as a vibrant check on government. In *Corporation of the Presiding Bishop of the Church of Jesus Christ of Latter-day Saints v. Amos*, the Court upheld a statutory exemption in the Civil Rights Act permitting religious discrimination in employment by religious organizations.[81] In upholding this exemption, the Court argued that it was not abandoning the principle of neutrality with respect to religion, stating that neutrality was served by alleviating significant governmental interference into the ability of religious organizations to carry out their missions.

Exemptions are also appropriate insofar as the granting of a religious exemption does not unduly expand government power. In *Mueller v. Allen*, the Court upheld a state income tax deduction for parents paying school tuition and other expenses associated with the enrollment of a child in a nonpublic elementary or secondary school of the parent's choice, including a religious school. Since the tax deduction was available only as a result of the private choice of individual parents to enroll their children in a religious school, the benefit provided to religion could not be attributable to government action. Thus, the benefit did not violate the neutrality principle. Furthermore, as the Court did in *Amos,* the *Mueller* Court dismissed the danger of excessive entanglement between government and religion, since the indirect nature of the benefit reduced the potential for intrusive government oversight of organized religion.

The Free Exercise Clause

Just as neutrality and equality have become governing principles for establishment clause cases, they have also been applied to the free exercise clause. With respect to the free exercise clause, the principle of equality means that all religious believers, regardless of their beliefs, should be treated equally under the law and that the government should not have the power to single out particular individuals or religious beliefs for discriminatory treatment.

The neutrality approach was adopted in *Employment Division v. Smith,* where the Court held that a law criminalizing the use of peyote, as applied to two American Indians, did not violate the free exercise clause, finding that the law was one of general applicability and was neutral regarding religious conduct.[82] The Court distinguished between laws that specifically target religion and neutral laws of general applicability, which, according to the Court, did not constitute an infringement of free exercise, no matter how substantial the burden on religious exercise.[83] Thus, through its focus on neutrality, the *Smith* Court moved its free exercise clause jurisprudence in the same direction as its free speech and establishment clause doctrines.

The emphasis on neutrality in *Employment Division v. Smith* marked a departure from the Court's previous free exercise "fundamental rights" jurisprudence. Prior to *Smith,* the Court's rule was that any government-imposed burden on religious practice presumptively violated the free exercise clause, and that such burdens could only be justified by a compelling government interest.[84] This doctrine was articulated in *Sherbert v. Verner* and *Wisconsin v. Yoder,* where the Court held that any state action substantially burdening religious exercise had to be strictly scrutinized.[85] But in *Smith,* the Court declared that neutral laws of general applicability burdening religious exercise do not require any heightened judicial review.[86] This rule—that the free exercise clause prohibited only deliberate governmental discrimination against religion—rested in part on a belief that the granting to religion of exemptions from neutral laws would pose too big of a risk of discrimination between religions.[87]

The *Smith* rule of equality, however, can sometimes be a difficult rule to fulfill, particularly depending on how one measures it. Laycock has outlined two different concepts of neutrality or equality in connection with the First Amendment religion clauses. The notion of "formal neutrality" would preclude formal or deliberate discrimination either between religions or between religion and nonreligion.[88] The other form of neutrality, according to Laycock, is "substantive neutrality"—a principle that examines whether the government's actions, even if formally neutral, have the actual effect of promoting or discouraging religion.[89]

According to Conkle, formal neutrality is the simplest means of implementing a policy of equal treatment for religion and nonreligion, and has become the dominant theme under both the free exercise and establishment clauses.[90] This notion of formal neutrality certainly prevailed in *Smith,* where the Court upheld a formally neutral, nondiscriminatory state law, even though that law resulted in a significant burden to a particular religious exercise. Thus, *Smith* changed free exercise from a substantive liberty to a comparative right, "in which the constitutionally required treatment of religious practices depends on the treatment of some comparable set of secular practices."[91] Whereas a personal-autonomy model of the free exercise clause would focus on burdens caused by laws infringing on religious exercise, *Smith* changed the focus to discrimination.

The Court elaborated on the *Smith* rule in the case of *Church of the Lukumi Babalu Aye, Inc. v. City of Hialeah,* which involved a challenge to several local ordinances that prohibited animal sacrifices.[92] Although the City argued that the laws reflected a generally applicable ban on those sacrifices, the Court found that the ban was targeted at religious uses, exempting any killings of animals for secular reasons. When taking into account both the laws and all their exemptions, it became clear to the Court that only the killing of animals for religious reasons— indeed, only the ceremonies of a particular sect, the Santeria religion—was subject to penalty.[93] Consequently, because the ordinances on animal sacrifice prohibited religious but not secular killings of animals, the Court found that there was objective evidence of governmental targeting religious conduct for discriminatory treatment.[94] According to Laycock, *City of Hialeah* is not about bad motive or reading a bad motive requirement into the *Smith* rule.[95] Bad motive may be one way to prove a violation, "but first and foremost *Smith-Lukumi* is about objectively unequal treatment of religion and analogous secular activities."[96] Thus, both *Smith* and *Lukumi* rely on the nondiscrimination principle to govern the right of free exercise of religion.[97]

In *Locke v. Davey,* the Court further explained the *Smith* legacy. In *Locke,* a Washington scholarship program allowed qualified recipients to use their scholarships to pursue a degree in any course of study except a devotional theology degree.[98] Davey sued, claiming that this program violated the free exercise clause because of its discriminatory purpose and effect. However, even though Washington discriminated against devotional theology students, the Supreme Court nonetheless upheld the program against a free exercise challenge.

While *Smith* banned facial discrimination against religion, *Locke* stated that, at least with respect to funding, facial discrimination against religion is presumptively unconstitutional if and only if the discrimination burdens a religious practice.[99] The *Locke* Court also held that a refusal to fund, by itself, does not burden religious exercise.[100] Thus, under the *Locke v. Davey* rule, a free exercise violation requires not only a discrimination but also a significant burden arising from that discrimination. This decision seems to move the Court away from its post-*Smith* emphasis on equality, allowing religious exercise to be targeted for special burdens, as long as those burdens are not considered significant. In *Locke* the Court did not focus on discrimination or equal protection; it focused on the nature of the burden imposed by the program, downplaying the facial discrimination against devotional theology students. This disregard of discrimination, by violating the equal protection approach, not only threatens free exercise rights but also erodes the limited-government principle by allowing the government to discriminate.

One change that would be affected by a wider application of the equal protection approach to free exercise cases involves zoning regulations on religious buildings. Currently, in the land-use area, courts review restrictions on religious buildings from a very deferential standpoint (that is, in the absence of statutory mandates such as the Religious Land Use and Institutionalized Persons Act, as well as various state laws that mirror the Religious Freedom Restoration Act).[101] However, if an equal protection approach were used, with the baseline that of religious uses of property, the regulations might be seen as unconstitutional. But if the baseline were all uses, both secular and religious, the regulations would be upheld, since the religious buildings would operate under the same restrictions as the secular buildings. However, as one scholar has argued, "Given the close association between a house of worship and religious expression, explicit restrictions on churches, synagogues, mosques and temples arguably constitute content discriminatory regulations of religious expression."[102]

The Free Speech Clause

Equal protection norms form the bedrock of the free speech clause. In *Arkansas Writers' Project, Inc. v. Ragland,* the Supreme Court indicated that any law singling out certain speakers for differential treatment was suspect under the First Amendment.[103]

An equal protection approach in the free speech area is already somewhat reflected in the Court's content-neutrality doctrine. Current First Amendment doctrine requires that any content-based law be subject to strict scrutiny.[104] Although this approach theoretically indicates that content regulations might be upheld if they are narrowly drawn and supported by a compelling governmental interest, in reality it allows virtually no content-based speech restriction to survive.[105]

The Court's content-neutrality doctrine was applied in *Schacht v. United States* (1970), where the Court overturned a law prohibiting soldiers from wearing their uniforms in theatrical productions if those productions treated the military with contempt.[106] Two years later, in *Police Department of Chicago v. Mosley,* the Court struck down a Chicago ordinance prohibiting all peaceful picketers, except peaceful labor picketers, from demonstrating near a school while that school was in session.[107] In both *Schacht* and *Mosley,* the Court's focus was on equality of treatment between all viewpoints. But the determination of this equality depends on what baseline is used for measuring such equality. Should a narrow or broad baseline be used? As will be explained later, when dealing with political speech, as broad a baseline as possible should be used.

According to Geoffrey Stone, *Schacht* and *Mosley* ushered in a new era of First Amendment jurisprudence. In the wake of those decisions, the initial focus of the Court in any free speech case has been on whether the challenged regulation is content based or content neutral.[108] In *Schacht* and *Mosley,* the equality principle prevailed over the speech principle. In both cases, the Court acknowledged that a content-neutral ban—prohibiting all soldiers from wearing their uniforms in theatrical productions, or prohibiting all protestors from picketing near schools— would be constitutional, even though such a ban would obviously be quite speech-restrictive. According to Stone, in each case "the government violated the First Amendment not because it limited Schacht's or Mosley's right to speak, but because it discriminated against them based on the content of their message."[109] The issue essentially was whether the government was treating all speakers and ideas equally, rather than whether it was restricting the marketplace of ideas.

To sustain various kinds of speech restrictions under a more permissive review than strict scrutiny, an intermediate level of scrutiny has been used for time-manner-place regulations found to be content neutral.[110] However, in its use of the content-neutrality rule as a prerequisite for employing intermediate scrutiny, the Court has often found that laws effectively singling out certain types of speech were in fact content neutral.[111] For instance, the following regulations have been found to be content neutral: laws governing the location of sexually explicit entertainment businesses;[112] laws governing the speech activities of abortion protestors;[113] regulations governing the solicitation activities of religious groups, even though those activities arise from the groups' religious beliefs;[114] and a law requiring cable television operators to carry, free of charge, the programming of local broadcast television stations.[115] Even though these laws and regulations were evaluated under the more deferential intermediate standard of review, they were effectively aimed at very specific groups of speakers. Consequently, given the subjective and inconsistent way in which the content-neutral principle has been applied, its future legitimacy falls into question. For this reason, a more simplified, all-encompassing approach is needed, such as the one provided by the equal protection approach.

There has always been a tenuous connection between the Court's content-neutral approach and the secondary-effects doctrine. But this latter doctrine can be explained through an equal protection approach to the First Amendment and an identification of the proper baseline. In *City of Renton v. Playtime Theatres Inc.,* the Court upheld a zoning ordinance that on its face singled out adult movie theaters for special restrictions on location.[116] The Court ruled that the ordinance was not content based because it was justified without reference to the content of the regulated speech, but instead was justified by the government's desire to alleviate "the secondary effects of such theatres on the surrounding community."[117] However, in reality, the zoning restrictions in the ordinance applied only to theaters that engaged in a particular expressive activity. But the decision can perhaps be more clearly explained in terms of baseline comparisons. The *Renton* Court was not looking at all movie theaters as the baseline comparison, but at businesses that cause certain dilapidating effects in surrounding neighborhoods. With this as the baseline, the theaters subject to the restrictions in *Renton* were treated with equality.

In *Young v. American Mini Theatres, Inc.,* the Court upheld a Detroit ordinance that prohibited two adult theaters or bookstores from operating within a thousand feet of one another.[118] In his concurring opinion, Justice Lewis Powell Jr. argued that the City was justified in regulating adult theaters differently than other theaters "because they have markedly different effects upon their surroundings."[119] Thus, to Powell, the relevant baseline was not speech but neighborhood effects. This baseline was used in part because of the Court's recognition that pornography is not entitled to the same degree of constitutional protection as political speech, since "society's interest in protecting this type of expression is of a wholly different, and lesser, magnitude than the interest in untrammeled political debate [and] few of us would march our sons and daughters off to war to preserve the citizen's right to see `Specified Sexual Activities' exhibited in the theatres of our choice."[120] As some scholars argue, pornographic speech is more like a sexual device than cognitive speech.[121]

However, when political speech is involved, the Court does not apply the secondary-effects doctrine, and hence uses a broader baseline. For instance, in *R.A.V. v. City of St. Paul,* the Court overturned an ordinance imposing additional penalties for violent crimes that convey a racist message.[122] According to the Court, even if racial hate crimes are likely to cause violent responses, that violence does not qualify as a secondary effect. Thus, the Court will not use narrow baselines— e.g., secondary effects—when political speech is involved. Similarly, in *Simon & Schuster Inc. v. Members of the New York State Crime Victims Board,* the Court overturned a law requiring convicted criminals who author books describing their crimes to share book royalties with the victims of their crimes.[123] The Court declined to review the law under the secondary-effects doctrine—e.g., the effect of allowing criminals to gain an economic benefit from their crimes. This was because the speech at issue could qualify as political speech—and the law not only singled out some political speech (speech about crimes), but singled out some speakers (convicted criminals) as well.

A problem with the current content-neutral approach is that it fails to adequately consider the actual burdens imposed on the subject speech by the subject law. Indeed, what could be more important when evaluating laws affecting individual rights than to examine the actual burdens being placed on the exercise of those rights? Not only does the Court often fail to take into account the actual degree of burden, but it also fails to distinguish between whether the law imposes a mere burden or a complete ban on the speech.[124] In reality, there is a substantial difference between a mere burden placed on speech being expressed in just one of many media channels, and a complete ban that effectively silences that speech in all communications venues.

The failure of the content-neutral approach to consider the actual and relative burdens on speech can be seen in the Supreme Court's decisions in *Denver Area* and *Playboy*. In *Denver Area Educational Telecommunications Consortium, Inc. v. FCC*, the Court struck down regulations requiring cable operators to place indecent programs on separate, blocked channels.[125] In its decision, the Court focused on the inconveniences to would-be viewers of indecent programming. However, none of these burdens amounted to an irreversible censorship. Viewers could get access to the desired programming by simply requesting access from the cable company.

Exemplifying the dramatic imbalance of burdens currently being allocated between commercial vendors of indecent programming and unwilling recipients of such programming is the Court's decision in *U.S. v. Playboy Entertainment Group*, striking down a provision in the Telecommunications Act of 1996 requiring cable channels "primarily dedicated to sexually-oriented programming" either to "fully scramble or otherwise fully block" their channels or to limit their transmission to the hours between 10 p.m. and 6 a.m., when children are unlikely to be among the viewing audience.[126] In dissent, Justice Stephen Breyer focused on the issue of relative burdens. He noted that the law in question placed only a burden on adult programmers, not a ban. According to Breyer, "adults may continue to watch adult channels, though less conveniently, by watching at night, recording programs with a VCR, or by subscribing to digital cable with better blocking systems."[127] As Justice Breyer argued, where tens of millions of children have no parents at home after school, and where children may spend afternoons and evenings watching television outside of the home with friends, the time-channeling law offered "independent protection for a large number of families."[128] He argued that the First Amendment was not intended to leave millions of parents helpless in the face of media technologies that bring unwanted speech into their children's lives.[129]

The Court's current approach treats all content-based regulations the same; it makes virtually no effort to determine whether a particular law imposes the kind of burden that threatens to drive an idea out of the marketplace of ideas. This approach—of invalidating laws found to be "content based," regardless of the actual burdens they impose—contrasts with the situation where a court determines a law to be content neutral and then sustains that law even though the burdens on speech caused by the law are readily apparent.

The Supreme Court's First Amendment jurisprudence, relying as it so often does on individual-autonomy considerations, has produced an inconsistent and even contradictory stance toward burdens on the unwilling recipient. Although *Denver Area* and *Playboy* gave almost no weight to the burdens being faced by unwilling recipients of nonpolitical speech (e.g., indecent media entertainment programming), other decisions issued under the guise of content neutrality have allowed significant burdens to be placed on traditional political speech for the benefit of the unwilling recipient.

In *Hill v. Colorado*, the Court upheld a Colorado statute creating a "floating buffer zone" prohibiting anyone from coming within eight feet of another person outside of an abortion clinic for the purpose of passing out a leaflet or engaging in oral protest or counseling.[130] Even though recognizing that the speech of the abortion protestors was of the type typically protected by the First Amendment and that the public sidewalks covered by the statute were "quintessential" public forums for free speech, the Court nonetheless relied on the "significant difference between state restrictions on a speaker's right to address a willing audience and those that protect listeners from unwanted communication."[131] It noted that the protection normally afforded to offensive speech would not always apply when the unwilling audience was unable to avoid the speech. In elaborating on the "right to be let alone," the Court stated that the case law has "repeatedly recogniz[ed] the interests of unwilling listeners in situations where the degree of captivity makes it impractical for the unwilling viewer to avoid exposure." Thus, according to the Court, the rights of the listener to be free of offensive speech "must be placed in the scales with the right of others to communicate."[132]

The dissent in *Hill* argued that the governmental interest in protecting people from unwanted communications had never before been extended to speech on public sidewalks. Moreover, as the dissent argued, the speech burdens imposed on the protestors were significant. As the dissent argued, "[I]t does not take a veteran labor organizer to recognize that leafletting will be rendered utterly ineffectual by a requirement that the leafletter obtain from each subject permission to approach. That simply is not how it is done, and the Court knows it."[133]

Contrary to the approach taken by the Court in its abortion-rights jurisprudence, there is often little consideration in current free speech jurisprudence of whether a regulation actually imposes an "undue burden" on the particular speech.[134] This ignoring of the degree of actual burden has resulted in the nullification of laws providing various child-protection safeguards on commercially provided pornography,[135] as well as laws requiring fundraisers to reveal the percentage of raised money that is actually provided to the charities for whom they are working.[136] It has also led courts to overturn every state regulation aimed at preventing minor children from being exposed to graphically violent video games.[137] Laws requiring parental consent before minors can obtain such games have been overturned on the grounds that those laws make content distinctions, even though the only burden imposed is on the ability of commercial vendors to sell those games to young children without their parents' knowledge or consent.[138]

A more balanced approach to burdens can be found in *Kovacs v. Cooper*, where the Court upheld an ordinance prohibiting the use of sound trucks that emitted "loud and raucous noises," reasoning that citizens in their homes should be protected from "aural aggression."[139] Although the statute essentially created a regulatory wall that blocked otherwise constitutionally protected speech, and hence infringed on the personal autonomy of the speaker, the Court noted that the "unwilling listener is practically helpless to escape this interference with his privacy by loud speakers except through the protection of the municipality."[140] It did not matter to the Court that not every person in the community wanted to keep out the information broadcast by the sound trucks, or that some might actually want to receive the information.[141]

This decision could also have been reached under an equal protection approach, with the baseline for equality being homeowner freedom to receive/not receive amplified speech. The regulations gave unreceptive listeners an ability to avoid such speech/noise that was approximately equal to their ability to access it. Under traditional First Amendment jurisprudence, courts dealing with free speech issues have required an opt-out scheme rather than an opt-in one.[142] Unwilling listeners must opt out of the unwanted speech environment. But an opt-in requirement, especially with respect to nonpolitical speech, would be an attempt to balance the burdens and equalize the situations of willing and unwilling listeners. This would entail the courts' use of a receptive/unreceptive baseline in cases regarding certain new technologies and nonpolitical speech. For instance, in judicial opinions sustaining restrictions on access to dial-a-porn services, ruling that such restrictions were necessary to protect the children of parents who did not wish them to hear this particular kind of speech, the courts in *Dial Information Services* and *Information Providers* not only found that the restrictions did not amount to a complete ban on the indecent speech, but also tried to equalize the burdens of accessing and avoiding such speech.[143]

Even though as a general rule content-based regulation is strictly scrutinized by the courts, content regulation has been allowed in certain media or conduits. Under an equal protection approach, such regulation can be explained by identifying the point of comparison or baseline to be used in determining equal treatment. For instance, the Court has determined that the print media constitute a completely separate baseline than do the broadcast media, with the former receiving a higher degree of First Amendment protection than the latter. However, within broadcasting, all entities are treated the same.

Courts have used the technological differences among media to justify the differing constitutional protections for speech within each medium. As the Supreme Court proclaimed in 1969, "Differences in the characteristics of new media justify differences in the First Amendment standards applied to them."[144] This assertion stems from Justice Robert Jackson's statement two decades earlier that each medium "is a law unto itself."[145]

Based on the notion of a scarce spectrum, the broadcast media receive the lowest degree of content protection.[146] This diminished constitutional protection was evident in *Red Lion Broadcasting Co. v. FCC*, which upheld a federal regulation called the Fairness Doctrine that forced broadcasters to give a right of reply to political figures criticized over the airwaves. This ruling subjected broadcasters to constraints that in any other medium would be unconstitutional.[147] Exemplifying this print/broadcast dichotomy, the Court later struck down essentially the same kind of law as applied to the print media.[148] The rationale given for the lower constitutional status of broadcasting is that a limited spectrum creates a natural monopoly, which in turn confers upon the government the need and duty to regulate it for the common good.[149]

In *FCC v. Pacifica Foundation,* upholding an FCC decision requiring broadcasters to channel indecent programming away from times of the day when there is a reasonable risk that children may be in the audience, the Court found that the broadcast media are intrusive and pervasive, and that they therefore should be their own separate baseline, not to be compared equally with the print media.[150] In reaffirming that the broadcast media should receive the most limited of content protections, the *Pacifica* Court held that the rights of the public to avoid indecent speech trump those of the broadcaster to disseminate such speech. The justifications for this ruling were twofold. First, the regulations were necessary because of the pervasive presence of broadcast media in American life, capable of injecting offensive material into the privacy of the home, where the right "to be let alone plainly outweighs the First Amendment rights of the intruder."[151] Second, broadcasting "is uniquely accessible to children, even those too young to read."[152] Stressing the need to preserve the home as a sanctuary, safe from unwanted speech or images, the *Pacifica* Court compared the broadcast audience to the *Kovacs* home-dwellers who were unable to escape the loudspeaker intrusion. The Court dismissed the argument that the offended listener or viewer could simply turn the dial and avoid the unwanted broadcast, reasoning that because the broadcast audience is constantly tuning in and out, prior warnings cannot protect the listener from unexpected program content.[153] These were all reasons that, to the Court, justified treating broadcast as a separate First Amendment baseline from print.

The print and broadcast models lie at the two ends of the spectrum of constitutional scrutiny, with cable television somewhere in between. Even though cable does not have the same kind of scarcity issues that broadcasting does, the courts have nonetheless regulated it more than the print media are regulated.[154]

In *Turner I,* the Court addressed the issues of whether to maintain the disparity in First Amendment treatment of the print and broadcast media, and then whether to apply the print or broadcast model to cable television.[155] Ever since *City of Los Angeles v. Preferred Communications Inc.,* the First Amendment status of cable television had been in a sort of legal limbo. In *Preferred Communications,* the Court stated that cable possessed First Amendment freedoms, but did not specify the exact nature of those freedoms.[156] Whereas the *Turner* Court affirmed that cable programmers are fully protected by the First Amendment, and that the scarcity rationale does not apply to cable, it nonetheless refused to apply the strict scrutiny used in the print model. Instead, the Court employed an intermediate level of scrutiny that amounted to a seeming compromise between the print and broadcast models.[157]

On remand, the Court in *Turner II* edged cable even closer to the broadcast model. Indeed, *Turner II* "shows a tolerance for speech-relevant regulatory constraints that is not far from the standard of *Red Lion,* notwithstanding the Court's earlier holding that the *Red Lion* standard was inapplicable to cable."[158] Factors that pushed cable toward the broadcast model and away from the print model include: the market power of cable operators, the fact that most cable systems operate as local monopolies, and the intrusiveness of television and its ability to exploit its audience.[159]

The *Turner* cases tried to piece together a third model or baseline to apply to cable television. Though the Court did not want to place the same kind of content restrictions on cable that exist for broadcast, it nonetheless continued to see a difference between the print and television media, and between the impact that each medium has on its audience. This uncertainty over exactly what regulatory standard (or baseline) to adopt for cable also appeared in *Denver Area Educational Telecommunications Consortium, Inc. v. FCC,* where Justice Breyer's plurality opinion retreated from any "rigid single standard" or analogy to any other media.[160] However, Justice Breyer did state that the *Pacifica* rationales—pervasiveness, invasion of the home, ineffectiveness of warnings, and accessibility to children—applied with equal force to cable television, thus justifying a less protective level of scrutiny than that typically associated with content-based regulation of the print media.[161]

With respect to the Internet, the Court has so far decided to treat it according to the print model.[162] Nonetheless, in *Ashcroft v. ACLU,* even though conferring the highest constitutional protections on the Internet, Justice Kennedy reiterated that the "unique characteristics" of "each mode of expression" should determine the constitutional coverage of that medium.[163] According to Kennedy, "[T]he economics and the technology of each medium affect both the burden of a speech restriction and the Government's interest in maintaining it."[164]

The Application of Equal Protection Norms

The limited-government model requires that a statute not violate the limited-government doctrine, and that it not fail an equal protection analysis regarding the exercise of a right specified in the Bill of Rights. For instance, a law imposing a special tax on newspaper ink may or may not violate the limited-government doctrine, but it does fail an equal protection analysis since the law would burden the First Amendment rights of a special group of speakers.[165] Any tax policy that seems oriented toward specially burdening the media or particular media entities is unconstitutional, even though another business or activity—e.g., home construction or horse racing—could be treated in a discriminatory manner.

Determining the relevant baseline to be used for comparison purposes is a crucial endeavor in any equal protection approach. This baseline issue has been a longstanding issue in the establishment clause area. The question is often whether the measure of equality should be between religion and nonreligion, or just between different religious sects. But since the First Amendment religion clauses are concerned with the protection of religious liberty in all its forms, and not with the protection of secular society from religious influences, the establishment clause baseline should be equality among religions, not equality between religion and nonreligion.[166]

In the free exercise area, the Court's change in doctrine from *Sherbert v. Verner* to *Employment Division v. Smith* can be explained in the change of baseline used. In *Sherbert v. Verner*, the Court in a way relied on neutrality principles to argue that an accommodation or exemption from regulation "reflects nothing more than the governmental obligation of neutrality in the face of religious differences."[167] The rule in *Sherbert* prohibited a state from denying unemployment benefits to a worker who had refused a job on the grounds that it would have required her to work on Saturdays, violating her Seventh Day Adventist convictions. In requiring the exemption, the Court said it was simply upholding the governmental obligation of neutrality in the face of religious differences; it was not treating Seventh Day Adventists specially, it was simply allowing them to practice their religion the same way that every other practitioner practiced his religion.

The same baseline used in *Sherbert* was later used in *Wisconsin v. Yoder*, where the Court rejected Wisconsin's attempt to enforce its compulsory-school-attendance law on members of the Amish religion. The Court again justified its decision in terms of a constitutional requirement for government neutrality: "A regulation neutral on its face may, in its application, nonetheless offend the constitutional requirement for governmental neutrality if it unduly burdens the free exercise of religion."[168] In both *Sherbert* and *Yoder*, the baseline for determining equality was the religious freedom of religious practitioners. If a law affected some religious practitioners more detrimentally than others, then the law was unconstitutional. However, in *Smith*, when the Court ruled that two American Indians were not exempt from an Oregon law forbidding the use of peyote, even when using it during religious observances, the baseline changed to all members of society, including the nonreligious. So if a law affected all of society neutrally, it was not unconstitutional, even if it differentially affected the religious activities or practices of some of society's citizens.

There is a strong argument that the baseline established in *Smith* is the wrong baseline and does not adequately protect or consider the unique needs of religious exercise. By establishing the baseline that it did, the *Smith* Court arguably did not sufficiently consider the convictions and needs of minority religions to the same degree that those of a mainstream religion would be protected by the political process. Since *Smith* may not adequately protect the unique practices of minority religions from the burdens of generally applicable neutral state laws, it can be argued that not all religions possess equal protection of their religious practices. The argument in opposition to *Smith* is that equality among religious practitioners, rather than equality between religious practitioners and secular citizens, should be the baseline used under the free exercise clause. If a different baseline had been used—namely, the ability of all religious practitioners to practice their religion equally—the case may have turned out differently.

A religious practitioner baseline was used in *Corporation of the Presiding Bishop of the Church of Jesus Christ of Latter-day Saints v. Amos,* where the Court exempted religious employers from a federal law against employment discrimination, allowing them to hire people of their faith for ministerial positions.[169] According to the Court, the nondiscrimination law was a potentially significant burden on a religious organization, and the exemption eliminated that burden. This relief of a potential burden served the goal of equal protection, allowing all religious organizations to be free of the unique burdens that nondiscrimination laws may have on particular religious sects. The baseline for comparison was not all of secular society, but all religious organizations. Under the holding in *Amos,* all religious organizations are to be given an equal chance to operate free of secular interference.

The effect of using a secular baseline is often to prevent benefits or special accommodations from going to religious organizations or believers. In *Estate of Thornton v. Caldor,* for instance, the Court ruled that a Connecticut law giving employees the right not to work on their religious Sabbath violated the establishment clause.[170] The statute violated the equal protection principle, since it granted an advantage to practitioners of those religions that believe in observing a Sabbath. In fact, the law violated equal protection norms on a couple of different levels. If the baseline in *Caldor* was all secular workers, then the law clearly violated equal protection norms, since religious employees who followed Sabbath requirements were treated differently from nonreligious workers, who did not have to go against their beliefs to work any certain day of the week. But the law may also have violated equal protection norms if the baseline were changed to all religious practitioners. This is because there are some religious workers who do not have a Sabbath. Therefore, the law treated some religious workers differently than others, favoring religious workers with a Sabbath.

In striking down the law in *Caldor,* the Court used a secular baseline rather than a religious one; it emphasized the strictly religious character of the accommodation and noted that the statute imposed costs on employers and on non-Sabbatarian employees, both of whom missed out on the statute's benefit and had to compensate for its costs.[171] Similarly, in *Texas Monthly v. Bullock,* where the Court struck down a sales-tax exemption for religious periodicals, the baseline used to measure equality was secular—namely, whether all secular periodicals received the same sales-tax exemption as that given to religious periodicals.

The Court's decision in *Caldor,* however, did not prevent it from ruling in favor of employees seeking benefits under a state's employment-compensation law in *Hobbie v. Unemployment Appeals Commission of Florida.*[172] In *Hobbie,* an employee was discharged when she refused to work on Saturday, her Sabbath. The Court sided with her, holding that the state's denial of unemployment compensation violated the free exercise clause. The employer in *Hobbie* had argued that to accommodate the employee's Sabbath would violate the establishment clause, citing the Court's earlier ruling in *Caldor*. But the Supreme Court distinguished *Caldor* from *Hobbie*, stating that Florida's provision of unemployment benefits to religious observers did not single out a particular class of such persons for favorable treatment. Rather, the provision of unemployment benefits generally available within the state to religious observers who lose their jobs because they cannot reconcile work demands with the demands of their religious beliefs is simply a neutral attempt to accommodate religious beliefs and practices.

In *Heffron v. International Society for Krishna Consciousness, Inc.*, the Court upheld Minnesota State Fair regulations prohibiting the distribution or sale of information materials, except from booths reserved for that specific purpose.[173] The Court upheld the regulation as a content-neutral time-manner-place restriction.[174] It could also have been upheld under an equal protection approach, but only if the baseline were all of secular society. In other words, the regulation clearly treated all people the same. However, if the baseline were religious practitioners or organizations, the outcome may have been different. Among religious sects, the regulation had a disparate effect. It clearly burdened the Krishna religion more than most other religions.

When political speech is involved, the baseline used must be that which allows for the maximum degree of protection. The search for the proper baseline in free speech cases often entails an identification of the relevant comparison group. Will it be a larger general public, or will it be a narrower, similarly situated First Amendment group? In *Minneapolis Star and Tribune Co. v. Minnesota Commissioner of Revenue*, the Court struck down a special ink and paper tax aimed at the print media (and indeed, at particular newspapers) and that was not applied to other businesses.[175] This was clearly an equal protection case, with the Court finding that the particular newspapers had been singled out for a discriminatory burden that the rest of society was not made to bear. Consequently, a broad or more protective baseline was used. In *Schneider v. State*, the Court struck down an ordinance that banned the distribution of leaflets on government property.[176] Again, a broad baseline was used, insofar as leaflets were compared with every other kind of expression that could be distributed on government property.[177]

On the other hand, in *Glickman v. Wileman Brothers and Elliott, Inc.*, the Court rejected a First Amendment challenge to marketing orders that required fruit producers to pay an assessment for generic advertising.[178] Looking at the assessment from the viewpoint of tree-fruit producers, all were asked to pay the same assessment. There was no equal protection problem from that perspective. But a broader comparison group—e.g., all of society—would have shown that a special tax was placed upon a particular segment of society to pay for a speech-related purpose. This would have been a more protective comparison group, but it was not used because political speech was not involved.

Determining the proper baseline or relevant comparison group for free speech purposes depends, just as it does under the religion clauses, on the primary purpose of the free speech clause. As argued previously, the free speech clause serves primarily to protect political speech.[179] Therefore, when political speech is involved, the courts should use the broadest baseline that ensures the greatest speech protections. When political speech is not involved, courts can choose narrower baselines, as with so-called low-value speech.[180]

Traditional free speech jurisprudence reflects the belief that courts should not make any subject-matter speech distinctions in terms of the constitutional protections given to speech. But without making some subject-matter (not viewpoint) distinctions, an equal protection approach is hardly possible, since there will be no meaningful comparisons to make. Moreover, given the vast amount of public speech in contemporary America, a refusal to recognize the various different types of speech is a refusal to recognize the realities of modern communications. Indeed, courts have already created categories of speech that, while warranting some constitutional protection, can be more easily regulated in the name of competing social interests. Examples of such categories include commercial speech,[181] speech that places individuals in a "false light,"[182] speech that discloses the private details of another person,[183] and child pornography.[184]

Only a differentiation of subject matters of speech, along with recognition of the kind of speech the First Amendment primarily seeks to protect, can realistically deal with the complex informational and media society that now exists in the United States. For instance, through its regulation of the securities market—a regulation commenced in the wake of the stock market crash of 1929—the government significantly regulates speech relating to financial securities.[185] Speech subject to securities regulation is not political speech aiming to express an opinion on a particular issue in the political arena. Rather, it is speech that simply aims to facilitate some financial transaction or investment. It is not "speech" as much as it is a necessary ingredient to some larger financial transaction. For the Court not to recognize a distinction between securities speech and political speech, and hence not to recognize that the First Amendment may apply differently to the two different kinds of speech, is to fatally disregard the nature of the economic and investment markets that have to function properly in order for a modern society to survive.

An examination of First Amendment case law reveals how the presence or absence of political speech should affect the identification of the relevant baseline. In *City of Erie v. Pap's A.M.*, the Court addressed the application to nude dancing establishments of a city ordinance forbidding public nudity.[186] The Court upheld the law's application, finding that it was a content-neutral law aimed at combating crime and other negative consequences caused by adult entertainment businesses.[187] But this holding can also be explained through an equal protection approach. The issue in the case can be seen as essentially one of whether the government was treating one kind of expressive nude behavior—e.g., nude dancing—differently than other kinds of nude behavior. The answer was that it was not. The City was treating all nudity, including nude dancing, in a similar fashion. The point of comparison was a very narrow and specific point—nudity. It was not the broader baseline of expressive behavior in general. This was because the type of expression at issue was not political speech.

A broad-baseline approach was applicable in *Metro Media Inc. v. City of San Diego,* where the Court overturned a law prohibiting all billboards in residential areas, even though it exempted a business's advertising at its own locations, along with other types of commercial advertising.[188] Although the law appeared to be content neutral, it obviously affected political speech. Indeed, in its operation, the ordinance gave preference to commercial over noncommercial speech. Moreover, the ordinance violated the broad baseline because it singled out billboards, as well as residential areas. And when political speech is at issue, the broadest baseline should be used, rather than some narrower baseline. Furthermore, the impact of this law may very well have had a disproportionate impact on political speech, especially if it was found that billboards were a prominent venue for political speech. In this respect, the Court should take into account not only the relative impact of the law, but the ability of speakers to shift to other means of expression.[189]

Under the First Amendment, political speech is given the highest priority and protections. However, with nonpolitical speech, a lower level of protection can be given. But all statutory restrictions still need to be measured by equal protection norms. In *Board of Trustees v. Fox,* the Court upheld a statute banning private companies from selling products on a state college campus. The Court upheld these commercial speech restrictions, even though it took "account of the difficulty of establishing with precision the point at which restrictions become more extensive than their objective requires." But because the speech involved was not political speech, the Court did not have to be overly concerned with the exact degree of burden. Nonetheless, the statute still measured up to equal protection norms, since all private companies were treated the same.

The judicial scrutiny of laws affecting speech relating to the democratic process should involve the identification of all possible baselines. For instance, more than one baseline was applicable in *City of Ladue v. Gilleo,* where the Court struck down an ordinance prohibiting homeowners from displaying political signs on their property.[190] Not only were political signs singled out from other signs, but homeowners were singled out from other kinds of property owners or citizens.

Under an equal protection approach to the First Amendment, the first line of inquiry should be whether the equality principle has been violated—in other words, whether one group of people or one set of ideas has been singled out and treated differently, in terms of their exercise of rights provided for in the Bill of Rights. If a discrimination has been found, the next line of inquiry should be whether that discrimination has significantly burdened a particular speaker or idea.[191] It is only when laws discriminate against First Amendment freedoms and significantly burden those freedoms that the courts should strictly scrutinize them.

In this respect, courts should look at whether the speaker has been left without any venue or means of communicating her idea.[192]

A similar approach has been adopted by the courts in their distinction between laws that have a direct effect on speech and laws that have only an incidental effect on speech.[193] An important element in the test of whether a discriminatory law substantially burdens a First Amendment right should be whether the person or group possesses an alternative way of exercising the right. If they do, then the burden might be reviewed under a more lenient standard of review. If the group has no alternative way of exercising the right, then the burden should be more strictly scrutinized.

Conclusion

The limited-government model of the First Amendment provides an interpretation that strives to be consistent not only with the original intent and meaning of the amendment, but also with the purpose and design of the original Constitution. This model may provide to the courts a more objective and workable approach than does the individual-autonomy model. Furthermore, the limited-government model may not involve the judiciary in the kind of unrestrained "lawmaking" that the individual-autonomy model does.

Because of the original-intent basis of the limited-government model and its consistency with the overall constitutional scheme, the Supreme Court has already incorporated it into much of its First Amendment jurisprudence, even if the Court has never explicitly articulated or even recognized this incorporation. But the Court's use of limited-government principles is by no means consistent, and the Court has never specifically recognized the limited-government model as controlling the interpretation of the First Amendment.

The area of election and campaign-finance laws is one area in which the limited-government model has had particularly confusing or ambiguous application. In *Citizens Against Rent Control v. City of Berkeley*, the Court struck down an ordinance that placed a $250 limitation on contributions to committees formed to support or oppose ballot measures submitted to a popular vote.[1] In so doing, the Court rejected the City's argument that the limitation was necessary to preserve the integrity of elections by reducing some speech that might otherwise have a disproportionate influence.[2] One could argue that *Citizens Against Rent Control* was decided on limited-government principles, protecting the freedom of citizens to control their government. However, one could also argue that the decision was based on a concern for autonomy interests of contributors.

In *McIntyre v. Ohio Elections Commission*, the Court struck down an Ohio law that prohibited the distribution of anonymous campaign literature.[3] The Court's focus was on the right of anonymous authors to engage in whatever speech they wanted, not on the extent of government power or on the doctrine of limited government. The Court in *McIntyre* concluded that the security of speakers would be preserved if the disclosure requirements were removed, which in turn would increase both the number of voices and the total amount of speech.[4] But the purpose of the First Amendment is not to increase the number of voices or the total amount of speech; it is to place appropriate limits on government power and authority. Yet again, *McIntyre* could be explained on the basis of the Court's concerns for the autonomy interests of anonymous speakers.

In *Republican Party of Minnesota v. White*, the Court found unconstitutional a section of Minnesota's Judicial Code of Conduct that prohibited a candidate for a judicial office, including an incumbent judge, from publicizing his or her opinions on legal or political issues.[5] This decision can be explained on limited-government grounds, since the proposed regulation was an attempt to have the government control in some way the outcome of the election and to prevent voters from having all the appropriate information. However, as with *McIntyre*, it could also be explained on autonomy grounds.

In *Nixon v. Shrink Missouri Government PAC*, the Court upheld state limits on contributions to candidates for state offices.[6] This decision was based upon *Buckley v. Valeo*, which upheld contribution limits but denied expenditure limits. This ruling stemmed from a finding that limiting contributions entails less of a restriction on speech rights because a contribution reflects just a general support for a candidate and not "the underlying basis of that support."[7] Contribution limits also more effectively serve the government interest in preventing corruption and the appearance of corruption resulting from large financial contributions. Limits on expenditures, on the other hand, have a more restrictive effect on political speech by directly curtailing how a candidate can communicate his or her message. Thus, expenditure limits threaten the limited-government principle, whereas contribution limits do not.

Furthermore, *Buckley* sustained contribution limits on the grounds of preventing political corruption, not on the grounds of promoting equality of speakers.[8] This position was reaffirmed in *FEC v. National Conservative PAC*, in which the Court stated that "preventing corruption or the appearance of corruption are the only legitimate and compelling interests thus far identified for restricting campaign finances."[9] However, a prevention of governmental corruption can be seen as a way of achieving limited government, since in preventing government corruption, society can induce the political process to operate more in tune with how the voters wish it to operate. An individual-autonomy approach, on the other hand, would tend to reject contribution limits. (However, at the same time, an autonomy approach could also be used to reject expenditure limits.) Prevention of government corruption is a limited-government concern, not an individual-autonomy concern.

The principle of limited government pervaded the opinion in *Buckley*, even if not directly recognized. On one hand, *Buckley* was concerned with limiting the government's power to infringe on political speech through regulations on expenditures. But *Buckley* was also concerned with limiting the government's ability to corrupt the election process and solidify its power through undemocratic means—hence the rule on contributions.

Since its decision in *Buckley,* the Supreme Court has focused on three government interests asserted to justify campaign-finance regulations: preventing corruption or the appearance of political corruption, promoting equality among political speakers, and allowing more opportunities for candidates to compete for political office by controlling skyrocketing campaign costs. However, of these three interests, the prevention of corruption is the only one allowed by the Court to support campaign-finance regulation. In *Davis v. FEC,* the Court explicitly rejected equalization of political opportunities as a justification for campaign-finance reform.[10] Furthermore, it recently restated in *Citizens United v. FEC* that any disparities or inequalities in the wealth of political speakers cannot justify burdens on First Amendment rights.[11]

The government interest in preventing political corruption or the appearance of political corruption is also the only interest that is related to the principle of limited government. The other two interests relate more to private rights of individual speakers or candidates, and hence would relate more to the individual-autonomy model of the First Amendment.

Even though the autonomy model could be used to explain some aspects of the Court's campaign-finance jurisprudence, the limited-government model may provide a more all-encompassing rationale. In *FEC v. Colorado Republican Federal Campaign Committee (Colorado I),* for instance, the Court struck down limitations on independent expenditures made by the Colorado Republican Party, reasoning that independent expenditures by political parties do not foster corruption any more than do independent expenditures by individuals.[12] However, in the subsequent case of *FEC v. Colorado Republican Federal Campaign Committee (Colorado II),* the Court upheld limitations on coordinated spending by political parties.[13] In *Colorado II,* the Court found that contributions to parties could be a means of avoiding limitations on contributions to individual candidates.[14] Furthermore, the Court found little evidence that such limitations infringed on the right of political parties to participate in elections.[15] With both *Colorado I* and *Colorado II,* the Court was primarily concerned about political corruption. This is because corruption significantly detracts from the public's opportunity to control and limit its government. In *Colorado I,* the Court gave political parties the freedom to participate in the political process and hence to control and limit government. However, in *Colorado II,* the Court declined the opportunity to use the First Amendment to give political parties additional powers, beyond that of participating in the political process on their own.

In *Randall v. Sorrel,* the Court struck down a Vermont statute imposing severe limits on political contributions, campaign expenditures, and independent expenditures.[16] Under the *Buckley* rule, the Court found that limitations on campaign expenditures were unconstitutional.[17] The Court also found that limitations on campaign contributions, although generally permissible under *Buckley,* could be so drastic as to violate the First Amendment.[18] In other words, the limitations could be so drastic as to prevent a candidate from being able to mount an effective campaign against an entrenched incumbent. The justification for the severe contribution limits in *Randall* was the belief that lawmakers had to spend too much time fundraising. But the Supreme Court held that the First Amendment limited government's power to regulate political speech so as to save legislators the trouble of fundraising. Indeed, while *Shrink Missouri Government* had seemed to spell the end to any judicial policing of government regulation of contributions, *Randall* reversed that course and put the judiciary back in the role of scrutinizing such regulation.[19] Moreover, *Randall* was not about personal autonomy as much as it was about marking out the boundaries of government's ability to control the election process.

Although the Bipartisan Campaign Reform Act of 2002 was upheld by the Court in *McConnell v. FEC,* the Court in subsequent cases, including *Randall,* has limited the reach of the BCRA.[20] In *FEC v. Wisconsin Right to Life,* the Court held that the BCRA's prohibitions on certain "electioneering communications" made during the sixty-day period before a federal general election were overly broad and unconstitutionally restricted free speech rights.[21] The Court found that issue ads that do not expressly advocate for a candidate could not be restricted as attempts to either prevent corruption or limit the effects of large corporate expenditures. This was a classic case of the Court's giving high protection to political speech, finding that the BCRA's provisions significantly restricted the ability of a nonprofit corporation to engage in political speech regarding the issues relevant to an upcoming or ongoing political controversy. A primary concern of the Court was whether the BCRA's regulations would serve to chill political debate. In its ruling, the *Wisconsin Right to Life* Court purported to follow *McConnell* by essentially crafting a very wide definition of "genuine issue advocacy," which under the BCRA was immune from the kind of regulations governing "express advocacy" ads for or against a particular candidate.

Later, in 2008, the Court in *Davis v. FEC* once again examined the intersection of campaign-finance regulations and the First Amendment.[22] The Court found that the BCRA's "millionaire's amendment," which provided different contribution and disclosure rules if any candidate in an election spent $350,000 or more of his or her own money, unconstitutionally discriminated against candidates who chose to spend their own money. Thus, in both *Wisconsin Right to Life* and *Davis,* it can be said that the Court struck down campaign-finance regulations that discouraged or inhibited outside groups from participating in or influencing the outcome of democratic elections, and that consequently inhibited the public's ability to control and limit the government.

In a recent decision on campaign finance, the Supreme Court in *Citizens United v. FEC* overturned a ban on corporate and union independent expenditures, from their corporate or union general treasuries, on express advocacy or any other kind of campaign speech. (However, the Court upheld the disclosure rules governing such corporate expenditures.)[23] In reaching its decision, the Court overturned its previous decision in *Austin v. Michigan Chamber of Commerce* and held that the First Amendment protects the right of unions and corporations to make independent expenditures advocating the election or defeat of a specific candidate in a political campaign. The BCRA had prohibited corporations and unions from using general treasury funds to make independent expenditures for certain "electioneering communications" mentioning a federal candidate. But in *Citizens United*, the Court reaffirmed *Buckley*, ruling that the only type of corruption that may give rise to a government interest in regulating speech is quid pro quo corruption.[24] The Court also stated that independent expenditures do not give rise to such corruption, and therefore Congress could not impose limitations on such expenditures.[25] Consequently, the Court invalidated those provisions of the BCRA that restrict such expenditures.

In striking down *Austin*, where the Court had upheld a Michigan law prohibiting corporate independent expenditures to support or oppose candidates, the Court in *Citizens United* adopted a bright-line rule rather than maintaining the balancing test of *Austin*. As the Court declared, "The First Amendment does not permit laws that force speakers to retain a campaign finance attorney, conduct demographic market research, or seek declaratory rulings before discussing the most salient political issues of our day."[26] For this reason, the Court overruled *Austin* and returned to the principle outlined in *Buckley*: that the government may not suppress political speech on the basis of the speaker's corporate identity. Again, the focus in the Court's decision was not on the speaker's identity, but on the principle of limited government.

Citizens United, in its refusal to make First Amendment distinctions based on the identity of the speaker—e.g., individual versus corporation—reflected the approach taken in *Boston v. Bellotti*, which invalidated a law banning corporations from making political expenditures on speech relating to referenda that do not materially affect the corporation's business.[27] The Court did not accept the argument that speech loses its constitutional protection just because its source is a corporation. However, if the First Amendment were to be interpreted under a personal-autonomy or natural-rights model, corporations could be singled out for special restrictions since they have no natural rights or personal-autonomy interests.

Since government is most importantly and effectively controlled through political elections in a democracy, the Court frequently strikes down campaign-finance regulations that interfere with this ability to control and limit government. Indeed, as the recent trend of Supreme Court case law demonstrates, campaign-finance regulations should be scrutinized heavily under the limited-government model, because these regulations are most threatening to the public's ability to maintain a limited government. Underlying these decisions is the assumption that legislators should not be given deference when they pass legislation under the banner of "reform" that in fact makes it more difficult for challengers to unseat them.[28]

Also underlying or supporting the recent post-*McConnell* trend of Supreme Court decisions on campaign finance is the realization that the complex regulatory regime of the McCain-Feingold Act has not at all slowed the growth in campaign spending, reduced the time that officeholders spend fundraising, or prevented government corruption.[29] In fact, the advocates of government regulation of political campaigns address the failures of McCain-Feingold by simply calling for more and more extensive regulations—e.g., of 527 organizations that currently operate outside the existing campaign-finance laws.

The election process is one of the most fundamental means by which a democratic society controls and directs (and yes, limits) its government. On one hand, the government cannot be allowed to manipulate this process, especially given the risk that political incumbents could use their power to immunize themselves from outside challenges. But on the other hand, the government does have a legitimate role in preventing corruption or corrupting influences, maintaining public confidence in the integrity of the electoral process, and encouraging widespread and informed public participation in the process. It is difficult for any one model of the First Amendment to address these various concerns, but an analysis of the existing case law suggests that the limited-government model may be the best-situated model for this task.

The limited-government model of the Bill of Rights evolves from a number of different constitutional considerations. First, it provides a consistency and harmony between the original Constitution and the Bill of Rights. To the framers of the original Constitution, the notion of limited government was an all-pervasive and ever-present concern. Constructing the foundation for a limited federal government and providing an intricate web of constitutional assurances for the maintenance of that limited government was a primary focus of the framers. The limited-government model of the Bill of Rights carries over this focus from the original Constitution to the Bill of Rights. It is logical to expect that the concerns of the framers did not radically change from the ratification of the original Constitution to the ratification of the Bill of Rights. It is also logical to expect that the fundamental principles that inspired the original Constitution would not have changed during the time leading up to and including the drafting and passage of the Bill of Rights.

The limited-government model recognizes the only consistent theme or principle that prevailed throughout the constitutional debates surrounding both the original Constitution and the Bill of Rights. Even when the framers of the Bill of Rights spoke in terms of natural rights or individual autonomy, the tangible principle or doctrine on which they relied was one of limited government. The notion and principle of limited government had become well defined throughout the constitutional period, and it was that principle that continued to be influential throughout the Bill of Rights period. The framers never did define or debate natural rights or individual autonomy in the same way that they did limited government. Natural rights and individual freedom may have been seen as a justification or a rationale, but they were never the core constitutional principles that could be predictably enforced and applied by the courts.

Perhaps the limited-government aspect of the Bill of Rights has become so obscured in recent decades because of what happened during the New Deal constitutional revolution. It was during that time that the principles and values of limited government in general were greatly discredited and dismissed. And only after those limited-government principles were discredited and dismissed did the Court then begin looking at the Bill of Rights in a different way. During the Warren era, for instance, the Court embarked on a new course of jurisprudence, in which it enforced the provisions of the Bill of Rights in a much different and more heightened manner. It was during that period that the Bill of Rights came to be identified with a personal-autonomy model. But this model was possible only after the New Deal constitutional revolution had virtually dismissed the limited-government scheme of the Constitution so carefully constructed by the framers.

Much has been made in this book about the debate between the Federalists and Anti-Federalists—a debate that led to the Bill of Rights. The reason the Federalists opposed a bill of rights is that they counted on republican checks on power and the way those checks would work as part of a political system created by the Constitution to protect liberty. This limited-government structure would preclude the need for a bill of rights, they believed. Indeed, one of the greatest concerns of the Founders was that Congress might ignore individual freedoms whenever a majority of the people had been unduly influenced to reject those claims of rights. For this reason, the Federalists believed the insertion of individual-rights provisions in a constitution would have little effect. A more reliable protector of liberty would be a more general constitutional structure limiting government from being able to commit such abuses in the first place. But this Federalist argument did not prevail. Instead, the Anti-Federalists were able to cast doubt upon how thoroughly the original Constitution had in fact been able to limit government. This became the real tipping point in the argument for a bill of rights—the argument that such a bill was needed so as to sufficiently limit the power of government. But the Anti-Federalists did not want to put the courts in charge of determining the degree of individual freedom enjoyed by the people. What the Anti-Federalists wanted were constitutional provisions limiting government from ever encroaching upon the areas outlined in the Bill of Rights.

What the limited-government model strives to do is to achieve a harmony between the original Constitution and the Bill of Rights. Instead of casting the two as antagonists—democratic will versus individual liberty—the limited-government model finds harmony. It does not pit the individual against the democratic community; instead, it simply outlines the bounds of power possessed by the democratic community. Its focus is not on a conflict between the individual and democratic society, but only on the singular subject of government power and its rightful boundaries. Indeed, the founding generation perceived the doctrine of popular sovereignty as at least as central or important as inalienable rights. They even saw the right of the people to self-govern as embodying a natural right.

The Constitution is not about setting out moral or natural-rights claims; it is about empowering a democratic people to govern itself and outlining the boundaries and limitations of that power. The Founders distrusted majority rule not because they saw it as inherently antagonistic to individual rights, but because they saw that it all too easily could transcend the boundaries placed on it by the rule of law. Yet the Founders were very mistrustful of protecting liberty simply through the insertion of individual-rights provisions in a constitution that would be up to the courts to apply. They did not trust the courts to do so, nor did they believe the courts had the power to do so when in opposition to a strong majority will. Therefore, what the Founders wanted was to build in constitutional structures that would limit and direct majority will in a way that would keep it from spilling outside its lawful boundaries and becoming oppressive to society. They wanted to protect liberty by controlling and limiting government, not by giving courts the unbounded power to enforce upon a democratic society a judicially defined vision of personal autonomy.

Notes

Introduction

1. For a discussion of *U.S. v. Carolene Products Co.,* 304 U.S. 144, 152 n.4 (1938), as well as the Court's New Deal jurisprudence, *see* PATRICK M. GARRY, AN ENTRENCHED LEGACY: HOW THE NEW DEAL CONSTITUTIONAL REVOLUTION CONTINUES TO SHAPE THE ROLE OF THE SUPREME COURT 102–8 (Penn. State Univ. Press 2009).

2. *See* Patrick M. Garry, *Liberty through Limits: The Bill of Rights as Limited Government Provisions,* 62 SMU L. Rev. 1745 (2009).

Chapter 1.
The Individual-Autonomy View of the Bill of Rights

1. HADLEY ARKES, CONSTITUTIONAL ILLUSIONS AND ANCHORING TRUTHS 8 (Cambridge Univ. Press 2010).

2. JOHN LOCKE, LOCKE'S SECOND TREATISE OF GOVERNMENT 77–79 (Lester DeKoster ed., W. B. Eerdmans 1978).

3. Steven Heyman, *Righting the Balance: An Inquiry into the Foundations and Limits of Freedom of Expression,* 78 B.U. L. Rev. 1275, 1282 (1998).

4. *Id.*

5. *Id.* at 1314.

6. Philip Hamburger, *Natural Rights, Natural Law, and American Constitutions,* 102 YALE L.J. 907, 919 (1993).

7. *Id.* at 919, 948.

8. Robert P. George, *Law and Moral Purpose,* FIRST THINGS 23 (January 2008).

9. The Declaration's reference to unalienable individual rights is said to reflect the natural-rights theories of the Founders. MICHAEL P. ZUCKERT, THE NATURAL RIGHTS REPUBLIC 234 (1996) (examining how natural-rights thinking pervaded and shaped the new republicanism of Jefferson and Madison, placing natural rights as being prior to and the precondition of republican government). *See also* Frederick Mark Gedicks, *An Originalist Defense of Substantive Due Process: Magna Carta, Higher-Law Constitutionalism, and the Fifth Amendment,* 58 EMORY L.J. 585, 622 (2009).

10. *See* Harry V. Jaffa, *Equality, Justice and the American Revolution,* in MODERN AGE: THE FIRST TWENTY-FIVE YEARS 312 (George Panichas ed., Liberty Press 1988).

11. *See* HARRY V. JAFFA , ORIGINAL INTENT AND THE FRAMERS OF THE CONSTITUTION 60 (Regnery Gateway 1994).

12. Gedicks, *An Originalist Defense,* 58 EMORY L.J. at 624 (2009).

13. *Id.* at 625.

14. JOHN LOCKE, TWO TREATISES OF GOVERNMENT 265, 269 (Peter Laslett ed., Cambridge Univ. Press 1988) (1691).

15. *Id.* at 330–31.

16. Gedicks, *An Originalist Defense,* 58 EMORY L.J. at 625 (2009) (stating that "a textual enumeration was not understood to have created the rights it listed").

17. Randy E. Barnett, *The Ninth Amendment: It Means What It Says,* 85 TEX. L. REV. 1, 14 (2006).

18. Randy Barnett, *A Law Professor's Guide to Natural Rights,* 20 HARV. J.L. & PUB. POL'Y 655, 669 (1997). Under one view, natural rights "are the set of concepts that define the moral space within which persons must be free to make their own choices and live their own lives if they are to pursue happiness while living in society." RANDY BARNETT, RESTORING THE LOST CONSTITUTION 80 (Princeton Univ. Press 2004).

19. Randy Barnett, *The Role of Natural Rights in Constitutional Adjudication,* 12 CONST. COMMENT 93, 106 (1995).

20. John McGinnis, *The Once and Future Property-Based Vision of the First Amendment,* 63 U. CHI. L. REV. 49, 56, 64 (1996).

21. Martin Redish, *The Value of Free Speech,* 130 U. PA. L. REV. 591, 593–94 (1982).

22. Darrel Menthe, *The Marketplace Metaphor and Commercial Speech Doctrine,* 38 HASTINGS CONST. L.Q. 131, 136, 142 (2010).

23. Gregory P. Magarian, *Substantive Due Process as a Source of Constitutional Protection for Nonpolitical Speech,* 90 MINN. L. REV. 247, 249 (2005).

24. *Palko v. State of Connecticut,* 302 U.S. 319 (1937).

25. *Corfield v. Coryell,* 6 F.Cas. 546, 551–552 (C.C.E.D. Pa. 1823) (No. 3230).

26. *Palko v. State of Connecticut,* 302 U.S. 319, 325 (1937).

27. JOHN PHILLIP REID, CONSTITUTIONAL HISTORY OF THE AMERICAN REVOLUTION 10–11 (1986).

28. Philip Hamburger, *Natural Rights,* 102 YALE L.J. 907, 926, 955 (1993).

29. *Id.* at 954.

30. RICHARD LABUNSKI, JAMES MADISON AND THE STRUGGLE FOR THE BILL OF RIGHTS 230–31 (Oxford Univ. Press 2006).

31. Mark Graber, *Enumeration and Other Constitutional Strategies for Protecting Rights,* 9 U. PA. J. CONST. L. 357, 387 (2007).

32. Hamburger, *Natural Rights,* 102 YALE L.J. at 910 (1993).

33. Michael McConnell, *Natural Rights and the Ninth Amendment,* 5 NYU J.L. & LIBERTY 1, 6 (2010).

34. THE DEBATES IN THE SEVERAL STATE CONVENTIONS, ON THE ADOPTION OF THE FEDERAL CONSTITUTION, VOL. 4 at 316 (January 18, 1788) (Jonathan Elliot ed., J. B. Lippincott 1941) (1836).

35. Graber, *Enumeration,* 9 U. PA. J. CONST. L. at 385 (2007).

36. *See* Howard J. Vogel, *The Ordered Liberty of Substantive Due Process and the Future of Constitutional Law as a Rhetorical Art,* 70 ALBANY L. REV. 1473, 1498 (2007).

37. Similar criticisms have attached to the Court's application of substantive due process (and its use of unenumerated fundamental rights), arguing that it "provides neither a sound starting point nor a directional push to proper legal analysis." Akhil Amar, *The Supreme Court, 1999 Term—Forward,* 114 HARV. L. REV. 26, 123 (2000). According to yet another critic, "[N]either historical evidence nor the doctrine of precedent support empowering courts to engage in the moral analysis required to discover, and then to impose, natural and inalienable rights and subjecting laws impacting on such rights to the strictest of judicial

scrutiny." Thomas McAffee, *Overcoming Lochner in the Twenty-first Century*, 42 U. RICH. L. REV. 597, 617 (2008).

38. Thomas B. McAffee, *Restoring the Lost World of Classical Legal Thought*, 75 U. CIN. L. REV. 1499, 1589 (2007).

39. *See Calder v. Bull*, 3 U.S. (3 Dall.) 386, 400 (1798).

40. *Id.* at 399.

41. McConnell, *Natural Rights*, 5 NYU J.L. & LIBERTY 3 (2010).

42. Thomas B. Griffith, *Was Bork Right about Judges?* 34 HARV. J.L. & PUB. POL'Y 157, 158 (2011). *See also* GERALD ROSENBERG, THE HOLLOW HOPE: CAN COURTS BRING ABOUT SOCIAL CHANGE? 336 (Univ. of Chicago Press 1991), for a study that supports a constrained view of judicial power, finding that "attempts to use the courts to produce significant social reform were mostly disappointing."

43. Diarmuid O'Scannlain, *The Natural Law in the American Tradition*, 79 FORDHAM L. REV. 1513, 1519 (2011). As one judge put it: "I do not believe that judges have the freestanding authority to enforce the natural law." *Id.* at 1522.

44. ROBERT BORK, THE TEMPTING OF AMERICA 66 (Free Press 1990).

45. Indeed, James Madison believed that state governments posed the greatest threat to individual rights. THE FEDERALIST NO. 10 at 78 (James Madison) (Clinton Rossiter ed., 1961).

46. *Barron v. Baltimore*, 32 U.S. 243 (1833).

47. Bryan Wildenthal, *Nationalizing the Bill of Rights: Revisiting the Original Understanding of the Fourteenth Amendment in 1866–1867*, 68 OHIO ST. L.J. 1509, 1530 (2007).

48. *See* 1 ANNALS OF CONG. 452, 458, 784 (June 8, 1789) (1st Cong., 1st Sess.)

49. Hamburger, *Natural Rights*, 102 YALE L.J. at 937 (1993).

50. *Id.* at 911.

51. LEONARD W. LEVY, LEGACY OF SUPPRESSION 114 (Belknap Press of Harvard Univ. Press 1960).

52. LARRY ELDRIDGE, A DISTANT HERITAGE: THE GROWTH OF FREE SPEECH IN EARLY AMERICA 5–6 (New York Univ. Press 1994).

53. *Id.* at 8.

54. *Id.* at 9.

55. Graber, *Enumeration*, 9 U. PA. J. CONST. L. at 368 (2007).

56. *Id.*

57. *Id.* at 370.

58. Robert P. George, *Natural Law*, 31 HARV. J.L. & PUB. POL'Y 171, 182 (2008) (arguing that the truths underlying natural rights must come from some source beyond the individual).

59. *See* Edward S. Corwin, *The Higher Law Background of American Constitutional Law*, 42 HARV. L. REV. 149, 153 (1928).

60. *Id.* at 184.

61. *See generally*, Daniel F. Piar, *A Welfare State of Civil Rights: The Triumph of the Therapeutic in American Constitutional Law*, 16 WM. & MARY BILL OF RTS. J. 649 (2008). In a therapeutic culture, the self is the moral order. *Id.* at 650.

62. *Id.* at 654, 670. But the therapeutic culture also "threatens to diminish individual autonomy by discouraging self-reliance and encouraging dependence on therapeutic authority. . . . Thus, while the therapeutic uses of law ostensibly expand individual liberty, they may also have the effect of increasing state power at the expense of the self-reliance and personal autonomy necessary for the democratic freedom." *Id.* at 673.

63. This "constitutional revolution" took the Court much further in its civil liberties jurisprudence than even a traditional libertarian like Justice Hugo Black "could allow." David O'Brien, *Justice Hugo Black, Liberal Legalism and Constitutional Politics*, 19 REVIEWS IN AMERICAN HISTORY 561–67, 562 (1991).

64. *See* Daniel F. Piar, *A Welfare State of Civil Rights*, 16 WM. & MARY BILL OF RTS. J. 649, 650 (2008).

65. *Id.* at 651. According to Leonard Levy in CONSTITUTIONAL OPINIONS: ASPECTS OF THE BILL OF RIGHTS, the Bill of Rights has taken on a romanticized and overly modern understanding. For instance, there is no "historical support" for the Court's *Miranda v. Arizona* ruling, in which the Court "expanded the right against self-incrimination beyond all precedent" 208.

66. *Lee v. Weisman*, 505 U.S. 577 (1992).

67. Philip Detweiler, *The Changing Reputation of the Declaration of Independence*, 19 WM. & MARY QUARTERLY 557, 558–65 (1962).

68. Hamburger, *Natural Rights*, 102 YALE L.J. at 915 (1993).

69. *Id.* at 919.

70. SCOTT DOUGLAS GERBER, TO SECURE THESE RIGHTS: THE DECLARATION OF INDEPENDENCE AND CONSTITUTIONAL INTERPRETATION 10, 40–56, 57–92 (New York Univ. Press 1995).

71. One of the scholars who argue that the Constitution was the means of implementing the Declaration's principles and statements of natural rights is Hadley Arkes. *See* HADLEY ARKES, BEYOND THE CONSTITUTION 40–46 (Princeton Univ. Press 1990).

72. JOHN HART ELY, DEMOCRACY AND DISTRUST: A THEORY OF JUDICIAL REVIEW 49 (Harvard Univ. Press 1980).

73. Lee J. Strang, *Originalism, the Declaration of Independence, and the Constitution: A Constitutional Right to Life?* 111 PENN. ST. L. REV. 413, 439 (2006).

74. *See* PAULINE MAIER, AMERICAN SCRIPTURE: MAKING THE DECLARATION OF INDEPENDENCE 169 (Vintage Books 1998).

75. *See* DANIEL BOORSTIN, THE GENIUS OF AMERICAN POLITICS 84 (Univ. of Chicago Press 1953).

76. According to the framing generation, one of the threats to liberty was the individual tendency toward licentiousness. *See* JOHN PHILLIP REID, THE CONCEPT OF LIBERTY IN THE AGE OF THE AMERICAN REVOLUTION (1988).

77. *See* 1 JOHN TRENCHARD & THOMAS GORDON, CATO'S LETTERS NO. 62 at 428 (Ronald Hamowy ed., Liberty Fund 1995) (1755).

78. 1 WILLIAM BLACKSTONE, COMMENTARIES ON THE LAWS OF ENGLAND 125 (St. George Tucker ed., Philadelphia: Young & Small 1803).

79. Hamburger, *Natural Rights*, 102 YALE L.J. at 919 (1993).

80. *Id.* at 927.

81. Heyman, *Righting the Balance*, 78 B.U. L. REV. at 1284, 1287, and 1291 (1998).

82. *Id.* at 1315–16.

83. JOHN LOCKE, TWO TREATISES OF GOVERNMENT 156 (Ian Shapiro ed., Yale Univ. Press 2003) (1689).

84. Barnett, *The Ninth Amendment*, 85 TEX. L. REV. 1, 77 (2006).

85. *Id.* at 14. For instance, the First Amendment speech clause does not preclude all time-manner-place regulations. The natural-rights model defines a "private domain within which persons may do as they please, provided their conduct does not encroach upon the rightful domain of others." BARNETT, RESTORING THE LOST CONSTITUTION 58.

86. *Id.* at 14. As Barnett argues, regulations of natural rights or liberty can be done so long

as such regulation is warranted to protect the liberties of others. Randy E. Barnett, *Who's Afraid of Unenumerated Rights?* 9 U. PA. J. CONST. L. 1, 18 (2006). Thus, the judicial inquiry should be "whether the regulation can be justified as necessary to protect the rights of others." *Id.* at 19. But this obviously requires that judges make such a determination. Judges will also have to determine what aspects of natural rights have been surrendered upon joining society. As Robert Barnwell maintained, a person gives up only "a part of our natural rights" when entering into society. THE DEBATES IN THE SEVERAL STATE CONVENTIONS, VOL. 4 at 295 (Jonathan Elliot ed., J. B. Lippincott 1941) (1836). James Madison made a similar point: "Individuals entering into society must give up a share of liberty to preserve the rest." JAMES MADISON, NOTES OF DEBATES IN THE FEDERAL CONVENTION OF 1787, 627 (1987).

87. Eighteenth-century notions of natural rights "never totally supplemented the seventeenth-century American belief in a community held together by substantive values reflected in moral legislation." McAffee, *Overcoming Lochner,* 42 U. RICH. L. REV. at 611. "An aspect of America's lack of a libertarian heritage is its consistent dedication to the idea that one purpose of government is to develop or promote a public morality." *Id.* at 612.

88. John Finnis outlines the limitations to which the exercise of natural rights is subject: "(i) to secure due recognition for the rights and freedoms of others; (ii) to meet the just requirements of morality in a democratic society; (iii) to meet the just requirements of public order in a democratic society; (iv) to meet the just requirements of the general welfare in a democratic society." JOHN FINNIS, NATURAL LAW AND NATURAL RIGHTS 213 (Clarendon Press 1980). Thus, a natural-rights model also envisions the existence of duties on the part of the rights holder. *Id.* at 219.

89. David Strauss, *Originalism, Conservatism and Judicial Restraint,* 34 HARV. J.L. & PUB. POL'Y 137, 140 (2011).

90. Barnett, *A Law Professor's Guide,* 20 HARV. J.L. & PUB. POL'Y 655, 669 (1997).

91. Ronald Dworkin, *Justice for Hedgehogs,* 90 B. U. L. REV. 469, 470 (2010).

92. *See* Isaiah Berlin, *Two Concepts of Liberty,* in FOUR ESSAYS ON LIBERTY 118, 155 (Oxford Univ. Press 1969).

93. Stanley Ingber, *Rediscovering the Communal Worth of Individual Rights: The First Amendment in Institutional Contexts,* 69 TEX. L. REV. No. 1, 37 (1990) (arguing that the resulting dominance of the individualist metaphor makes retrieval of common values increasingly difficult).

Chapter 2.
Limited Government in the Overall Constitutional Scheme

1. The structures also reflected a states' rights tradition "that extolled the ability of local governments to protect citizens against abuses by central authorities." AKHIL REED AMAR, THE BILL OF RIGHTS: CREATION AND RECONSTRUCTION 4 (Yale Univ. Press 1998). To late-eighteenth-century Americans, according to JOHN PHILLIP REID in THE CONCEPT OF LIBERTY IN THE AGE OF THE AMERICAN REVOLUTION, the greatest threat to liberty was legislative power without restraint.

2. *See* Bradford R. Clark, *Separation of Powers as a Safeguard of Federalism,* 79 TEX. L. REV. 1321, 1339 (2001). "Although federal lawmaking procedures are generally regarded as integral parts of the constitutional design for the separation of powers, they also preserve federalism both by making federal law more difficult to adopt, and by assigning lawmaking power solely to actors subject to the political safeguards of federalism." *Id.* at 1324. The

Constitution also protects federalism by ensuring small-state equality of representation in the U.S. Senate and by giving states a prominent role in the selection of the president. *Id.* at 1343, 1368.

3. *Id.* at 1341.

4. *Id.* at 1340.

5. Like separation of powers, federalism served to check the abuse of power and the infringements on individual liberty. THE FEDERALIST NO. 9, 72 (Alexander Hamilton).

6. According to Charles L. Black, the Constitution creates governing structures and then addresses the relationships between and within those structures, federalism and separation of powers being the most prominent. CHARLES BLACK, STRUCTURE AND RELATIONSHIP IN CONSTITUTIONAL LAW 10–11 (Louisiana State Univ. Press 1969). As the Court stated in *Bowsher v. Synar,* a general principle of separation of powers can be constructed from various provisions in the Constitution: "Even a cursory examination of the Constitution reveals the influence of Montesquieu's thesis that checks and balances were the foundation of a structure of government that would protect liberty." *Bowsher v. Synar,* 478 U.S. 714, 723 (1986).

7. According to Lawrence Sager, "[O]ur constitutional text and jurisprudence respond in part to concerns of political justice by architecting and protecting structural features of government–the horizontal separation of powers and the vertical distribution of authority within a federal structure." LAWRENCE G. SAGER, JUSTICE IN PLAINCLOTHES: A THEORY OF AMERICAN CONSTITUTIONAL PRACTICE 154–55 (Yale Univ. Press 2004).

8. The Constitution does not contain any language mandating the separation of the three branches of government. Instead, it simply states affirmatively the powers of each branch, and then creates a system of numerous specific checks and balances–such as veto power for the president, etc. John Roberts, *Are Congressional Committees Constitutional?* 52 CASE W. RES. L. REV. 489, 512 (2001). Thus, separation of powers is more an informal descriptor of how the Constitution works, in terms of checks and balances, rather than a reflection of precise constitutional provisions.

9. These two structural features also support each other. For instance, the separation-of-powers requirements of bicameralism and presentment in Article I, Section 7 restrain federal lawmaking, and hence federal intrusion into state lawmaking, by making it more difficult to pass laws. *See* Bradford R. Clark, *Separation of Powers as a Safeguard of Federalism,* 79 TEX. L. REV. 1321, 1341 (2001).

10. Daryl Levinson, *Empire-Building Government in Constitutional Law,* 118 HARV. L. REV. 915, 949 (2005) (arguing that, to the framers, the competition among branches would result in "a balanced equilibrium, in which no branch can accumulate a potentially monarchical or tyrannical quantum of power, try as each of them will").

11. The structural provisions for separation of powers in the Constitution were seen by the framers as necessary to protect individual liberty by limiting government. Larry Kramer, *Putting the Politics Back into the Political Safeguards of Federalism,* 100 COLUM. L. REV. 215, 268 (2000).

12. Akhil Reed Amar, *Of Sovereignty and Federalism,* 96 YALE L.J. 1425, 1450 (1987).

13. THE FEDERALIST NO. 51, 291 (James Madison) (Clinton Rossiter ed., 1999). While federalism allows the two levels of state and federal government to monitor each other, the separation-of-powers doctrine allows each level to check itself. *Id.*

14. This two-tiered system is what James Madison called the Constitution's "double security" for individual rights. THE FEDERALIST NO. 51, 67 (James Madison) (Lester DeKoster ed., 1976).

15. *See* Steven G. Calabresi and Kevin H. Rhodes, *The Structural Constitution: Unitary Executive, Plural Judiciary,* 105 HARV. L. REV. 1153, 1155 (1992).

16. Steven Gey, *The Procedural Annihilation of Structural Rights*, 61 HASTINGS L.J. 1, 6 (2009).

17. Amar, *Of Sovereignty and Federalism*, 96 YALE L.J. at 1495 (1987).

18. *Id.* at 1502.

19. James Madison, *Speech in Congress Opposing the National Bank* (February 2, 1791), in JAMES MADISON, WRITINGS 480, 481 (Jack Rakove ed., Library of America 1999).

20. Kurt Lash, *James Madison's Celebrated Report of 1800*, 74 GEO. WASH. L. REV. 165, 171 (2006).

21. *Id.* at 173.

22. *Id.* at 177.

23. *See Buckley v. Valeo*, 424 U.S. 1, 122 (1976) (stating that a system of separated powers is "a self-executing safeguard against the encroachment or aggrandizement of one branch at the expense of the other").

24. *See Bowsher*, 478 U.S. at 721 (1986) (stating that the separation of powers was meant to "diffuse power the better to secure liberty").

25. Alison LaCroix, *The Authority for Federalism*, 28 LAW & HIST. REV. 451, 485 (2010).

26. Benjamin Madison, *Rico, Judicial Activism, and the Roots of Separation of Powers*, 43 BRANDEIS L.J. 29, 74 (2004). As James Madison wrote, "If angels were to govern men, neither external nor internal controls in government would be necessary." THE FEDERALIST No. 51, 354 (James Madison) (J. B. Lippincott 1866).

27. THORNTON ANDERSON, CREATING THE CONSTITUTION: THE CONVENTION OF 1787 AND THE FIRST CONGRESS 50–51 (Penn. State Univ. Press 1993). 28. THE FEDERALIST No. 47 (James Madison). Madison believed that human nature required constraints on power: "It may be a reflection on human nature, that such devices should be necessary to control the abuses of government." THE FEDERALIST No. 51 (James Madison).

29. M.J.C. VILE, CONSTITUTIONALISM AND THE SEPARATION OF POWERS 133 (Oxford: Clarendon Press 1967). By 1776, the separation of powers had emerged as the only viable basis for a constitutional system of limited government. *Id.* at 147.

30. Madison, *Rico, Judicial Activism*, 43 BRANDEIS L.J. 29, 74 (2004).

31. *Id.*

32. Hugo Black, *The Bill of Rights*, 35 NYU L. Rev. at 869 (1960).

33. Baron de Montesquieu, *The Spirit of Laws*, bk. XI, ch. 6 at 151–52 (Thomas Nugent trans., Hafner 1949).

34. FORREST MCDONALD, NOVUS ORDO SECLORUM: THE INTELLECTUAL ORIGINS OF THE CONSTITUTION 81 (Univ. Press of Kansas 1985) (stating that "American republican ideologies could recite the central points of Montesquieu's doctrine as if it had been a catechism").

35. ANDERSON, CREATING THE CONSTITUTION 50–51 (1993). The framers "turned to the separation of powers as a fundamental principle of free government." Vile, CONSTITUTIONALISM at 126.

36. THE FEDERALIST No. 73 at 444 (Alexander Hamilton) (Clinton Rossiter ed., 1961).

37. Vile, CONSTITUTIONALISM at 151.

38. *Id.* at 152.

39. *Id.* at 154.

40. Federalism reflects the balancing of power between the states and national government. *See Younger v. Harris*, 401 U.S. 37, 44 (1971) (suggesting that the constitutional scheme envisions a federal structure in which states are equal partners with the national government). As David Walker describes it, "[F]ederalism is a governmental system that includes a central government and at least one major subnational tier of governments; that

assigns significant substantive powers to both levels initially by the provisions of a written constitution; and that succeeds over time in sustaining a territorial division of powers by judicial, operational, representational and political means." DAVID WALKER, THE REBIRTH OF FEDERALISM: SLOUCHING TOWARD WASHINGTON 20 (Chatham House 1995).

41. Amar, *Of Sovereignty and Federalism,* 96 YALE L.J. at 1466 (1987).

42. *Id.* at 1492. As one scholar has noted, the Constitution embodied the innovation that the sovereign people(s) could delegate their authority on a limited basis to more than one government operating within the same territory. Because the delegation to the federal government was to be limited in scope, the states and the people thereof would retain significant residual powers, but the federal government's laws would be supreme within its delegated sphere. John Manning, *Federalism and the Generality Problem in Constitutional Interpretation,* 122 HARV. L. REV. 2003, 2059–60 (2009).

43. The Tenth Amendment states that "the powers not delegated to the United States by the Constitution, nor prohibited by it to the States, are reserved to the States respectively, or to the people." U.S. CONST. amend. X.

44. William H. Pryor, *Madison's Double Security: In Defense of Federalism, the Separation of Powers, and the Rehnquist Court,* 53 ALA. L. REV. 1167, 1175 (2002).

45. Alexander Hamilton argued that the "necessity of local administrations for local purposes, would be a complete barrier against the oppressive use of such a power." THE FEDERALIST NO. 32 at 197 (Alexander Hamilton) (Clinton Rossiter ed., 1961). A "state/federal division of authority protects liberty–both by restricting the burdens that government can impose from a distance and by facilitating citizen participation in government that is closer to home." *United States v. Morrison,* 529 U.S. 598, 655 (2000) (Breyer, J., dissenting).

46. *See Younger v. Harris,* 401 U.S. 37, 44 (1971). A federalism structure, codified in the Tenth Amendment to the U.S. Constitution, helps protect the independent integrity and lawmaking authority of the states. *See* Amar, *Of Sovereignty and Federalism,* 96 YALE L.J. at 1466 (1987). Sovereign power is divided between that given to the federal government by the U.S. Constitution and that reserved to the states through the Tenth Amendment. *Id.* at 1492. For a general discussion of federalism and the role it plays in limiting the power of government, *see* Patrick M. Garry, *A One-Sided Federalism Revolution: The Unaddressed Constitutional Compromise on Federalism and Individual Rights,* 36 SETON HALL L. REV. 851 (2006).

47. *See* GARY WILLS, EXPLAINING AMERICA: THE FEDERALIST 108–11 (1981). According to Amar, state governments would serve as monitors against abuses committed by the federal government. Amar, *Of Sovereignty and Federalism,* 96 YALE L.J. at 1504 (1987). Amar provides a number of examples in which states are able to provide remedies against federal abuses of individual rights. *Id.* at 1509.

48. *See, e.g.,* THE FEDERALIST NO. 26 at 172 (Alexander Hamilton); Amar, *Of Sovereignty and Federalism,* 96 YALE L.J., at 1501 (1987).

49. Federalism offers a structure of "overlapping legal remedies for constitutional wrongs." *Id.* at 1504. Although recent history focuses most attention on instances where the federal government has stepped in to remedy state violations of civil rights, there have also been times when the states have been called upon to address federal abuses. *Id.* at 1506. Prior to *Bivens v. Six Unknown Federal Agents,* for example, only the state law of trespass was available to persons whose homes had been illegally searched by federal agents. 403 U.S. 388 (1971). Furthermore, in the early state habeas corpus cases, states provided a means by which those who were incarcerated in federal prisons and in violation of their federal constitutional rights could obtain their freedom. Amar, *Of Sovereignty and Federalism,* 96 YALE L.J., at 1509 (1987).

50. *United States v. Morrison,* 529 U.S. 598, 655 (2000) (Breyer, J., dissenting). Federalism

establishes a system of dual sovereignty, under which the states can be a localized control on the centralized federal government. Cass Sunstein, *Constitutionalism after the New Deal*, 101 HARV. L. REV. 421, 504 (1987). The principle of dual sovereignty also protects against a consolidation of power that could lead to a tyrannous federal government. *See Gregory v. Ashcroft*, 501 U.S. 452, 458–64 (1991).

51. Larry D. Kramer, *Putting the Politics Back into the Political Safeguards of Federalism*, 100 COLUM. L. REV. 215, 252 (2000). In *United States v. Lopez*, the Court described federalism as a "first principle." 514 U.S. 549, 552 (1995).

52. The Eleventh Amendment states that the "[j]udicial power of the United States shall not be construed to extend to any suit in law or equity, commenced or prosecuted against one of the United States by Citizens of another State, or by Citizens or Subjects of any Foreign State." U.S. CONST. amend. XI.

53. Michael B. Rappaport, *Reconciling Textualism and Federalism: The Proper Textual Basis of the Supreme Court's Tenth and Eleventh Amendment Decisions*, 93 NW. U. L. REV. 819, 821, 831–34 (1999).

54. *Id.* at 821. According to Nicholas Rosenkranz, the structure of the Constitution and its recognition of the states both work to establish federalism as a "constitutional default rule." Nicholas Rosenkranz, *Federal Rules of Statutory Interpretation*, 115 HARV. L. REV. 2085, 2097 (2002).

55. *See* U.S. CONST. art. I, § 1, 8; Jay S. Bybee, *The Tenth Amendment among the Shadows: On Reading the Constitution in Plato's Cave*, 23 HARV. J.L. & PUB. POL'Y 551, 555 (2000).

56. THE FEDERALIST No. 45 (James Madison) (Jacob Cooke ed., 1961) 312.

57. *U.S. Term Limits, Inc. v. Thornton*, 514 U.S. 779, 838 (1995) (Kennedy, J., concurring). The Constitution created a structure of "two orders of government, each with its own direct relationship . . . to the people who sustain it and are governed by it." *Id.*

58. *New York v. United States*, 505 U.S. 144, 181 (1992).

59. *See Gregory*, 501 U.S. 458–64.

60. Steven Calabresi, *A Government of Limited and Enumerated Powers*, 94 MICH. L. REV. 752, 770 (1995).

61. Amar, *Of Sovereignty and Federalism*, 96 YALE L.J. at 1425, 1426 (1987). As the Court explained in *New York v. United States*, federalism "secures to citizens the liberties that derive from the diffusion of sovereign power." *New York*, 505 U.S. at 181. The Court also stated that a "healthy balance of power between the States and the Federal Government will reduce the risk of tyranny and abuse from either front." *Id.*

62. THE FEDERALIST No. 51 at 67 (James Madison) (Lester DeKoster ed., 1976). The interstate competition fostered by federalism can also promote liberty. The ability of citizens to move from one state to another, to "vote with their feet," will "discipline government in the same way in which consumer choice . . . disciplines producers." MICHAEL S. GREVE, REAL FEDERALISM: WHY IT MATTERS, HOW IT COULD HAPPEN 3 (AEI Press 1999). In this same way, the competitive system of federalism devised by the framers "leads to the protection of liberty" by allowing citizens to move from a state where they feel tyrannized to one with less tyrannous laws. Calabresi, *A Government of Limited and Enumerated Powers*, 94 MICH. L. REV. at 776 (1995).

63. *See, e.g.*, THE FEDERALIST No. 46 (James Madison) (Clinton Rossiter ed., 1961) (arguing that the states "will, in all possible contingencies, afford complete security against invasions of the public liberty by the national authority"); *see also* AMAR, THE BILL OF RIGHTS (Yale Univ. Press 1998) (arguing that bolstering the states as bulwarks against federal tyranny was the primary motivation behind the adoption of the Bill of Rights).

64. The framers believed that the states would serve to check any encroachments by the

national government on the liberties of the people. *See, e.g.*, THE FEDERALIST NO. 51 at 322–23 (James Madison) (Clinton Rossiter ed., 1961). It was foreseen that the separation of powers alone would offer little protection to the states, since it was presumed that all the federal branches would share an interest in expanding national power. John C. Yoo, *The Judicial Safeguards of Federalism,* 70 S. Cal. L. Rev. 1311, 1390–91 (1997).

65. THE FEDERALIST NO. 28 at 179 (Alexander Hamilton) (Jacob E. Cooke ed., 1961).

66. *See, e.g.*, THE FEDERALIST NOS. 9, 51 (Alexander Hamilton) (Jacob E. Cooke ed., 1961) (referencing the distinction between free governments and republican governments).

67. Bradford P. Wilson, *Separation of Powers and Judicial Review,* in SEPARATION OF POWERS AND GOOD GOVERNMENT 68 (Bradford P. Wilson & Peter W. Schramm eds., Rowman & Littlefield 1994).

68. *Id.*

69. Levinson, *Empire-Building,* 118 HARV. L. REV. at 915, 919 (2005).

70. Gey, *The Procedural Annihilation of Structural Rights,* 61 HASTINGS L.J. 1, 6 (2009).

71. *See* THE FEDERALIST NO. 51 (James Madison) (J. B. Lippincott 1866).

72. Gary Lawson, *Prolegomenon to Any Future Administrative Law Course: Separation of Powers and the Transcendental Deduction,* 49 ST. LOUIS U. L.J. 885 (2005).

73. Calabresi and Rhodes, *The Structural Constitution,* 105 HARV. L. REV. 1153, 1155 (1992).

74. Carl H. Esbeck, *Uses and Abuses of Textualism and Originalism in Establishment Clause Interpretation,* UTAH L. REV. 489, 502 (2011) (also arguing that the meaning of the Bill of Rights needs to be interpreted in light of the Constitution's overall frame of government).

75. ROBERT A. GOLDWIN, FROM PARCHMENT TO POWER: HOW JAMES MADISON USED THE BILL OF RIGHTS TO SAVE THE CONSTITUTION 65 (National Affairs Inc. 1997).

76. Graber, *Enumeration,* 9 U. PA. J. CONST. L. at 372 (2007).

77. *Id.* at 379.

78. *Id.*

79. *Id.* at 380.

80. *Id.* at 386.

81. *See generally* GARRY, AN ENTRENCHED LEGACY (2009).

82. VILE, CONSTITUTIONALISM at 14 (1969).

83. Lash, *James Madison's Celebrated Report,* 74 GEO. WASH. L. REV. 165, 178, 189 (2006).

84. *United States v. Darby,* 312 U.S. 100, 115, 119 (1941).

85. Kurt Lash, *The Lost Jurisprudence of the Ninth Amendment,* 83 TEX. L. REV. at 597, 601–2 (2005).

86. *Id.* at 663–64.

87. The New Deal constitutional revolution, in the way it upheld the New Deal legislative agenda, led to "the death of our federal system." DAVID P. CURRIE, THE CONSTITUTION IN THE SUPREME COURT: THE SECOND CENTURY, 1888–1986 (Univ. of Chicago Press 1990), 236.

88. LARRY D. KRAMER, THE PEOPLE THEMSELVES: POPULAR CONSTITUTIONALISM AND JUDICIAL REVIEW 219–20 (Oxford Univ. Press 2004). Because of this "settlement," federalism became a dead doctrine until the Rehnquist Court. WALKER, REBIRTH OF FEDERALISM at 96.

89. *Palko v. Connecticut,* 302 U.S. 319 (1937).

90. *U.S. v. Carolene Products Co.,* 304 U.S. 144, 152–53 n.4 (1938) (rejecting a due process challenge to federal regulations of interstate shipments of skimmed milk) ("There may be narrower scope for operation of the presumption of constitutionality when legislation appears on its face to be within a specific prohibition of the Constitution, such as those of

the first ten amendments, which are deemed equally specific when held to be embraced with the Fourteenth").

91. WALKER, REBIRTH OF FEDERALISM at 96 (1995).

92. Levinson, *Empire-Building,* 118 HARV. L. REV. at 971 (2005).

93. Michael B. Rappaport, *It's the O'Connor Court: A Brief Discussion of Some Critiques of the Rehnquist Court and Their Implications for Administrative Law,* 99 NW. U. L. REV. 369, 375 (2004) (arguing that "the two-tiered approach of vigorous judicial review concerning individual rights, but deferential review of structural matters, is of relatively recent vintage").

94. *Miranda v. Arizona,* 384 U.S. 436 (1966) (creating new procedural safeguards for criminal defendants subjected to custodial interrogation).

95. *Loving v. Virginia,* 388 U.S. 1 (1967) (striking down Virginia's ban on interracial marriage).

96. *New York Times v. Sullivan,* 376 U.S. 254 (1964) (limiting the liability of defendants in a defamation action).

97. *Roe v. Wade,* 410 U.S. 113 (1973) (recognizing a constitutional right to abortion).

98. *Craig v. Boren,* 429 U.S. 190 (1976) (striking down gender-based discrimination).

99. *Furman v. Georgia,* 408 U.S. 238 (1972) (ruling that the death penalty as imposed in the cases at hand amounted to cruel and unusual punishment in violation of the Eighth and Fourteenth Amendments).

100. *Goldberg v. Kelly,* 397 U.S. 254 (1970) (holding that a termination of welfare benefits requires a due process hearing).

101. Arthur Hellman, *The Business of the Supreme Court under the Judiciary Act of 1925: The Plenary Docket in the 1970s,* 91 HARV. L. REV. 1711 (1978).

102. *Id.* at 1741. The number of individual-rights cases was nearly double the number the Court had heard during the 1959–1964 period. *Id.* at 1750.

103. *Id.* at 1761.

104. This skewed focus is evident in the Court's handling of deportation orders of the Immigration and Naturalization Service. Even though Congress has exclusive power to legislate in the area of immigration and naturalization, U.S. CONST. art I, § 8, cl. 4, and even though Congress has delegated some of those powers to the executive branch (the INS), the Court has taken a judicially active and intrusive stance to immigration matters that affect or involve issues of individual rights. Rather than showing deference to Congress and to separation-of-powers concerns, the Court has actively reviewed and scrutinized congressional laws dealing with the INS's detention of deportable aliens. *See Zadvydas v. Davis,* 533 U.S. 678 (2001).

105. MARY ANN GLENDON, RIGHTS TALK: THE IMPOVERISHMENT OF POLITICAL DISCOURSE 4 (Free Press 1991) (arguing that the traditional theory was that individual freedom was protected mainly through these structural features of our political regime).

106. *Id.* at 5.

107. Daniel J. Hulsebosch, *Bringing the People Back In,* 80 NYU L. REV. 653, 658 (2005). Much of the legal academy favors the relatively recent norm of expansive readings of the Bill of Rights. Saikrishna B. Prakash, *Branches Behaving Badly: The Predictable and Often Desirable Consequences of the Separation of Powers,* 12 CORNELL J.L. & PUB. POL'Y 543, 546 (2003). Substantive individual rights appear to be the only place where the legal academy favors limitations on government.

108. Hulsebosch, *Bringing the People Back In,* 80 NYU L. REV. at 660 (2005).

109. *See generally* GARRY, AN ENTRENCHED LEGACY (2009).

110. Thomas McAffee, *The Federal System as Bill of Rights,* 43 VILL. L. REV. 17, 22 (1998).

111. Kramer, *Putting the Politics Back,* 100 COLUM. L. REV. 215, 266 (2000).

112. *Id.* at 24–25.

113. *Id.*

114. *See* GARRY, AN ENTRENCHED LEGACY (2009).

115. Jack Wade Nowlin, *The Rehnquist Court and the "New Federalism,"* appearing in THE ASHGATE RESEARCH COMPANION TO FEDERALISM 551–67 (Ann Ward and Lee Ward eds., Ashgate 2009).

Chapter 3.
The Impetus for the Bill of Rights

1. According to John Phillip Reid in CONSTITUTIONAL HISTORY OF THE AMERICAN REVOLUTION: THE AUTHORITY OF RIGHTS, the eighteenth-century American claim to rights was based far less on natural-rights philosophy than on the English constitutional tradition of limits on government. The eighteenth-century view of rights was conceived "not in the modern sense, as instruments for liberating individuals, but in the early modern sense as restraints on arbitrary government." Jack Green, *The Salience of Rights in the Origins of the American Revolution*, REVIEWS IN AMERICAN HISTORY 198–203, 202 (1988).

2. Esbeck, *Uses and Abuses of Textualism and Originalism*, UTAH L. REV. 489, 605 (2011).

3. *Id.* at 606.

4. Thomas B. McAffee, *Inalienable Rights, Legal Enforceability, and American Constitutions: The Fourteenth Amendment and the Concept of Unenumerated Rights*, 36 WAKE FOREST L. REV. 747, 777–78 (2001).

5. JACK N. RAKOVE, ORIGINAL MEANINGS: POLITICS AND IDEAS IN THE MAKING OF THE CONSTITUTION 288 (Vintage 1997).

6. *Id.* at 289.

7. As Stephen Macedo has theorized, the Constitution established islands of governmental powers "surrounded by a sea of individual rights," not islands of rights "surrounded by a sea of governmental powers." STEPHEN MACEDO, THE NEW RIGHT V. THE CONSTITUTION 97 (Cato Institute 1987).

8. ERVIN POLLACK, JURISPRUDENCE 74 (Ohio State Univ. Press 1979).

9. Randy Barnett, *The Separation of People and State*, 32 HARV. J.L. & PUB. POL'Y 451, 452.

10. Letter from William R. Davie to James Madison (June 10, 1789), in CREATING THE BILL OF RIGHTS: DOCUMENTARY RECORD FROM THE FIRST CONGRESS 245–46 (Helen E. Veit et al. eds., The Johns Hopkins Univ. Press 1991).

11. Gary Lawson, *A Truism with Attitude: The Tenth Amendment in Constitutional Context*, 83 NOTRE DAME L. REV. 469, 471 (2008).

12. *Id.* at 472.

13. Graber, *Enumeration*, 9 U. PA. J. CONST. L. at 329 (2007).

14. Lawson, *A Truism with Attitude*, 83 NOTRE DAME L. REV. at 491 (2008).

15. James Madison, *Speech in Congress Proposing Constitutional Amendments* (June 8, 1789), in 12 THE PAPERS OF JAMES MADISON 196, 202 (Charles F. Hobson & Robert A. Rutland eds., Univ. Press of Virginia 1979).

16. 1 ANNALS OF CONG. 437 (Joseph Gales ed., 1834) (June 8, 1789).

17. RAKOVE, ORIGINAL MEANINGS at 336.

18. James Madison, *Speech to House of Representatives* (June 8, 1789), in CREATING THE BILL OF RIGHTS at 81 (Helen Veit et al. eds., 1991).

19. RICHARD LABUNSKI, JAMES MADISON AND THE STRUGGLE FOR THE BILL OF RIGHTS 178–255 (Oxford Univ. Press 2006).

20. *See* George Mason, Objections to the Constitution of Government Formed by the Convention (1787), in 2 The Complete anti-Federalist 11, 13 (Herbert J. Storing & Murray Dry eds., Univ. of Chicago Press 1985).

21. Another aspect of the limited-government nature of the Constitution was the fact that the Constitution did not impose any substantial obligations on government—for instance, the Constitution did not mandate that it act in certain manners. For a general discussion of the structural design of the Constitution and the goals of the framers, *see generally* Joseph J. Ellis, American Creation: Triumphs and Tragedies in the Founding of the Republic (A. A. Knopf 2007).

22. McConnell, *Natural Rights,* 5 NYU J.L. & Liberty at 18 (2010).

23. McAffee, *Restoring the Lost World,* 75 U. Cin. L. Rev. at 1562 (2007). In fact, a number of the Constitution's critics argued that a reservation of all the powers not granted by the Constitution could be an adequate alternative to a bill of rights. *Id.* at 1562, n.319. "That such an argument could be made . . . reflects that such an anti-federalist position was not rooted in reading federal powers through the lens of inherent rights assumptions." *Id.* During the debate over ratification, for instance, Thomas Jefferson argued that there was no specific assurance in the proposed Constitution that in all cases where specific powers had not been delegated to the federal government those powers had been retained by the states. Robert Allen Rutland, The Birth of the Bill of Rights: 1776 to 1791 at 129 (Univ. of North Carolina Press 1955).

24. *Letters from the Federal Farmer* (October 9, 1787), *reprinted in* Origins of the American Constitution 272 (Michael Kammen ed., Penguin 1986); *Brutus, Essay of November 1, 1787, reprinted in* Origins of the American Constitution 313, 315 (Michael Kammen ed., Penguin 1986).

25. Michael Dorf, *Incidental Burdens on Fundamental Rights,* 109 Harv. L. Rev. 1175, 1189 (1996).

26. *Id.* (arguing that by "juxtaposing affirmative powers with negative limits, the Constitution's architecture assumed that, even when the government pursues a permissible goal, the government might sometimes violate individual rights—and thus, the negative limits prohibit otherwise valid exercises of power").

27. *Id.* at 1191.

28. *Id.* at 1229.

29. In a similar vein, Jed Rubenfeld has suggested that the right of privacy should protect against "a particular kind of creeping totalitarianism." Jed Rubenfeld, *The Right of Privacy,* 102 Harv. L. Rev. 737, 784 (1989).

30. *See* Leonard W. Levy, Freedom of Speech and Press in Early American History: A Legacy of Suppression at xxi–xxii (Harper Row 1963).

31. *See* Paul Finkelman, *Intentionalism: The Founders and Constitutional Interpretation,* 75 Texas L. Rev. 435, 461–63 (1996).

32. *See* Merrill Jensen, *Book Review,* 75 Harv. L. Rev. 456, 458 (1961); Finkelman, *Intentionalism,* 75 Texas L. Rev. at 464 (1996).

33. Rakove, Original Meanings at 149.

34. *Id.* at 148.

35. *Id.* at 323.

36. *Id.* at 151.

37. *Id.* at 293.

38. As Thomas McAffee argues, "Modern commentators' dichotomy between power allocative and rights protective provisions is foreign to the thinking of the founders." McAffee, *Restoring the Lost World,* 75 U. Cin. L. Rev. at 1529. What has been lost in the

contemporary debate on the Bill of Rights "is the crucial Madisonian insight that localism and liberty can sometimes work together rather than at cross-purposes." AMAR, THE BILL OF RIGHTS at 7.

39. RAKOVE, ORIGINAL MEANINGS at 324. To the Anti-Federalists, "because of the attenuated chain of representation, Congress would be far less trustworthy than state legislatures." AMAR, THE BILL OF RIGHTS at 11. Their highest concern with the Bill of Rights was "the idea of limiting federal power." *Id.* at 14.

40. RAKOVE, ORIGINAL MEANINGS at 325.

41. *See* David DeWolf, *Ten Tortured Words,* 85 DENV. U. L. REV. at 443, 448 (2007).

42. Letter from Hardin Burnley to James Madison (Nov. 28, 1789), in 2 THE BILL OF RIGHTS: A DOCUMENTARY HISTORY 1188 (Bernard Schwartz ed., Chelsea House Pub. 1971) (arguing that protecting the rights set out in the Bill of Rights is a means of further limiting governmental power by preventing it from improper extension).

43. RALPH KETCHAM, FRAMED FOR POSTERITY: THE ENDURING PHILOSOPHY OF THE CONSTITUTION at 104 (Univ. Press of Kansas 1993).

44. GOLDWIN, FROM PARCHMENT TO POWER at 124.

45. *Id.* at 144. Moreover, the fact that the Bill of Rights was aimed strictly at the power of the federal government can be seen from the fact that the Senate deleted with hardly any debate a proposed article that applied various rights in the Bill of Rights to the states-proposed Article 14, which stated, "No state shall infringe the equal rights of conscience, nor the freedom of speech, or of the press, nor of the right of trial by jury in criminal cases." *Id.* at 161.

46. *Id.* at 105.

47. *See* Patrick Henry, *Debates in the Convention of the Commonwealth of Virginia on the Adoption of the Federal Constitution* (June 14, 1788), in 3 JONATHAN ELLIOT & JAMES MADISON, THE DEBATES IN THE SEVERAL STATE CONVENTIONS 446 (J. B. Lippincott, Taylor & Maury 1836–59).

48. *See Letter from the Federal Farmer* XVI (January 20, 1788), *reprinted in* 2 HERBERT J. STORING, ED., THE COMPLETE ANTI-FEDERALIST 323–26 (Univ. of Chicago Press 1981).

49. McAffee, *The Federal System as Bill of Rights,* 43 VILL. L. REV. at 129 (1998).

50. MADISON'S REPORT ON THE VIRGINIA RESOLUTIONS, *reprinted in* THE DEBATES IN SEVERAL STATE CONVENTIONS, VOL. 3 at 546, 561–68.

51. McAffee, *The Federal System as Bill of Rights,* 43 VILL. L. REV. at 133 (1998).

52. *Id.* at 138.

53. *See Letters of Centinel* No. 2, in 2 THE COMPLETE ANTI-FEDERALIST at 143–44 (Herbert J. Storing ed., 1981); *Speech of Patrick Henry in Virginia Ratifying Convention,* in THE DEBATES IN THE SEVERAL STATE CONVENTIONS, VOL. 3 at 449 (Jonathan Elliot ed., 2d ed. 1836).

54. *See* James Madison, *Report on the Virginia Resolutions* (January 1800), *reprinted in* THE FOUNDERS' CONSTITUTION, VOL. 5 at 145 (Philip B. Kurland & Ralph Lerner eds., Univ. of Chicago Press 1987).

55. Ketcham, FRAMED FOR POSTERITY at 40.

56. Terrance Sandalow, *Social Justice and Fundamental Law,* 88 NW. U. L. REV. 461, 465 (1993). A primary concern of many of the framers involved how "to reconcile the power of government with the liberty of citizens." JAMES H. READ, POWER VERSUS LIBERTY: MADISON, HAMILTON, WILSON AND JEFFERSON 4 (Univ. of Virginia Press 2000).

57. JOHN PHILLIP REID, RULE OF LAW: THE JURISPRUDENCE OF LIBERTY IN THE SEVENTEENTH AND EIGHTEENTH CENTURIES 4–6 (N. Illinois Univ. Press 2004).

58. *Id.* at 78–79.

59. Ketcham, Framed for Posterity at 96.

60. When eighteenth-century Americans used the term *liberty,* they used it to refer to several different but complementary concepts: a community's right of self-determination, an individual's right to participate in civic affairs, a right to the protection of property and certain other specified freedoms, and the concept of natural rights. However, these concepts of liberty never reached the modern concept of unbounded personal autonomy because of the pervasive eighteenth-century belief in civil order based on reverence for history and traditional social authority. Jack Greene, *Jeffersonian Republicans and the Modernization of American Political Consciousness,* Reviews in American History 37–42, 38 (1985).

61. Ketcham, Framed for Posterity at 133.

62. *Id.* at 143.

63. *Id.* at 73.

64. *Id.* at 99.

65. Robert Delahunty, *Letters from the Founders,* 1 U. St. Thomas J.L. & Pub. Pol'y 1, 68 (2007). In The Federalist No. 38 at 235, James Madison argued that the Bill of Rights "ought to be declaratory, not of the personal rights of individuals, but of the rights reserved to the states in their political capacity" (Clinton Rossiter ed., 1961). Likewise, in The Federalist No. 84 at 515, Alexander Hamilton argued that "one object of the Bill of Rights is to declare and specify the political privileges of the citizens in the structure and administration of the government" (*id.*).

66. Amar, The Bill of Rights at xiii; *see also* Amar, *Intratextualism,* 112 Harv. L. Rev. at 133 (1999).

67. Amar, The Bill of Rights at xii. Amar argues that during the constitutional period liberty "was still centrally understood as public liberty of democratic self-government—majoritarian liberty rather than liberty against popular majorities." *Id.* at 159.

68. *Id.* at 120.

69. Mark Rahdert, *In Search of a Conservative Vision of Constitutional Privacy,* 51 Vill. L. Rev. 859, 882 (2006).

70. *Id.* at 882.

71. In summing up his argument that the Ninth Amendment served to protect the autonomy of the states, Madison argued that overly broad readings of federal power should not be allowed to infringe on state autonomy. 1 Annals of Cong., 1951 (Joseph Gales ed., 1834) (statement of Representative Madison).

72. James Madison, *Speech on the Constitutionality of the Bank of the United States* (February 2, 1791), in James Madison: Writings at 480, 489 (Jack Rakove ed., 1999). In the debate over the bank charter in 1791, James Madison argued that the power to charter a bank reflected an attempt to construe the enumerated powers of the federal government in such a way as to alter the essential nature of limited government, and that this violated the Ninth and Tenth Amendments. James Madison, *Speech in Congress Opposing the National Bank* (February 2, 1791), in *id.* at 489. *See also Memorandum from Roger Sherman to James Madison* (February 4, 1791), in Thirteen, The Papers of James Madison 382 (Charles F. Hobson & Robert A. Rutland eds., 1981).

73. Kurt Lash, *The Inescapable Federalism of the Ninth Amendment,* 93 Iowa L. Rev. 801, 805 (2008).

74. *Id.* at 809.

75. For a reference to James Madison's views about the danger to individual rights posed by local majorities, *see* Letter from James Madison to Thomas Jefferson (October 17, 1788), in 1 Letters and Other Writings of James Madison, 4th President of the United States 425 (J. B. Lippincott 1867).

76. Lash, *The Inescapable Federalism,* 93 IOWA L. REV. at 854. The protection of individual rights was not the single or even primary goal of the Ninth Amendment. *Id.* at 853. According to Amar, the Ninth Amendment "explicitly sought to protect liberty by preventing Congress from going beyond its enumerated powers." AMAR, THE BILL OF RIGHTS at 123.

77. Lash, *Three Myths of the Ninth Amendment,* 56 DRAKE L. REV. at 880 (2008).

78. Lash, *The Lost Jurisprudence,* 83 TEX. L. REV. at 637–42, 669–73 (2005).

79. *See generally Wickard v. Filburn,* 317 U.S. 111 (1942).

80. *See generally* THOMAS B. MCAFFEE, INHERENT RIGHTS, THE WRITTEN CONSTITUTION AND POPULAR SOVEREIGNTY: THE FOUNDERS' UNDERSTANDING (Greenwood Press 2000); McAffee, *Inalienable Rights,* 36 WAKE FOREST L. REV. at 792–93 (2001).

81. THOMAS B. MCAFFEE, THE "FOUNDATIONS" OF ANTI-FOUNDATIONALISM—OR TAKING THE NINTH AMENDMENT LIGHTLY: A COMMENT ON FARBER'S BOOK ON THE NINTH AMENDMENT at 240 (The Berkeley Electronic Press Selected Works 2007).

82. AMAR, THE BILL OF RIGHTS 127, 143 (1998).

83. AMAR, THE BILL OF RIGHTS 104. Robert Palmer has similarly written that the jury trial was seen as a better means for maintaining local control than for protecting individual liberties. Robert Palmer, *Liberties as Constitutional Provisions,* in WILLIAM E. NELSON, LIBERTY AND COMMUNITY: CONSTITUTION AND RIGHTS IN THE EARLY AMERICAN REPUBLIC 55, 101 (Oceana Publications 1987).

84. Kurt Lash, *The Inescapable Federalism,* 93 IOWA L. REV. at 806 (2008).

85. *Id.* at 809.

86. In *Griswold,* the Court applied a kind of individual-rights model. Concurring, Justice Goldberg wrote that the rights protected by the Ninth Amendment were those sufficiently rooted in the traditions and collective conscience of the nation. 381 U.S. at 493.

87. Kurt Lash, *A Textual-Historical Theory of the Ninth Amendment,* 60 STAN. L. REV. 895, 897 (2008).

88. *Id.*

89. *Id.* at 903.

90. *Id.* at 920.

91. Ryan Williams, *The Ninth Amendment as a Rule of Construction,* 111 COLUMBIA L. REV. 498, 501, 509 (2011).

92. *Id.* at 513.

93. Letter from Hardin Burnley to James Madison (Nov. 28, 1789), in 5 DOCUMENTARY HISTORY OF THE CONSTITUTION OF THE UNITED STATES 1786–1870 at 219 (Dept. of State ed., 1905).

Chapter 4.
Balancing Judicial Restraint and Democratic Rule

1. *Missouri v. Jenkins,* 515 U.S. 70, 126 (1995) (Thomas, J., concurring) (discussing concerns that were raised during the drafting and ratification of the Constitution regarding the federal judiciary's power).

2. *Id.* at 128.

3. THE FEDERALIST NO. 78, 394 (Alexander Hamilton) (Buccaneer Books 1992).

4. THE FEDERALIST NO. 49, 257 (James Madison) (Buccaneer Books 1992).

5. KEITH WHITTINGTON, CONSTITUTIONAL INTERPRETATION: TEXTUAL MEANING, ORIGINAL INTENT, AND JUDICIAL REVIEW 6 (1999).

6. Frederick Schauer, Free Speech: A Philosophical Inquiry 19–29 (Cambridge Univ. Press 1982).

7. Owen Fiss, *Free Speech and Social Structure*, 71 Iowa L. Rev. 1405 (1986).

8. *Roper v. Simmons*, 543 U.S. 551 (2005).

9. *Id.* at 605.

10. *See* John O. McGinnis, *The Federalist Approach to the First Amendment*, 31 Harv. J.L. & Pub. Pol'y 127, 127 (2008) (arguing that "the First Amendment should be applied much more stringently against the federal government than it is against the states"). According to McGinnis, "[S]o long as constitutional law protects free movement and the free flow of core political speech among the states, individuals are free to exit if the balance between liberty and license becomes radically off kilter." *Id.* at 129. A federalist approach to the First Amendment would accomplish the following: allowing states to react creatively to technological change; helping to diffuse tension among people with different views; and a lessening of partisanship by creating a structure that facilitates the study of the consequences of moral principles. *Id.* at 131.

11. As George Anastaplo observes, courts are "unlikely to be able to uphold the liberties of a people if they are, for a long period, the only source of support for such liberties." George Anastaplo, The Constitutionalist: Notes on the First Amendment 231 (Southern Methodist Univ. 1971).

12. Heyman, *Righting the Balance*, 78 B.U. L. Rev. 1275, 1316 (1998).

13. *Id.* at 1332–33.

14. 274 U.S. 357, 375 (1927) (Brandeis, J., concurring).

15. See, for example, *Ward v. Rock*, 491 U.S. 781, 791 (stating that the regulations must also be "narrowly tailored to serve a significant government interest").

16. *Id.* However, the Court might not allow a content-neutral regulation if it is seen as completely shutting off an entire means of communicating an idea. *See City of Ladue v. Gilleo*, 512 U.S. 43 (1994). In *Gilleo*, the Court struck down an ordinance that prohibited homeowners from displaying any and all political signs, holding that the ordinance eliminated an entire channel of expressing constitutionally protected speech. *Id.* at 54–59. Indeed, the Court did not even address the issue of whether the ordinance was content based or content neutral. *Id.* at 51–53.

17. *Heffron v. International Society for Krishna Consciousness, Inc.*, 452 U.S. 640, 647 (1981). Similarly, In *International Society for Krishna Consciousness v. Lee*, a regulation prohibiting society members from soliciting at airports was upheld. 505 U.S. 672 (1992).

18. 512 U.S. 753 (1994).

19. *Members of the City Council of the City of Los Angeles v. Taxpayers for Vincent*, 466 U.S. 789 (1984).

20. *See City of Renton v. Playtime Theatres, Inc.*, 475 U.S. 41, 47 (1986) (upholding a local law requiring adult movie theaters to be a certain distance from residential neighborhoods, churches, parks, and schools); *Young v. Am. Muni Theatres, Inc.*, 427 U.S. 50, 63 (1976) (upholding an ordinance banning a concentration of adult businesses). *See also City of Los Angeles v. Alameda Books, Inc.*, 535 U.S. 425 (2002) (upholding a zoning ordinance limiting the number of adult businesses that can operate in a single building).

21. *See, e.g., Ward*, 491 U.S. at 791 (1989) (stating that the government "may impose reasonable restrictions on time, place, or manner of protected speech, provided the restrictions are justified without reference to the content of the regulated speech, that they are narrowly tailored to serve a governmental interest, and that they leave open ample alternative channels for communication"); *Virginia State Board of Pharmacy v. Virginia Citizens Consumer Council*, 425 U.S. 748, 771 (1976) (stating that content-neutral time-

manner-place constraints are valid if they serve an important government interest and leave open ample alternative channels of communication).

22. For an argument setting forth the connections between place and manner restrictions and the content of speech, *see generally* Timothy Zick, *Speech and Spatial Tactics,* 84 TEX. L. REV. 581, 583 (2006). According to Zick, the Court has never recognized the "power of place to facilitate First Amendment freedoms." *Id.* at 613. And because of the relationship between the place of speech and the content of speech, according to Zick, not all place regulations are content neutral in their effect. "The time, place, and manner doctrine applies only where the state is neutral with regard to content, the presumption being that place itself has nothing to do with the substance of speech." *Id.* at 616. "Each type of place raises discrete speech issues, touches upon different expressive traditions, and constitutes a distinct part of our expressive topography." *Id.* at 618.

23. *Coal. to Protest the Democratic Nat'l Convention v. City of Boston,* 327 F.Supp.2d 61, 66 (D. Mass. 2004); *aff'd sub nom. Black Tea Soc'y v. City of Boston,* 378 F.3d 8 (1st Cir. 2004). Four years earlier, at the 2000 Democratic National Convention in Los Angeles, a free speech zone kept protestors almost 300 yards from any convention delegate. *See Serv. Employee Int'l Union v. City of Los Angeles,* 114 F.Supp.2d 966, 972 (C.D. Cal. 2000) (enjoining the use of this zone, not because it was designed to restrict protest but because its size was insufficiently tailored to the state's interest).

24. *See Menotti v. City of Seattle,* 409 F.3d 1113, 1124–26, 1167 (9th Cir. 2005).

25. Julia Preston, *Court Backs Police Department in Curbs on Labor Tactics,* NEW YORK TIMES, August 26, 2004, at B7.

26. *See Hill v. Colorado,* 530 U.S. 703 (2000). The Court upheld a state law requiring protestors to stay eight feet away from anyone entering or leaving an abortion clinic. *Id.* at 719 (holding this law to be a content-neutral "regulation of the places where some speech may occur"). In *Madison v. Women's Health Center,* the Court approved a "speech-free buffer zone" banning all protests within thirty-six feet of an abortion clinic. 512 U.S. 753, 770 (1994). This regulation essentially banned all anti-abortion protestors, and yet the Court still ruled that, as a time-manner-place restriction it did not violate the First Amendment. *Id.* at 770.

27. *Hill v. Colorado,* 503 U.S. 703, 723, 726 (2000).

28. *Id.* at 756. As the dissent argued, "[I]t does not take a veteran labor organizer to recognize that leafletting will be rendered utterly ineffectual by a requirement that the leafletter obtain from each subject permission to approach. That simply is not how it is done, and the Court knows it." *Id.*

29. *See, e.g., Clark v. Community for Creative Non-Violence,* 468 U.S. 288, 293 (1984) (holding that place restraints on political protests "are valid provided that they are justified without reference to the content of the regulated speech, that they are narrowly tailored to serve a significant government interest, and that they leave open ample alternative channels for communication of the information").

30. 327 F.Supp.2d at 66, 67–68, 74 (D. Mass. 2004).

31. *Id.* at 74–76 (stating that "given the constraints of time, geography, and safety, I cannot say that the design itself is not narrowly tailored in light of other opportunities for communication available under the larger security plan"). However, these alternative opportunities were not available in physical "places" for the protestors to gather, but in conveying their messages through the mass media. *See Black Tea Soc'y,* 378 F.3d at 14 (1st Cir. 2004).

32. *See Black Tea Soc'y,* 378 F.3d at 14 (1st Cir. 2004) (arguing that, given the option of expressing their protest messages through the mass media, "viable alternative means

existed to enable protestors to communicate their messages to the delegates").

33. Forcing convention protestors to resort to the mass media to convey their messages could well violate the First Amendment freedom of association. *See* 1 ALEXIS DE TOCQUEVILLE, DEMOCRACY IN AMERICA 196 (Phillips Bradley trans., Vintage Books 1990) (1840) (stating that the "most natural privilege of man, next to the right of acting for himself, is that of combining his exertions with those of his fellow creatures and of acting in common with them").

34. 381 U.S. 479 (1965) (holding that a right of privacy exists).

35. *Id.* at 484, 485.

36. *Id.* at 484.

37. 431 U.S. 678 (1977) (overturning state law banning the distribution of contraceptives to minors under 16 years of age).

38. *Id.* at 684.

39. 410 U.S. 113, 155 (1973). A woman's right to have an abortion was now included within the zone of privacy created in *Griswold. Roe* was reaffirmed in *Planned Parenthood of Southeastern Pennsylvania v. Casey,* 505 U.S. 833, 846–47 (1992) (stating that a woman's right to choose an abortion is grounded in the concept of liberty protected by the due process clause of the Fourteenth Amendment).

40. *Casey,* 505 U.S. at 851.

41. A further development in the expansion of privacy rights to cover the abortion decision occurred in *Stenberg v. Carhart,* where the Supreme Court struck down a Nebraska law prohibiting partial-birth abortion. *Stenberg v. Carhart,* 530 U.S. 914 (2000).

42. *Planned Parenthood v. Casey,* 505 U.S. 833, 851 (1992). Under the Court's privacy rulings, a judicially articulated national value on sexual privacy can trump all other community values or morals.

43. *Bartnicki v. Vopper,* 532 U.S. 514, 525 (2001) (ruling that the media are immune from civil damages suits brought under the Wiretap Act). Aside from the media, the government also participates in the erosion of personal privacy. For instance, nearly every state includes a date encryption on its driver's licenses. John Cross, *Age Verification in the Twenty-first Century,* 23 J. MARSHALL J. COMPUTER & INFO. L. 363, 372 (2005). However, when the license is swiped through a digital scanner (e.g., for age-verification purposes), the private data stored on the card's magnetic strip is susceptible to theft. Millions of Americans are victimized by identity theft, and the driver's license is a frequent means by which this theft occurs. *Id.* at 394.

44. Evidence that the framers did not recognize or even contemplate any kind of right to sexual privacy can be seen in the plethora of eighteenth- and nineteenth-century laws punishing adultery. *See generally* Carolyn B. Ramsey, *Sex and Social Order: The Selective Enforcement of Colonial American Adultery Laws in the English Context,* 10 YALE J.L. & HUMAN. 191, 208–13 (1998).

45. ROBERT F. NAGEL, THE IMPLOSION OF AMERICAN FEDERALISM (Oxford Univ. Press 2002).

46. *Id.* at 67.

47. 1 WILLIAM BLACKSTONE, COMMENTARIES ON THE LAWS OF ENGLAND 121–22 (Univ. of Chicago Press 1979) (1765).

48. Isaac Adams, *Growing Pains: The Scope of Substantive Due Process Rights of Parents of Adult Children,* 57 VAND. L. REV. 1883, 1889 (2004)

49. *Id.* at 1890.

50. John Hart Ely, *The Supreme Court, 1977 Term–Forward: On Discovering Fundamental Values,* 92 HARV. L. REV. 5, 39 (1978). Ely notes that the problems that arise from relying

on tradition involve those of cultural geography, time, competing tradition, and levels of generality. *Id.* at 39–40.

51. *See Furman v. Georgia,* 408 U.S. 238, 470 (Rehnquist, J., dissenting).

52. *Bowers v. Hardwick,* 478 U.S. 186, 192 (1986). Under this approach, the court protects only those rights and liberties that have been historically recognized in American culture and legal tradition. Thus, historical tradition is used by the court to protect unenumerated rights.

53. Daniel Conkle, *Three Theories of Substantive Due Process,* 85 N.C. L. Rev. 63, 99–100 (2006).

54. *See Casey,* 505 U.S. at 849.

55. *Id.* at 853.

56. Conkle, *Three Theories,* 85 N.C. L. Rev. at 107.

57. *Id.* at 112. Conkle also argues that "The theory of reasoned judgment calls for a decision-making methodology that is radically at odds with the principle of majoritarian self-government and that severely tests the limits of judicial objectivity and competence." *Id.* at 114–15.

58. *Lawrence v. Texas,* 539 U.S. at 572.

59. *Id.* at 576–77.

60. 521 U.S. 702, 720–21, 735 (1997) (rejecting due process challenges to Washington's law banning assisted suicide).

61. *Poe v. Ullman,* 367 U.S. 497, 545–46 (1961) (Harlan, J., dissenting).

62. *See Cruzan v. Director, Mo. Dept. of Health,* 497 U.S. 261, 293–94 (1990) (Scalia, J., concurring in the holding that a competent person has a constitutional right to refuse lifesaving measures).

63. *Glucksberg,* 521 U.S. at 727.

64. *Id.* at 2271.

65. 497 U.S. at 281.

66. *Bowers,* 478 U.S. at 190, 192; *Lawrence,* 539 U.S. at 575, 584.

67. *Bowers,* 478 U.S. at 190, 192. The Court found that sodomy was a common-law crime at the time the Bill of Rights was ratified, as well as when the Fourteenth Amendment was adopted. *Id.* at 192–93.

68. *Lawrence,* 539 U.S. at 571–72.

69. *Id.* at 598 (Scalia, J., dissenting).

70. *Id.* at 589. Scalia called the decision an example of judicial activism that seeks to declare homosexuality a fundamental right, even though "the court does not have the boldness" to say so. *Id.* at 594, 604–5.

71. *Lochner v. New York,* 198 U.S. 45, 61 (1905) (ruling that labor regulations "are meddlesome interferences with the rights of individuals"). The Court struck down a limitation imposed by the New York state legislature on the maximum hours per week that bakers could work, explaining that the due process clause gave heightened protection to one specific aspect of liberty, economic liberty, because it was fundamental to the Constitution's understanding of a free life. Peter Berkowitz, *The Court, the Constitution, and the Culture of Freedom,* Policy Review No. 132 (August 1, 2005).

72. According to some scholars, the *Lochner* Court "equated due process with laissez-faire economics." Jeffrey M. Shaman, *On the 100th Anniversary of Lochner v. New York,* 72 Tenn. L. Rev. 455, 506 (2005).

73. 198 U.S. at 53.

74. 165 U.S. 578, 589–90 (1897).

75. *Lochner,* 198 U.S. at 53.

76. *See* Shaman, *100th Anniversary,* 72 TENN. L. REV. at 496–97 (arguing that "the Court made active and frequent use of the Due Process Clause to strike down laws that the Court perceived as interfering with its favorite fundamental right").

77. *See, e.g., U.S. v. Carolene Products Co.,* 304 U.S. 144 (1938).

78. *See* Shaman, *100th Anniversary,* 72 TENN. L. REV. at 457.

79. *West Coast Hotel Co. v. Parrish,* 300 U.S. 379, 391–92 (1937).

80. *Id.* at 475.

81. 505 U.S. 833, 851 (1992).

82. *Id.* at 861–62.

83. Economic rights were once considered the pillar of human dignity and independence, just as noneconomic rights now seem to be. In the *Slaughterhouse Cases* of 1872, 83 U.S. 36, 83 (1872) (Field, J., dissenting), the dissenters provided the impetus for the substantive due process epitomized by *Lochner.* Justice Stephen Johnson Field, referencing the liberty protected by the Fourteenth Amendment, described the sanctity of private property as circumscribing a person's freedom. This view was restated even more clearly in *Munn v. Illinois,* 94 U.S. 113, 136 (1876) (Field, J., dissenting).

84. *Kelo v. City of New London,* 125 S.Ct. 2655 (2005), where the Supreme Court held that a city's exercise of eminent domain power in furtherance of an economic development plan, even if used to transfer property from one private party to another, satisfies the constitutional "public use" requirement. This ruling obviously threatens the most sacred of American domains–the home. Furthermore, the homes were marked for eminent domain not because they were blighted, but because they were needed to ensure an economic development that would increase the city's tax base. *Id.* at 2664–65. And the justification for this decision rested on a very broad reading of the term *public use* in the Fifth Amendment's provision that private property could "be taken for public use" on payment of just compensation. *Id.* at 2665–66. Writing for the Court, Justice John Paul Stevens ruled that courts should be highly deferential to government decisions to displace one private property owner in favor of another private party in the name of economic development. *Id.* But even if economic compensation is given, the first owner is not compensated for any subjective losses incurred as a result of not wanting to be forced out of a home in which he or she has many emotional attachments. *Id.* at 2686 (Thomas, J., dissenting). The decision was met with much protest. *See* Timothy Egan, *Ruling Sets Off Tug of War Over Private Property,* N.Y. TIMES, July 30, 2005, at A1 (stating that the decision "set off a storm of legislative action and protest, as states have moved to protect homes and businesses from the expanded reach of eminent domain").

85. *See NLRB v. Jones L. Laughlin Steel Corp.,* 301 U.S. 1, 41 (1937), where the Court refused to scrutinize, using a substantive due process analysis, legislation regulating labor relations. Instead, the Court merely deferred to the congressional finding that there was a rational basis for the regulations and that the regulated activities had a substantial economic effect. Prior to 1937, property rights were seen by the *Lochner*-era Court (*Lochner v. New York,* 198 U.S. 45 [1905]) as fundamental to the Constitution's view of a free and independent life. But the New Deal constitutional revolution abandoned the doctrine of substantive due process (that had been applied exclusively to property rights). Later, with the creation of privacy rights, the doctrine was revived; but this time, the nature of liberty that was found essential under the Constitution for individual freedom and to which the Court gave heightened protection was not economic liberty but autonomy in intimate relations.

Chapter 5.
Applying the Bill of Rights as Government-Limiting Provisions

1. *See* Thomas Cooley, *A Treatise on the Constitutional Limitations which Rests upon the Legislative Power of the States of the American Union* 422 (Legal Classics ed. 1987) (1868) (arguing that obscenity and defamation are not related to public issues on which citizens need to form opinions).

2. 221 U.S. 418, 436–37 (1911).

3. *See also* DAVID M. RABBAN, FREE SPEECH IN ITS FORGOTTEN YEARS 176 (Cambridge Univ. Press 1997) (outlining the courts' frequent use of property rights as grounds for defeating free speech defenses).

4. 326 U.S. 1, 20 (1945) (stating that "the widest possible dissemination of information from diverse and antagonistic sources is essential to the welfare of the public").

5. LOCKE, THE SECOND TREATISE OF GOVERNMENT at 221–43 (Thomas P. Peardon ed., 1952).

6. THE DEBATES IN THE SEVERAL STATE CONVENTIONS, VOL. 3 at 48, 52, 169, 386 (Jonathan Elliot ed., Ayer 1987) (1836).

7. AMAR, THE BILL OF RIGHTS at 53–54.

8. *Id.* at 61.

9. *Id.* at 62 (arguing that as illustrated by the Third Amendment, the federalism and separation-of-powers implications of the Bill of Rights often go unnoticed because of our modern-day fixation on individual rights).

10. 128 S.Ct. 2783 (2008).

11. Clark M. Neily, *The Right to Keep and Bear Arms in the States,* 33 HARV. J.L. & PUB. POL'Y 185, 186.

12. *Heller,* 128 S.Ct. at 2823.

13. J. Harvie Wilkinson, *Of Guns, Abortions, and the Unraveling Rule of Law,* 95 VA. L. REV. 253, 264 (2009).

14. *Id.*

15. GOLDWIN, FROM PARCHMENT TO POWER at 128.

16. KETCHAM, FRAMED FOR POSTERITY at 101 (1993).

17. AMAR, THE BILL OF RIGHTS at 46.

18. *See Blakely v. Washington,* 542 U.S. 296; *Melendez-Diaz v. Massachusetts,* 129 S.Ct. 2527 (2009).

19. 411 U.S. 1, 35 (1973).

20. 424 U.S. 507, 520 (1976); *see also Lloyd Corporation v. Tanner,* 407 U.S. 531, 570 (1972) (holding that a privately owned shopping center not dedicated to public use was not under First Amendment obligation to allow protests on its premises).

21. The Fourth Amendment states that "the right of the people to be secure in their persons, houses, papers, and effects, against unreasonable searches and seizures, shall not be violated, and no warrants shall issue, but upon probable cause, supported by oath or affirmation, and particularly describing the place to be searched, and the persons or things to be seized." U.S. CONST. amend. IV. The Seventh Amendment states that "in suits at common law, where the value in controversy shall exceed twenty dollars, the right of trial by jury shall be preserved, and no fact tried by a jury, shall be otherwise reexamined in the court of the United States, than according to the rules of the common law." U.S. CONST. amend. VII.

22. AMAR, THE BILL OF RIGHTS at 83 (arguing that juries, guaranteed in no fewer than three amendments, were at the heart of the Bill of Rights).

23. *Id.* at 97.

24. The jury trial was fundamentally more "a question of government structure, than one of 'individual right.'" *Id.* at 104.

25. *See* Suja Thomas, *A Limitation on Congress: "In Suits at Common Law,"* 71 Ohio St. L.J. 1071, 1073, 1084 (2010).

26. 1 Alexis de Tocqueville, Democracy in America 293–94 (Bradley Phillips ed., Vintage 1945).

27. Amar, The Bill of Rights at 106.

28. Letter from Thomas Jefferson to Thomas Paine (July 11, 1789) in 15 The Papers of Thomas Jefferson 269 (Julian P. Boyd ed., 1958).

29. Raymond Shih Ray Ku, *Privacy Is the Problem,* 19 Widener L.J. 873, 876 (2010).

30. *Id.* at 884.

31. *Id.* at 885.

32. *Id.* at 891.

33. *See* Arnold H. Loewy, *The Fourth Amendment: History, Purpose and Remedies,* 43 Tex. Tech. L. Rev. 1, 3 (2010).

34. George C. Thomas, *Stumbling toward History: The Framers' Search and Seizure World,* 43 Tex. Tech L. Rev. 199, 221 (2010).

35. Thomas Davies, *Can You Handle the Truth? The Framers' Preserved Common Law Criminal Arrest and Search Rules and Due Process of Law,* 43 Tex. Tech L. Rev. 51, 56 (2010).

36. *Id.* at 59.

37. 2 Legal Papers of John Adams 142–44 (L. Kinvin Wroth & Hiller B. Zobel eds., Belknap Press of Harvard Univ. Press 1965).

38. Davies, *Can You Handle the Truth?* 43 Tex. Tech L. Rev. at 85 (2010).

39. *Id.* at 86.

40. *See* Oliver M. Dickerson, *Writs of Assistance as a Cause of the Revolution,* in The Era of the American Revolution 40 (Richard Morris ed., Columbia Univ. Press 1939).

41. *See* George Thomas, *Time Travel, Hovercrafts and the Framers: James Madison Sees the Future and Rewrites the Fourth Amendment,* 80 Notre Dame L. Rev. 1451, 1475–77 (2005).

42. Davies, *Can You Handle the Truth?* 43 Texas Tech L. Rev. at 99 (2010).

43. Thomas Davies, *Recovering the Original Fourth Amendment,* 98 Mich. L. Rev. 547, 699–701 (1999).

44. Thomas Davies, *How the Post-Framing Adoption of the Bare Probable Cause Standard Drastically Expanded Government Arrest and Search Power,* 73 J.L. & Cont. Problems 1, 31–38 (2010).

45. *Id.* at 36–41.

46. Thomas, *Stumbling toward History,* 43 Tex. Tech L. Rev. 199, 206 (2010).

47. *See* William Cuddihy, The Fourth Amendment: Origins and Original Meaning 674–79 (2009).

48. *See* Patrick Henry, Virginia Ratification Convention, June 5, 1788, in The Debates in the Several State Conventions, Vol. 3 at 57 (Jonathan Elliot ed., 2d ed., J. B. Lippincott 1836).

49. *Id.* at 209 (George Mason, June 11, 1788, Virginia Ratification Convention).

50. *See* Cuddihy, The Fourth Amendment at 677.

51. Thomas, *Stumbling toward History,* 43 Tex. Tech. L. Rev. at 208 (2010).

52. *Id.* at 209.

53. Davies, *Can You Handle the Truth?* 43 Tex. Tech L. Rev. at 83 (2010).

54. *See United States v. Villamonte-Marquez,* 462 U.S. 579, 588 (1983).

55. 519 U.S. 33, 39 (1996).

56. The reasonableness standard could also support an individual-autonomy model of the Fourth Amendment, but that model might tend to look more at the harm to the individual or intrusion into the individual's property rather than the reasonableness of the government action.

57. 497 U.S. 177 (1990).

58. Jack Wade Nowlin, *The Warren Court's House Built on Sand,* MISSISSIPPI L. J. (forthcoming).

59. *Id.*

60. 131 S.Ct. 1849, 1858 (2011). The Court's balancing approach to reasonableness, weighing the individual interests against the state interests in crime control, was also evident in *Michigan v. Summers* (452 U.S. 692 [1981]) and *Michigan Department of State Police v. Sitz* (496 U.S. 444 [1990]).

61. Nowlin, *The Warren Court's House,* MISSISSIPPI L. J. (forthcoming).

62. Thomas Clancy, *The Fourth Amendment as a Collective Right,* 43 TEX. TECH L. REV. 255, 276 (2010).

63. *See, e.g., Maryland v. Wilson,* 519 U.S. 408 (1997) (police protection); *Michigan v. Clifford,* 464 U.S. 287 (1984) (fighting fires); *Hudson v. Palmer,* 468 U.S. 517 (1984) (prisoners' cells); *Michigan v. Summers,* 452 U.S. 692 (1981) (detention during warrant execution); *South Dakota v. Opperman,* 428 U.S. 364 (1976) (inventory searches); *Board of Education v. Earls,* 536 U.S. 822 (2002) (public school students and student drug testing); *O'Connor v. Ortega,* 480 U.S. 709 (1987) (governmental workplaces); *New Jersey v. T. L. O.,* 469 U.S. 325 (1985) (public school students).

64. *See Delaware v. Prouse,* 440 U.S. 648 (1979); *Illinois v. Lidster,* 540 U.S. 419 (2004) (informational checkpoints); *Michigan Dept. of State Police v. Sitz,* 496 U.S. 444 (1990) (sobriety checkpoints).

65. *See United States v. Aukai,* 497 F.3d 955, 956 (9th Cir. 2007).

66. *See Herring v. United States,* 129 S.Ct. 695 (2009). For instance, in 1971, the Court held that the Fourth Amendment is not violated when an officer makes a reasonable, good faith mistake about the identity of the person he is arresting. *Hill v. California,* 401 U.S. 797 (1971).

67. *Brigham City v. Stuart,* 547 U.S. 398, 403 (2006).

68. *Mincey v. Arizona,* 437 U.S. 385, 392 (1978).

69. 468 U.S. 897, 922 (1984).

70. *See* Van Vechten Veeder, *Freedom of Public Discussion,* 23 HARV. L. REV. 413–14 (1910) (noting that the process of continual readjustment between the needs of society and the protection of individual rights is nowhere more conspicuous than in the history of the law of defamation).

71. CLINTON ROSSITER, SEEDTIME OF THE REPUBLIC 443, 442 (Harcourt Brace 1953).

72. 395 U.S. 444, 447 (1969).

73. 315 U.S. 568, 572 (1942).

74. *Id.*

75. 467 U.S. 649 (1984).

76. 467 U.S. at 651, 655 (1984).

77. *See* Laurence Rosenthal, *The New Originalism Meets the Fourteenth Amendment: Original Public Meaning and the Problem of Incorporation,* 18 J. CONTEMP. LEGAL ISSUES 361 (2009) (arguing against the claim that the Fourteenth Amendment incorporated the Bill of Rights against the states); Michael Kent Curtis, *The Bill of Rights and the States: An*

Overview from One Perspective, 18 J. CONTEMP. LEGAL ISSUES 3, 5 (2009) (arguing in favor of the Fourteenth Amendment's incorporation of the Bill of Rights against the state, and discussing the historical opposition to such incorporation). For a reference to the debate on incorporation, *see* AMAR, THE BILL OF RIGHTS; MICHAEL KENT CURTIS, NO STATE SHALL ABRIDGE: THE FOURTEENTH AMENDMENT AND THE BILL OF RIGHTS (Duke Univ. Press 1986); RAOUL BERGER, GOVERNMENT BY JUDICIARY: THE TRANSFORMATION OF THE FOURTEENTH AMENDMENT (2d ed., Liberty Fund 1997).

78. Barry Friedman, *Reconstructing Reconstruction: Some Problems for Originalists,* 11 U. PA. J. CONST. L. 1201, 1205 (2009).

79. Richard Aynes, *The 39th Congress (1865–1867) and the 14th Amendment: Some Preliminary Perspectives,* 42 AKRON L. REV. 1019, 1019 (2009).

80. *Slaughterhouse Cases,* 83 U.S. 36, 78 (1872).

81. 1 BRUCE ACKERMAN, WE THE PEOPLE: FOUNDATIONS 102–3 (Belknap Press of Harvard Univ. Press 1991).

82. Gerard Magliocca, *Why Did the Incorporation of the Bill of Rights Fail in the Late Nineteenth Century?* 94 MINN. L. REV. 102, 103 (2009).

83. *See Gideon v. Wainwright,* 372 U.S. 335 (1963) (Sixth Amendment right to counsel incorporated); *Malloy v. Hogan,* 378 U.S. 1 (1964) (Fifth Amendment right to be free of compelled self-incrimination); *Klopfer v. North Carolina,* 386 U.S. 213 (1967) (Sixth Amendment right to a speedy and public trial); *Duncan v. Louisiana,* 391 U.S. 145 (1968) (Sixth Amendment right to a jury trial); *Mapp v. Ohio,* 367 U.S. 643 (1961) (Fourth Amendment right to be free from unreasonable searches and seizures and the right to have illegally seized evidence excluded from evidence at trial). Indeed, these cases make up what has been called the Warren Court's "famous transformation of American criminal procedure." Risa L. Goluboff, *Dispatch from the Supreme Court Archives: Vagrancy, Abortion, and What the Links between Them Reveal about the History of Fundamental Rights,* 62 STAN. L. REV. 1361, 1376 (2009). But it is also a transformation that has led to "perverse consequences." *Id.*

84. *Id.* at 133.

85. Lash, *A Textual-Historical Theory,* 60 STAN. L. REV. 895, 919–20 (2008).

86. *Id.* at 924.

87. *See* GEORGE ANASTAPLO, THE CONSTITUTIONALIST 193 (S. Methodist Univ. Press 1971) (arguing that the Fourteenth Amendment reflected the belief that the states were no better than the federal government, and hence that they should be subject to the same restraints as the federal government).

88. Aynes, *The 39th Congress (1865–1867),* 42 AKRON L. REV. 1019, 1027 (2009).

89. *Id.* at 1034.

90. Richard Aynes, *Enforcing the Bill of Rights against the States,* 18 J. CONTEMP. LEGAL ISSUES 77, 85 (2009).

91. Aynes, *The 39th Congress (1865–1867),* 42 AKRON L. REV. 1019, 1038 (2009).

92. *Id.* at 1040.

93. *Id.* at 1046.

94. *See Slaughterhouse Cases* 83 U.S. 36, 129 (1872) (Swayne, J., dissenting) (stating that "[b]y the Constitution, as it stood before the war, ample protection was given against oppression by the Union, but little was given against wrong and oppression by the states. That want was intended to be supplied by this amendment").

95. Aynes, *The 39th Congress (1865–1867),* 42 AKRON L. REV. 1019, 1041 (2009).

96. William Rich, *Why "Privileges for Immunities"? An Explanation of the Framers' Intent,* 42 AKRON L. REV. 1111 (2009).

97. Elizabeth Reilly, *The Union as It Wasn't and the Constitution as It Isn't*, 42 AKRON L. REV. 1081, 1083 (2009).

98. *Id.* at 1086.

99. CIVIL RIGHTS CASES 109, U.S. 3 (1883) (finding the Civil Rights Act of 1875 an unconstitutional exercise of power to reach conduct other than state action).

100. *U.S. v. Cruikshank*, 92 U.S. 542 (1875).

101. According to William E. Nelson in THE FOURTEENTH AMENDMENT: FROM POLITICAL PRINCIPLE TO JUDICIAL DOCTRINE (1988), the Fourteenth Amendment sought to end Southern resistance to giving equality to the freed slaves, to combat the harassment of Northerners in the South, and to revise the "three-fifths" clause made obsolete by the Thirteenth Amendment. But in response to claims that the Fourteenth Amendment gave sweeping and overriding power to the federal government, the Republicans asserted that there was no intent to abrogate state autonomy.

102. 521 U.S. 507 (1997).

103. *See Board of Trustees of University of Alabama v. Garrett*, 531 U.S. 356 (2001); *United States v. Morrison*, 529 U.S. 598 (2000); *Kimel v. Florida Board of Regents*, 528 U.S. 62 (2000).

104. *City of Boerne*, 521 U.S. at 519.

105. *Id.* at 528.

106. *See Katzenbach v. Morgan*, 384 U.S. 641, 668 (1966) (Harlan, J., dissenting).

107. *City of Boerne*, 521 U.S. at 532, 534.

108. Jennifer Mason McAward, *The Scope of Congress' Thirteenth Amendment Enforcement Power after City of Boerne v. Flores*, 88 WASH. U. L. REV. 77, 101 (2010).

109. *Id.*

110. *See Slaughterhouse Cases*, 83 U.S. 36, 49–54 (1872).

111. *See Slaughterhouse Cases*, 83 U.S. at 67–73 (1872).

112. *Id.* at 78.

113. *Id.* at 71–72. *See also* Wilson Huhn, *The Legacy of Slaughterhouse, Bradwell and Cruikshank*, in *Constitutional Interpretation*, 42 AKRON L. REV. 1051, 1074 (2009).

Chapter 6.
The Free Speech Clause as a Limited-Government Provision

1. 130 S.Ct. 876 (2010).

2. 130 S.Ct. at 917 (Roberts, C.J., concurring) (stating that infringements on corporate speech would subvert "the vibrant public discourse that is at the foundation of our democracy").

3. *Broadrick v. Oklahoma*, 413 U.S. 601, 615 (1973).

4. AMAR, THE BILL OF RIGHTS at 21.

5. According to Amar, the "right of the people to assemble does not simply protect the ability of self-selected clusters of individuals to meet together; it is also an express reservation of the collective rights . . . to assemble in a future convention and exercise our sovereign right to alter or abolish our government." *Id.* at 26. This right is the right of the people to "bring wayward government to heel by assembling in convention." *Id.*

6. *Id.* at 31. One way to achieve citizen control over the central government is to have free social institutions that provide for citizen education. *Id.* at 133.

7. KETCHAM, FRAMED FOR POSTERITY at 120–21.

8. *Id.*

9. *Id.* at 125.

10. John Trenchard & Thomas Gordon, Cato's Letters No. 15 (Ronald Hamowy ed., Liberty Fund 1995).

11. 515 U.S. 753 (1995).

12. 454 U.S. at 265–66. The Court held that "religious worship and discussion" are "forms of speech and association protected by the First Amendment." *Id.* at 269.

13. *Lamb's Chapel v. Center Moriches Union Free School District,* 508 U.S. 384, 387 (1993).

14. *Id.* The group was denied access to the public school building because it wanted to show a film series and lecture that was religious in nature.

15. 466 U.S. 789, 810–12 (1984).

16. 518 U.S. 727 (1996). In addition to these restrictions, the regulations also required the programmers of leased channels to alert cable operators of their intent to broadcast indecent material at least thirty days before the scheduled broadcast date.

17. 58 F.3d 654 (D.C. Cir. 1995).

18. *Id.* at 663.

19. *Id.* at 667. The decision, however, applied only to broadcast television, not to cable.

20. 96 F.3d 380, 382 (9th Cir. 1996).

21. *Id.* at 385–89.

22. *Frisby v. Schultz,* 487 U.S. 474, 484 (1988). *See also Moser v. FCC,* 46 F.3d 970 (9th Cir. 1995), where the court noted that a ban on auto-dialing machines still left abundant alternatives open to advertisers.

23. *Hill v. Colorado,* 530 U.S. 703 (2000).

24. *Schenck v. Pro-Choice Network,* 519 U.S. 357, 385 (1997).

25. And in *Urofsky v. Gilmore,* where a group of university professors challenged the constitutionality of a statute restricting state employees from accessing sexually explicit material on computers owned by the state, the court noted that the statute did not prohibit all access to such materials, since an employee could always get permission from their agency head to access the material. 167 F.3d 191, 194 (4th Cir. 1999).

26. *See Clark v. Community for Creative Non-Violence,* 468 U.S. 288 (1984).

27. *Christian Legal Society v. Martinez,* 130 S.Ct. 2971, 2994 (2010).

28. *Ward v. Rock Against Racism,* 491 U.S. 937 (1989).

29. *Madsen v. Women's Health Center,* 512 U.S. 753 (1994).

30. As the Supreme Court once observed, because of "constantly proliferating new and ingenious forms of expression, we are inescapably captive audiences for many purposes." 422 U.S. at 210–11.

31. In *Dial Info. Svcs. v. Thornburgh* and *Info. Providers' Coalition v. FCC,* the Second and Ninth Circuits ruled that the restrictions in the so-called "Helms Amendment," 47 USC □□ 223(b) et seq., did not violate the First Amendment. *Dial Info. Svcs. v. Thornburgh,* 938 F.2d 1535 (2d Cir. 1991); *Info. Providers' Coalition v. FCC,* 928 F.2d 866 (9th Cir. 1991).

32. *Sable Communications v. FCC,* 492 U.S. 115 (1989).

33. 88 F.3d 729 (9th Cir. 1996). The case involved a challenge to a California law regulating automatic dialing and announcing devices. The law prohibited the use of the devices unless a live operator first identified the calling party and obtained the called party's consent to listen to the prerecorded message. *Id.* at 731.

34. *Id.* at 733.

35. *Id.* at 736.

36. 408 U.S. 665, 690–91 (1972).

37. *Id.* 691. As the Court stated, the "crimes of news sources are no less reprehensible and threatening to the public interest when witnessed by a reporter than when they are not." *Id.* Moreover, the Court refused to release subpoenaed reporters from the same testimonial

obligations owed by any other citizen. *Id.* at 686–88.

38. *Id.* at 690. Justice White also noted that "we remain unclear how often and to what extent informers are actually deterred from furnishing information when newsmen are forced to testify before a grand jury." *Id.* at 693.

39. *Id.* at 694.

40. *Id.* at 694–95, 693.

41. *See Branzburg,* 408 U.S. at 744–45 (Stewart, J., dissenting).

42. *See Miller v. Transamerican Press,* 621 F.2d 721, 726 (5th Cir. 1980) (applying the three-part test); *Riley v. City of Chester,* 612 F.2d 708, 716–17 (3d Cir. 1979) (also applying the three-part balancing test articulated in the *Branzburg* dissent). In *LaRouche v. National Broadcasting System,* 780 F.2d 1134 (4th Cir. 1986), the Fourth Circuit employed the following test: "(1) whether the information is relevant, (2) whether the information can be obtained by alternative means, and (3) whether there is a compelling interest in the information." *Id.* at 1139. As another court put it in a slightly different context, the balancing of interests will tip in favor of disclosure where: (1) the information sought is material, relevant, and necessary; (2) there is a strong showing that it cannot be obtained by alternative means; and (3) the information is crucial to the plaintiff's case. This same test was used in *Shoen v. Shoen,* 48 F.3d 412, 415 (9th Cir. 1995) and *Bauer v. Gannett Co., Inc.,* 557 N.W.2d 608, 611 (Minn. Ct. App. 1997), where the court added an additional factor to this case-by-case balancing test: whether the reporter or news organization is a party to the litigation. "When the reporter is a party to the litigation, the balance may tip more in favor of disclosure than when the reporter is not a party." *Id.*

43. *See* Erik Ugland, *The New Abridged Reporter's Privilege: Policies, Principles, and Pathological Perspectives,* 71 OHIO L.J. 1, 33 (2010).

44. *Id.* at 39–40.

45. 376 U.S. 254, 279–80 (1964). The actual malice standard requires either knowing or reckless disregard of the falsity of the information. *Id.* This showing must be made by clear and convincing evidence. *See Church of Scientology International v. Behar,* 238 F.3d 168, 174 (2d Cir. 2001). The actual malice standard does not measure malice in the sense of ill will or animosity, but by the speaker's subjective doubts about the truth. *See Masson v. New Yorker Magazine, Inc.,* 501 U.S. 496, 510 (1991). The reckless conduct needed to show actual malice "is not measured by whether a reasonably prudent man would have published, or would have investigated before publishing," but by whether there is evidence "to permit the conclusion that the defendant in fact entertained serious doubts as to the truth of his publication." *St. Amant v. Thompson,* 390 U.S. 727, 731 (1968)

46. *New York Times,* 376 U.S. at 270.

47. 441 U.S. 153, 160 (1979).

48. *Id.* at 169.

49. *Id.* at 171.

50. 472 U.S. 749 (1985).

51. *New York Times Co. v. Sullivan,* 376 U.S. 254 (1964); *Gertz v. Robert Welch, Inc.,* 418 U.S. 323 (1974).

52. 521 U.S. 844 (1997).

53. *Id.* at 880.

54. 504 U.S. 191 (1992).

55. *See Virginia State Board of Pharmacy v. Virginia Citizens Consumer Counsel, Inc.,* 425 U.S. 748, 770 (1976) (stating that "some forms of commercial speech regulation are surely permissible"). To judge whether regulatory restrictions on commercial speech are permissible, the court has evolved a four-part test that is less stringent than the strict-

scrutiny test used to evaluate restrictions on political speech. *See Central Hudson Gas & Electric Corporation v. Public Services Commission*, 447 U.S. 557, 566 (1980).

56. *Unites States v. Edge Broad. Co.*, 509 U.S. 418, 430 (1993).

57. *Ohralik v. Ohio State Bar Ass'n*, 436 U.S. 447, 456 (1978). Courts have "upheld the ability of government to categorically exclude ordinary business corporations from participation in core political speech, an exclusion that would be unthinkable with respect to an individual citizen wishing to participate in a public debate." James Weinstein, *Speech Categorization and the Limits of First Amendment Formalism*, 54 CASE W. RES. L. REV. 1091, 1115–16 (2004).

58. *Central Hudson Gas & Electric Corp. v. Public Service Commission*, 447 U.S. 557 (1980).

59. 501 U.S. 1030 (1991).

60. *See* Antony Page, *Taking Stock of the First Amendment's Application to Securities Regulation*, 58 S.C. L. REV. 789, 789–790 (2007).

61. For an articulation of the government speech doctrine, *see Pleasant Grove v. Summum*, 129 S.Ct. 1125 (2009); *Rust v. Sullivan*, 500 U.S. 173 (1991) (upholding against a First Amendment challenge a federal law requiring doctors who received federal funding to refrain from discussing abortion with their patients).

62. *See Garcetti v. Ceballos*, 547 U.S. 410 (2006).

63. 524 U.S. 569, 574–75 (1998).

64. 539 U.S. 194, 201 (2003).

65. *Id.* at 212.

66. 520 U.S. 351, 366 (1997).

67. 395 U.S. 367, 394 (1969).

68. 453 U.S. 367 (1981).

69. 319 U.S. 190, 218–24 (1943).

70. *Arkansas Educational Television Commission v. Forbes*, 523 U.S. 666 (1998).

71. 337 U.S. 1, 4 (1949).

72. *See generally* ALEXANDER MEIKLEJOHN, FREE SPEECH AND ITS RELATION TO SELF-GOVERNMENT (Harper 1948); ALEXANDER MEIKLEJOHN, POLITICAL FREEDOM: THE CONSTITUTIONAL POWERS OF THE PEOPLE (Oxford Univ. Press 1965).

73. For an analysis of Meiklejohn's views, *see* PATRICK M. GARRY, THE AMERICAN VISION OF A FREE PRESS 74–80 (Garland Publishing 1990).

74. MEIKLEJOHN, POLITICAL FREEDOM: THE CONSTITUTIONAL POWERS OF THE PEOPLE 79 (Harper 1960).

75. The First Amendment model of Alexander Meiklejohn views the U.S. constitutional system as one of deliberative democracy. It seeks to promote reflective and deliberative debate. This Madisonian model sees the right of free expression as a key part of the system of public deliberation. Consequently, government may impose some controls on the information market that seek to sustain and uplift our system of deliberative democracy. In particular, it may promote political speech at the expense of other forms of speech; and it may discourage some forms of entertainment, if such entertainment comes to crowd out political speech. Obviously, in the Madisonian view, educational and public-affairs programming has a special place. The marketplace view, however, can confuse notions of the individual as consumer with those of the individual as citizen. To Meiklejohn, the First Amendment "is not the guardian of unregulated talkativeness." ALEXANDER MEIKLEJOHN, POLITICAL FREEDOM: THE CONSTITUTIONAL POWERS OF THE PEOPLE 26 (Greenwood Press 1979).

76. *See* RODNEY SMOLLA, SMOLLA AND NIMMER ON FREEDOM OF SPEECH 1–30 (Matthew Bender 1994–)(2003).

77. For example *see* ALEXANDER M. BICKEL, THE MORALITY OF CONSENT 62 (Yale Univ. Press 1975) (declaring that "the First Amendment should protect and indeed encourage speech so long as it serves to make the political process work"); Lillian R. BeVier, *The First Amendment and Political Speech: An Inquiry into the Substance and Limits of Principle,* 30 STAN. L. REV. 299, 358 (1978); Harry Kalven Jr., *The New York Times Case: A Note on the Central Meaning of the First Amendment,* 1964 S. CT. REV. 191, 208 (1964) (arguing that the First Amendment "has a central meaning—a core of protection of speech without which democracy cannot function").

78. BeVier, *The First Amendment and Political Speech,* 30 STAN. L. REV. at 358 (1978).

79. 504 U.S. 191, 196 (1992).

80. 468 U.S. 364, 383, 381 (1984).

81. 424 U.S. 1, 14 (1976).

82. 384 U.S. 214, 218 (1966).

83. *See* SMOLLA, SMOLLA AND NIMMER ON FREEDOM OF SPEECH at 1–33 (2003); *see also Fed. Election Comm'n v. Nat'l Conservative Political Action Comm.,* 470 U.S. 480, 493 (1985) ("There can be no doubt that the expenditures at issue in this case [expenditures by independent political committees supporting reelection of President Reagan] produce speech at the core of the First Amendment"); *Red Lion Broadcasting Co. v. FCC,* 395 U.S. 367, 390 (1969) ("[T]he essence of self-government . . . " [quoting *Garrison v. Louisiana,* 379 U.S. 64, 75–75 (1964)]); *Roth v. United States,* 354 U.S. 476, 484 (1957) ("The protection given speech and press was fashioned to assure unfettered interchange of ideas for the bringing about of political and social changes desired by the people"). In *Connick v. Myers,* an action brought by an ex-government employee who claimed she was fired in retaliation for criticisms she made about her employer, the Court focused on whether the speech was political in character and whether it addressed "a matter of public concern." 461 U.S. 138, 146 (1983). The Court stated that if the speech was not of public concern, there was no First Amendment protection against dismissal. *Id.* at 146.

84. *See Minneapolis Star and Tribune Co. v. Minnesota Commissioner of Revenue,* 460 U.S. 575, 578 (1983).

85. 529 U.S. 803, 806–7 (2000).

86. *Id.* at 806.

87. *Id.* at 807.

88. *Id.*

89. *Id.* at 845.

90. *Id.*

91. *Id.* at 842.

92. Stanley Ingber, *Rediscovering the Communal Worth of Individual Rights: The First Amendment in Institutional Contexts,* 69 TEX. L. REV. 1, 19 (1990).

93. *Id.* at 20. As Ingber argues, "[N]one of the traditional justifications of free speech is likely to be convincing when viewed exclusively from an individualist perspective." *Id.* According to Ingber, the moral relativism of the self-realization thesis hides beneath the illusion that the competition of the marketplace "will shed the bad and save the good." *Id.* at 41.

94. Jon M. Garon, *Entertainment Law,* 76 TUL. L. REV. 559, 634.

95. 130 S.Ct. 876, 906.

96. Darrel Menthe, *The Marketplace Metaphor and Commercial Speech Doctrine,* 38 HASTINGS CONST. L.Q. 131, 159 (2010).

97. Not only is the type and volume of speech in our public media space growing, but so is the type and volume of media entities that might claim First Amendment protection for

their business activities. If we do not confine the highest First Amendment protections to political speech, virtually any regulation applying to a media company might be subject to constitutional scrutiny because it would have the effect of reducing the financial ability to speak.

98. As Cass Sunstein notes, "[T]here is no way to operate a system of free expression without drawing lines. Not everything that counts as words or pictures is entitled to full constitutional protection. The question is not whether to draw lines, but how to draw the right ones." Cass R. Sunstein, *Free Speech Now,* 59 U. Chi. L. Rev. 255, 308 (1992).

99. Sunstein defines political speech as speech "both intended and received as a contribution to public deliberation about some issue." Cass R. Sunstein, Democracy and the Problem of Free Speech 130 (Free Press 1993).

100. "The only difference between speech and other behavior is speech's capacity to communicate ideas in the effort to reach varieties of truth." Robert Bork, Slouching towards Gomorrah 148 (Regan Books 1996). According to James Weinstein, previous case law has held that if a particular medium is essential to democratic communication, then any particular message in that medium is essential to democratic communication, then any particular message in that medium is constitutionally protected. Weinstein, *Speech Categorization,* 54 Case W. Res. L. Rev. at 1121 (2004). But this presumes that any communication in a medium essential to democratic rule will convey information relevant to democratic decision making. *Id.* Furthermore, for the medium to serve its democratic purpose, it must appeal to the rationality of its audience and must not mislead its audience into matters "unconnected with democratic decisionmaking." *Id.* It is assumed "that the audience of media essential to public discourse consists of independent rational agents involved in a dialogue about how we should govern ourselves, rather than dependent and vulnerable persons addressed monologically." *Id.* at 1122. This also assumes that the medium is capable of facilitating rational, interactive debate.

101. Sunstein would not give constitutional protection to words or expressions that are made "in a way that is not plausibly part of social deliberation about an issue." Cass R. Sunstein, *Free Speech Now,* 59 U. Chi. L. Rev. at 312 (1992).

102. Eugene Volokh, *Freedom of Speech and Information Privacy: The Troubling Implications of a Right to Stop People from Speaking about You,* 52 Stan. L. Rev. 1049, 1099 (2000).

103. *Id.*

104. Steven Heyman, *Ideological Conflict and the First Amendment,* 78 Chi.-Kent L. Rev. 531, 605 (2003).

105. Robert Bork, *Neutral Principles and Some First Amendment Problems,* 47 Ind. L.J. 1, 20 (1971).

106. *Id.* at 28.

107. Sunstein makes a similar argument. He argues that "[r]estrictions on political speech have the distinctive feature of impairing the ordinary channels for political change." Sunstein, Democracy at 306. As long as there is freedom of political speech, controls on other kinds of speech can always be protested. For instance, "[i]f the government bans violent pornography, citizens can continue to argue against the ban. But if the government forecloses political argument, the democratic corrective is unavailable. Controls on nonpolitical speech do not have this uniquely damaging feature." *Id.*

108. According to Judge Bork, "One of the freedoms, the major freedom, of our kind of society is the freedom to choose to have a public morality." Robert Bork, Tradition and Morality in Constitutional Law 9 (American Enterprise Institute for Public Policy Research 1984). He decries the entry into First Amendment law of what he describes as the "old, and incorrect, view that the only kinds of harm that a community is entitled to

suppress are physical and economic injuries. . . . The result of discounting moral harm is the privatization of morality, which requires the law of the community to practice moral relativism." *Id.* at 3.

109. ANASTAPLO, THE CONSTITUTIONALIST at 15 (1971).

110. *Id.* at 109.

111. *Id.* at 166.

112. If individual autonomy is to justify speech protections, if everyone has an equal right to express anything, then speech itself has ceased being something special. When everyone has an equal right to utter anything, then speech "becomes the equivalent of noise, and free speech theory becomes unintelligible." G. Edward White, *The First Amendment Comes of Age: The Emergence of Free Speech in Twentieth-Century America,* 95 MICH. L. REV. 299, 391 (1996).

113. *Abrams v. U.S.,* 250 U.S. 616 (1919).

114. White, *The First Amendment Comes of Age,* 95 MICH. L. REV. at 325 (1996).

115. Gregory P. Magarian, *Regulating Political Parties under a "Public Rights" First Amendment,* 44 WM. & MARY L. REV. 1939, 1951.

116. *Turner Broadcasting System, Inc. v. FCC,* 512 U.S. 622 (1994).

117. Martin Redish, *The Value of Speech,* 130 U. PA. L. REV. 591, 593–95.

118. THOMAS I. EMERSON, THE SYSTEM OF FREEDOM OF EXPRESSION 5 (Little Brown 1967).

119. 221 U.S. 418 (1911).

120. *Kovacs v. Cooper,* 336 U.S. 77 (1949).

121. 478 U.S. 675 (1986).

122. *Id.* at 681.

123. *City of Renton v. Playtime Theatres,* 475 U.S. 41, 48 (1986).

124. *Id.* at 48.

125. 391 U.S. 367 (1968).

126. *Id.* at 377.

127. 490 U.S. 401, 402 (1989).

128. *Id.* at 404.

129. *Zacchini v. Scripps-Howard Broadcasting Co.,* 47 Ohio St. 2d 224 (1976); *Zacchini v. Scripps-Howard Broadcasting Co.,* 433 U.S. 562 (1977).

130. *Florida Star v. B.J.F.,* 491 U.S. 524 (1989).

Chapter 7.
The Religion Clause and Limited Government

1. E. Gregory Wallace, *Justifying Religious Freedom: The Western Tradition,* 114 PENN. ST. L. REV. 485, 488, 491 (2009).

2. *See* Steven Smith, *The Rise and Fall of Freedom in Constitutional Discourse,* 140 U. PA. L. REV. 149, 157–58 (1991).

3. *See* JAMES MADISON, A MEMORIAL AND REMONSTRANCE AGAINST RELIGIOUS ASSESSMENTS (June 20, 1785), *reprinted in* 5 THE FOUNDERS CONSTITUTION 82 (Philip Kurland & Ralph Learner eds., 1987).

4. KETCHAM, FRAMED FOR POSTERITY at 95.

5. *See, e.g.,* STEPHEN L. CARTER, THE CULTURE OF DISBELIEF 33–43 (Basic Books 1993); BETTE NOVIT EVANS, INTERPRETING THE FREE EXERCISE OF RELIGION 132–37, 162 (Univ. of North Carolina Press 1997).

6. *Walz v. Tax Commission,* 397 U.S. 664 (1970).

7. James Hitchcock, *The Enemies of Religious Freedom,* FIRST THINGS 26 (February 2004).

8. 494 U.S. 872, 876 (1990).

9. *Id.* at 874.

10. 494 U.S. at 886 (upholding, without applying even minimal scrutiny, a law that bans all use of peyote, even though the law incidentally burdens religious practice). Under the *Smith* analysis, a court must first determine whether a law that burdens religion is neutral or whether on its face it targets religion; and the next step requires a determination if the law is "generally applicable," or if the law takes aim at religion through its "design, construction, or enforcement." *Id.* at 878–79. But if the law is neutral and of general applicability, then the exercise of religion will receive no constitutional protection from that law. No matter how seriously such a law burdens the exercise of religion, it will be upheld under a rational basis review. *Id.* at 882. For instance, in *Jimmy Swaggart Ministries v. Board of Equalization of California,* the Court held that California's imposition of sales- and use-tax liability on sales of religious materials does not violate the free exercise clause, since those taxes impose no constitutionally significant burden on religious practice or beliefs. 493 U.S. 378, 392 (1990).

11. Prior to *Smith,* free exercise cases had been governed by the doctrine of *Sherbert v. Verner,* 374 U.S. 398 (1963) (holding that laws burdening religious exercise had to be justified by a compelling state interest). *See also Wisconsin v. Yoder,* 406 U.S. 205, 214 (1972) (holding that the individual liberty of Amish superseded the State's interest in education).

12. *City of Boerne v. Flores,* 521 U.S. 507, 548 (1997) (O'Connor, J., dissenting).

13. Gerald Bradley, *Beguiled: Free Exercise Exemptions and the Siren Song of Liberalism,* 20 HOFSTRA L. REV. 245 (1991).

14. *Id.* at 307.

15. *Smith,* 494 U.S. at 889.

16. Nathan Oman, *Natural Law and the Rhetoric of Empire,* 8 WASH. L. REV. 661, 664–67, 669 (2011).

17. *Id.* at 689.

18. Michael McConnell, *Accommodation of Religion: An Update and a Response to the Critics,* 60 GEO. WASH. L. REV. at 725–26.

19. *Id.*

20. *See* Kathleen A. Brady, *Religious Group Autonomy: Further Reflections about What Is at Stake,* 22 J.L. & RELIGION 153, 168, 178 (2006) (arguing that a "broad right of autonomy for religious groups" is necessary to protect the ability of "religious communities to generate and communicate new and progressive ideas for civil and social life," and that "religious group autonomy is essential to support robust freedom of belief").

21. Richard Garnett, *Religious Freedom, Church Autonomy, and Constitutionalism,* 57 DRAKE L. REV. 901, 907 (2009).

22. For a discussion of the view that the establishment clause serves to protect a secular society from the political divisiveness that religion can cause, *see* Garnett, *Religion,* 94 GEO. L.J. at 1667 (2006).

23. *See* Carl H. Esbeck, *The Establishment Clause as a Structural Restraint on Governmental Power,* 84 IOWA L. REV. 1, 44–45 (1998).

24. *See* PATRICK M. GARRY, WRESTLING WITH GOD: THE COURTS' TORTUOUS TREATMENT OF RELIGION at 134, 140 (Catholic Univ. of America Press 2006).

25. *See Id.* at 45–52.

26. For a discussion on the primacy of the free exercise clause, see Patrick M. Garry, *Religious Freedom Deserves More than Neutrality: The Constitutional Argument for*

Nonpreferential Favoritism of Religion, 57 FLA. L. REV. 1, 42–44 (2005).

27. Several decades ago, when the Court was more firmly committed to a separationist stance, the separationist fear was over the threat of government capture by a religion or religions. *See* Calvin Massey, *The Political Marketplace of Religion,* 57 HASTINGS L.J. 1, 13 (2005). But later, as that threat seemed increasingly unlikely, the focus of the separationists turned more to a desire to protect society from the presumed social divisiveness caused by religious beliefs.

28. Michael McConnell, *Religion and Its Relation to Limited Government,* 33 HARV. J.L. & PUB. POL'Y 943, 944.

29. *See* McConnell, *Accommodation of Religion,* 60 GEO. WASH. L. REV. at 690 (1992).

30. *Id.* at 718. "Anti-accommodationists object to 'singling out' religion for special protection under the Free Exercise Clause, but they typically have no qualms about 'singling' out religion for special prohibitions under the Establishment Clause. . . . The anti-accommodationists seemingly take the position that the government must never 'advance' religion, but may inhibit, penalize, and punish it." *Id.* at 718–19. Although the anti-accommodationists view their position as neutral, it is neutral only for those "who believe that full religious practice can occur in the 'private' realm." Mark D. Rosen, *Establishment, Expressivism, and Federalism,* 78 CHI.-KENT L. REV. 669, 676 (2003). There are many, however, who believe that a full religious life is possible only if one's religious beliefs infuse every aspect of one's life, both private and public. *See Lee v. Weisman,* 505 U.S. 557, 645 (1992) (Scalia, J., dissenting).

31. Herbert J. Storing ed., *Charles Turner Speech at the Massachusetts Ratifying Convention,* February 5, 1788, *appearing in* 4 THE COMPLETE ANTI-FEDERALIST 221 (1981).

32. Herbert J. Storing, *Essay by Deliberator,* PHILADELPHIA FREEMAN'S JOURNAL, February 20, 1788, *appearing in* 3 THE COMPLETE ANTI-FEDERALIST 179 (1981).

33. Michael McConnell, *Religion and Its Relation to Limited Government,* 33 HARV. J.L. & PUB. POL'Y 943, 944.

34. *Id.* at 948.

35. According to Vincent Munoz, the Anti-Federalists who pushed for the First Amendment opposed religious establishments "only in connection with a consolidated, unlimited national government." Vincent Phillip Munoz, *The Original Meaning of the Establishment Clause and the Impossibility of Its Incorporation,* 8 U. PA. J. CONST. L. 585, 617 (2006).

36. *Id.* at 615–17. *See also* Kyle Duncan, *Subsidiarity and Religious Establishments in the United States Constitution,* 52 VILL. L. REV. 67, 121 (2007) (arguing that the establishment clause relates to federalism, that it concerns "the assignment of competences among constituent governmental structures," and that it serves as "a negative provision vis-à-vis the federal government").

37. *See generally* STEVEN D. SMITH, FOREORDAINED FAILURE: THE QUEST FOR A CONSTITUTIONAL PRINCIPLE OF RELIGIOUS FREEDOM 29 (Oxford Univ. Press 1995); *see also* Gerard V. Bradley, *The No Religious Test Clause and the Constitution of Religious Liberty: A Machine that Has Gone of Itself,* 37 CASE W. RES. L. REV. 674, 678 (1987). According to Smith, "[T]he Framers of the Establishment Clause did not intend to adopt any particular right or principle of religious freedom, but rather intended simply to reconfirm in writing the jurisdictional arrangement that preexisted the Constitution and that no one wanted to alter: this was an arrangement in which religion was a subject within the domain of the states, not the national government." Smith, *The Jurisdictional Establishment Clause,* 81 NOTRE DAME L. REV. at 1843 (2006). This jurisdictional interpretation "holds that the core purpose of the Establishment Clause was to confirm that jurisdiction over religion–or at least over the central concerns of religious establishment and free exercise of religion–

would remain with the states." *Id.* at 1870. However, as Smith also recognizes, now that the establishment clause has been incorporated through the Fourteenth Amendment, "a return to the federalist jurisdictional arrangement for religion that the First Amendment originally contemplated is not only undesirable, but impossible. It simply is not going to happen." *Id.* at 1892. For another view of the jurisdictional interpretation of the establishment clause, *see* Akhil Reed Amar, *Anti-Federalists, the Federalist Papers, and the Big Argument for Union*, 16 HARV. J.L. & PUB. POL'Y 111, 115 (1993) (arguing that the First Amendment language "shall make no law" constitutes a jurisdictional clause insofar as it is a denial of power). *See also* Ira C. Lupu and Robert W. Tuttle, *Federalism and Faith*, 56 EMORY L.J. 19, 42–43 (2006) (noting the argument that the First Amendment did not create a national religion policy, but simply left the whole matter to the states).

38. Daniel O. Conkle, *Toward a General Theory of the Establishment Clause*, 82 Nw. U. L. REV. 1113, 1134 (1988).

39. *Id.* at 1135.

40. *See* Akhil Reed Amar, *The Bill of Rights and the Fourteenth Amendment*, 101 YALE L.J. 1193 (1992).

41. GERARD BRADLEY, CHURCH-STATE RELATIONSHIPS IN AMERICA 92 (Greenwood Press 1987).

42. SMITH, FOREORDAINED FAILURE 30 (1995).

43. AMAR, THE BILL OF RIGHTS at 246 (1998).

44. *Id.* at 45.

45. THE DEBATES IN THE SEVERAL STATE CONVENTIONS, VOL. 3 at 330 (Jonathan Elliot ed., 2d ed. 1836).

46. THE DEBATES IN THE SEVERAL STATE CONVENTIONS, VOL. 4 at 194–95 (Jonathan Elliot ed., 2d ed. 1836).

47. James J. Knicely, *First Principles and the Misplacement of the Wall of Separation*, 52 DRAKE L. REV. 171, 173 (2004).

48. Stuart D. Poppel, *Federalism, Fundamental Fairness, and the Religion Clauses*, 25 CUMB. L. REV. 247, 250 (1995).

49. John C. Jeffries and James E. Ryan, *A Political History of the Establishment Clause*, 100 MICH. L. REV. 279, 287 (2001).

50. 330 U.S. 1 (1947).

51. Conkle, *Toward a General Theory*, 82 Nw. U. L. REV. at 1136. There is "specific evidence that the framers and ratifiers of the fourteenth amendment, whatever their intentions with respect to the Bill of Rights generally, at least did not intend to incorporate the establishment clause for application to the states. In 1875 and 1876, after the adoption of the fourteenth amendment, Congress considered, but rejected, a resolution that was specifically designed to make the religion clauses of the first amendment applicable to the states." *Id.* at 1137.

52. *See* Knicely, *First Principles*, 52 DRAKE L. REV. 171, 225 (2004); William K. Lietzau, *Rediscovering the Establishment Clause: Federalism and the Rollback of Incorporation*, 39 DEPAUL L. REV. 1191, 1193 (1990).

53. Note, *Rethinking the Incorporation of the Establishment Clause: A Federalist View*, 105 HARV. L. REV. 1700, 1715 (1992). Many federalism critics of incorporation argue that the framers intended states to have leeway in their own church-state relations, and that states should be free to shape those relations so as to allow for greater experimentation in education and public benefits programs. *Id.*

54. *See Elk Grove Unified School District v. Newdow*, 542 U.S. 1, 45, 49 (2004) (Thomas, J., concurring) (proposing a federalist construction of the establishment clause). Such a federalist view is necessary, according to Munoz, because "the Founders did not share

a uniform understanding of the proper relationship between church and state," and the establishment clause was drafted to quell concerns that the new federal government would "impose one form of church-state relations throughout the nation." Munoz, *The Original Meaning*, 8 U. PA. J. CONST. L. at 604 (2006). As a consequence of viewing the establishment clause as a structural or federalism provision, rather than one that protects individual rights, Amar concludes that the establishment clause should not have been incorporated through the Fourteenth Amendment to apply to the states. *See* Akhil Reed Amar, *The Bill of Rights as a Constitution*, 100 YALE L.J. 1131, 1157–61 (1991); Akhil Reed Amar, *Some Notes on the Establishment Clause*, 2 ROGER WILLIAMS U. L. REV. 1, 5 (1996); *see also* Munoz, *The Original Meaning*, 8 U. PA. J. CONST. L. at 631 (arguing that because the establishment clause did not constitutionalize a personal right of nonestablishment it should not have been incorporated).

55. 124 S.Ct. 2301, 2328 (2004) (Thomas, J., concurring).

56. *Id.* at 2330.

57. *School District of Abington Township v. Schempp*, 374 U.S. 203, 309 (1963) (Stewart, J., dissenting).

58. Esbeck, *Uses and Abuses of Textualism and Originalism*, UTAH L. REV. 489, 586 (2011).

59. *Id.* at 600.

60. According to Conkle, the Supreme Court has used the establishment clause "to enforce a wavering, but relatively strict, separation of church and state at all levels of American government." Conkle, *Toward a General Theory*, 82 Nw. U. L. REV. at 1117 (1988). According to the Court in *Lynch v. Donnelly*, when courts enforce a strict separation of church and state, they assault the freedom of religious exercise as guaranteed in the First Amendment. 465 U.S. at 668.

61. *Lee v. Weisman*, 505 U.S. 577 (1992).

62. *County of Allegheny*, 492 U.S. 573 (1989).

63. *Santa Fe Independent School Dist. v. Doe*, 530 U.S. 290 (2000).

64. *McCreary County v. ACLU*, 545 U.S. 844 (2005).

65. Brian J. Serr, *A Not-So-Neutral "Neutrality": An Essay on the State of the Religion Clauses on the Brink of the Third Millennium*, 51 BAYLOR L. REV. 319, 320 (1999). The Court's establishment clause decisions "mandate a government `neutrality' of hypersensitivity toward even the most limited acknowledgments of religion in public life." *Id.*

66. 437 F.3d 1, 6–7 (2d Cir. 2006).

67. *Id.* at 6–8.

68. *Santa Fe Independent School Dist. v. Doe*, 530 U.S. 290 (2000).

69. *Id.* at 294.

70. *Id.* at 320. The Court held that the practice created "the perception of encouraging the delivery of prayer at a series of important school events." *Id.*

71. *Id.* at 311–12.

72. *Lee*, 505 U.S. 577, 586 (1992).

73. *Lee*, 505 U.S. 577 at 586 (1992).

74. *Id.* at 586.

75. Michael Stokes Paulsen, *Lemon Is Dead*, 43 CASE W. RES. L. REV. 795, 832 (1993).

76. *Lee*, 505 U.S. at 594–98.

77. *Lee*, 505 U.S. at 597. For a discussion of why the Court should have applied the exercise clause in *Lee* and *Santa Fe*, rather than the establishment clause, *see* Patrick M. Garry, *The Institutional Side of Religious Liberty: A New Model of the Establishment Clause*, 2004 UTAH L. REV. 1155, 1167–71 (2004).

78. 465 U.S. 668 (1984).

79. Alberto B. Lopez, *Equal Access and the Public Forum: Pinette's Imbalance of Free Speech and Establishment*, 55 BAYLOR L. REV. 167, 195 (2003). Since *County of Allegheny* (1989), which confirmed the endorsement test as the Court's preferred method of analysis, the Court has continued its reliance on the endorsement test for establishment clause cases. The Court, 492 U.S. at 593–94, recently applied the test in *Santa Fe*, 530 U.S. 290, 316 (2000).

80. *County of Allegheny*, 492 U.S. 593 (1989). See *Lynch*, 465 U.S. at 690 (O'Connor, J., concurring) (discussing the endorsement test and the importance of determining what message government communicates in its activities).

81. 492 U.S. 573 (1989).

82. *Id.* at 600–602, 619–20.

83. *Id.* at 620–21.

84. 492 U.S. at 598–603.

85. *Id.* at 620.

86. *Lynch*, 465 U.S. at 692 (1984) (O'Connor, J., concurring).

87. *Id.* at 688. To Justice O'Connor, the endorsement test functioned to prevent government from "making a citizen's religious affiliation a criterion for full membership in the political community." *Id.* at 690 (O'Connor, J., concurring).

88. Steven G. Gey, *When Is Religious Speech Not "Free Speech"?* 2000 U. ILL. L. REV. 379, 444 (2000). They also argue that religious speech can be socially and politically divisive and hence, should be discouraged from entering the public sphere. See Douglas Laycock, *Freedom of Speech That Is Both Religious and Political*, 29 U.C. DAVIS L. REV. 793, 794–801 (1996).

89. *Capital Square Review & Advisory Bd. v. Pinette*, 515 U.S. 753, 777 (O'Connor, J., concurring in part and concurring in judgment).

90. Lopez, *Equal Access*, 55 BAYLOR L. REV. at 218–19 (citing examples of threats and harassment made against religious dissenters and those who take court action to oppose public displays of religion).

91. *Id.* at 219.

92. *Id.* at 224.

93. *Id.* at 221–22.

94. See *Lynch*, 465 U.S. at 690 (O'Connor, J., concurring).

95. *Allegheny*, 492 U.S. at 599–600.

96. *Id.* at 620.

97. See Steven D. Smith, *Symbols, Perceptions, and Doctrinal Illusions: Establishment Neutrality and the "No Endorsement" Test*, 86 MICH. L. REV. 266, 301 (1987).

98. *Am. Jewish Cong. v. City of Chi.*, 827 F.2d 120, 129 (7th Cir. 1987) (Easterbrook, J., dissenting).

99. 492 U.S. at 674 (Kennedy, J., concurring in part and dissenting in part).

100. *Allegheny*, 492 U.S. at 669 (Kennedy, J., concurring in part and dissenting in part).

101. *Id.* at 674 (Kennedy, J., concurring in part and dissenting in part).

102. *Id.* at 664 (Kennedy, J., concurring in part and dissenting in part).

103. *Id.* at 655, 664 (Kennedy, J., concurring in part and dissenting in part).

104. *Skarin v. Woodbine Community Sch. Dist.*, 204 F.Supp.2d 1195, 1198 (S.D. Iowa 2002).

105. *Id.*

106. 921 F.2d 1047, 1049 (10th Cir. 1990).

107. 926 F.2d 1066 (11th Cir. 1991).

108. In *Capital Square Review & Advisory Board v. Pinette*, 515 U.S. 753 (1995), involving

a private group's placement of a cross in a public plaza next to the state capitol, the court ruled that the display did not violate the establishment clause. *Id.* at 770. However, the plurality left open the possibility that the establishment clause might be violated if the government "fostered or encouraged" the mistaken attribution of private religious speech to the government. *Id.* at 766. Justice O'Connor noted that "an impermissible message of endorsement can be sent in a variety of contexts, not all of which involve direct government speech or outright favoritism." *Id.* at 774 (O'Connor, J., concurring in part and concurring in judgment). This may occur "even if the governmental actor neither intends nor actively encourages [the endorsement]." *Id.* at 777 (O'Connor, J., concurring in part and concurring in judgment). Thus, the establishment clause imposes on the government "affirmative obligations that may require a State, in some situations, to take steps to avoid being perceived as supporting or endorsing a private religious message." *Id.* Consequently, even though Justice O'Connor joined in the majority opinion, which stated that "private religious speech . . . is as fully protected under the Free Speech Clause as secular private expression," *Id.* at 760, she also announced that the establishment clause limits the free speech clause's protection of private religious speech when that speech occurs on government property or in other contexts in which the speech becomes associated with the government. *Id.* at 777 (O'Connor, J., concurring in part and concurring in judgment). The problem is, of course, how to determine when private speech "becomes associated" with the government.

109. 489 U.S. 1, 5, 15 (1991).

110. In the plurality opinion, Justice Brennan noted that "we in no way suggest that all benefits conferred exclusively upon religious groups or upon individuals on account of their religious beliefs are forbidden by the Establishment Clause unless they are mandated by the Free Exercise Clause." 489 U.S. at 18 n.8. Yet one is left with the conclusion that *Texas Monthly* stands for the proposition that government benefits to religion can only be sustained if those benefits flow to a large number of nonreligious groups as well as religious entities, or if the accommodation is aimed only at alleviating a free exercise infringement.

111. Thus, accommodation should not be allowed to favor one religion over another. Indeed, "it is exceedingly impractical to treat accommodations of religion as categorically unconstitutional." McConnell, *Accommodation of Religion,* 60 GEO. WASH. L. REV. at 715. If a legislature, for instance, concluded that religious organizations had better success at certain social welfare functions, such as drug rehabilitation, then there should be nothing to stop those legislatures from providing funding in a way that might favor those religious organizations.

112. *See* JAMES E. CURRY, PUBLIC REGULATION OF THE RELIGIOUS USE OF LAND 3 (Michie 1964).

113. ANSON PHELPS STOKES, CHURCH AND STATE IN THE UNITED STATES 369, n.94 (Harper 1950).

114. *Id.* at 369, 419.

115. Alexis de Tocqueville likewise observed that the early Americans considered religion "indispensable to the maintenance of republican institutions." 1 ALEXIS DE TOCQUEVILLE, DEMOCRACY IN AMERICA 305–6 (Everyman's Library ed. 1994) (1835). He came to agree with this position, arguing that religion was desperately needed in a democratic republic. *Id.* at 307. Jefferson, in his *Notes on Virginia,* expressed the sentiment that belief in divine justice was essential to the liberties of the nation: "And can the liberties of a nation be thought secure when we have removed their only firm basis, a conviction in the minds of the people that these liberties are of the gift of God?" THOMAS JEFFERSON, NOTES ON VIRGINIA, *reprinted in* THE LIFE AND SELECTED WRITINGS OF THOMAS JEFFERSON 187–278 (Adrienne Koch & William Peden eds., Random House 1944).

116. For a discussion on the influence of republican thought on the writing of the Constitution, *see generally* THOMAS L. PANGLE, THE SPIRIT OF MODERN REPUBLICANISM: THE MORAL VISION OF THE AMERICAN FOUNDERS AND THE PHILOSOPHY OF LOCKE (Univ. of Chicago Press 1988).

117. Letter from John Adams to the Officers of the First Brigade of the Third Division of the Militia of Massachusetts, *in* 9 THE WORKS OF JOHN ADAMS, SECOND PRESIDENT OF THE UNITED STATES 228, 229 (Charles Frances Adams ed., Little, Brown 1854).

118. Letter from John Adams to Benjamin Rush (Aug. 28, 1811), *in* THE SPUR OF FAME: DIALOGUES OF JOHN ADAMS AND BENJAMIN RUSH 1805–1813 at 191, 192 (John A. Schutz & Douglass Adair eds., The Huntington Library 1966). According to Benjamin Rush, "The only foundation for a useful education in a republic is to be laid in religion. Without it there can be no virtue, and without virtue there can be no liberty, and liberty is the object and life of all republican governments." Brian C. Anderson, *Secular Europe, Religious America*, PUB. IN., at 143, 152 (Spring 2004).

119. STOKES, CHURCH AND STATE at 515 (1950).

120. David Barton, *The Image and the Reality: Thomas Jefferson and the First Amendment*, 17 NOTRE DAME J. LAW, ETHICS & PUB. POL'Y 399, 428 (2003). George Washington saw religion as an incubator for the kind of civic virtue on which democratic government had to rely. JOSEPH P. VITERITTI, CHOOSING EQUALITY: SCHOOL CHOICE, THE CONSTITUTION, AND CIVIL SOCIETY 127 (Brookings Inst. Press 1999).

121. George Washington, Farewell Address (Sept. 17, 1796), *in* 1 A COMPILATION OF THE MESSAGES AND PAPERS OF THE PRESIDENTS 205, 212 (James D. Richardson ed., published by authority of Congress 1897). The framers believed, as for instance did George Washington, that religion and morality were the "indispensable supports" for democratic government. *Id.*

122. J. William Frost, *Pennsylvania Institutes Religious Liberty*, 1862–1860, in ALL IMAGINABLE LIBERTY: THE RELIGIOUS LIBERTY CLAUSES OF THE FIRST AMENDMENT 33, 45 (Francis Graham Lee ed., Univ. Press of America 1995).

123. Michael McConnell, *Why Is Religious Liberty the "First Freedom"?* 212 CARDOZO L. REV. 1243, 1253 (2000); *see also* JOHN G. WEST JR., THE POLITICS OF REVELATION AND REASON: RELIGION AND CIVIC LIFE IN THE NEW NATION, 11–78 (Univ. Press of Kansas 1996). Through the middle of the nineteenth century, it was common practice for religious schools to be supported by state-generated revenue. CARL F. KAESTLE, PILLARS OF THE REPUBLIC: COMMON SCHOOLS AND AMERICAN SOCIETY, 1780–1860, at 166–67 (Hill and Wang 1983).

124. Michael W. McConnell, *Establishment and Disestablishment at the Founding, Part I: Establishment of Religion*, 44 WM. & MARY L. REV. 2105, 2197 (2003).

125. ELLIS SANDOZ, A GOVERNMENT OF LAWS: POLITICAL THEORY, RELIGION, AND THE FOUNDING 216–17 (Louisiana State Univ. Press 1990).

126. DANIEL L. DREISBACH, REAL THREAT AND MERE SHADOW: RELIGIOUS LIBERTY AND THE FIRST AMENDMENT 151 (Crossway Books 1987).

127. Northwest Ordinance of 1787, *reprinted in* 1 U.S.C. lii–lv (2000); Edwin S. Gaustad, *Religion and Ratification, in* THE FIRST FREEDOM, RELIGION AND THE BILL OF RIGHTS 41, 55 (James E. Wood Jr. ed., J. M. Dawson Institute of Church-State Studies 1990).

128. JOHN WITTE JR., RELIGION AND THE AMERICAN CONSTITUTIONAL EXPERIMENT 58 (Westview Press 2000).

129. RODNEY K. SMITH, PUBLIC PRAYER AND THE CONSTITUTION: A CASE STUDY IN CONSTITUTIONAL INTERPRETATION 66 (Scholarly Resources 1987).

130. Act of Aug. 7, 1789, ch. 8, 1 Stat. 50. The Northwest Ordinance was originally enacted by the Continental Congress in 1787, and then reenacted and adopted in 1789 by

the First Congress. *Id.* at 747.

131. SMITH, PUBLIC PRAYER at 103.

132. 1 ANNALS OF CONG., 90 (Joseph Gales ed., 1834). Beginning with the first session of the Continental Congress in 1774, the legislature opened its sessions with prayer, and the First Congress in 1789 established the office of Congressional Chaplain. Kurt T. Lash, *Power and the Subject of Religion,* 59 OHIO ST. L.J. 1069, 1070, 1124 (1998).

133. ANSON PHELPS STOKES & LEO PFEFFER, CHURCH AND STATE IN THE UNITED STATES 87–88 (Harper & Row 1964). Public religious proclamations were common in the post-constitutional period, from George Washington's first inaugural address, in which he referred to the role of divine providence in guiding the formation of the United States, to the opening of sessions of Congress with a prayer. SMITH, PUBLIC PRAYER at 103 and n.80.

134. DREISBACH, REAL THREAT AND MERE SHADOW at 150.

135. *Id.* at 151.

136. James M. O'Neill, *Nonpreferential Aid to Religion Is Not an Establishment of Religion,* 2 BUFFALO L. REV. 242, 255 (1952) (quoting George Washington, Instructions to the Commissioners for Treating with the Southern Indians [Aug. 29, 1789], *in* 4 AMERICAN STATE PAPERS: INDIAN AFFAIRS 65, 66 [Walter Lowrie & Matthew St. Clair Clark eds., Washington, D.C.: Gales & Seaton 1832]).

137. *See* 3 JOSEPH STORY, COMMENTARIES ON THE CONSTITUTION OF THE UNITED STATES, § 1868, at 726 (Brown, Shattuck 1833). Story argues that "at the time of the adoption of the Constitution, and of the [first] amendment to it . . . , the general, if not the universal sentiment in America was, that Christianity ought to receive encouragement from the state, so far as was not incompatible with the private rights of conscience, and the freedom of religious worship." *Id. See also* THOMAS M. COOLEY, THE GENERAL PRINCIPLES OF CONSTITUTIONAL LAW IN THE UNITED STATES OF AMERICA 205–6 (Boston: Little, Brown 1880). Cooley maintains that it "was never intended that by the Constitution the government should be prohibited from recognizing religion, or that religious worship should never be provided for in cases where a proper recognition of Divine Providence in the working of government might seem to require it, and where it might be done without drawing any invidious distinctions between different religious beliefs, organizations, or sects." *Id.*

138. MARK DEWOLFE HOWE, THE GARDEN AND THE WILDERNESS 31 (Univ. of Chicago Press 1965). *See also* LEONARD W. LEVY, CONSTITUTIONAL OPINIONS: ASPECTS OF THE BILL OF RIGHTS 142 (Oxford Univ. Press 1986) (observing that "[m]any contemporaries [of the Constitutional Convention] believed that governments could and should foster religion").

139. DREISBACH, REAL THREAT AND MERE SHADOW at 84; *see also* ROBERT ALLEN RUTLAND, THE BIRTH OF THE BILL OF RIGHTS 127, 166–67, 184, 209 (Univ. of North Carolina Press 1955).

140. JOHN WITTE JR., THE REFORMATION OF RIGHTS: LAW, RELIGION, AND HUMAN RIGHTS IN EARLY MODERN CALVINISM (Cambridge Univ. Press 2007).

141. McConnell, *Accommodation of Religion,* 60 GEO. WASH. L. REV. 685, 690 (1992) (stating that "the concern of the Religion Clauses is with the preservation of the autonomy of religious life"); *see also* Paulsen, *Lemon Is Dead,* 43 CASE W. RES. L. REV. 795, 798 (1993). Paulsen argues: "If nonestablishment and free exercise are understood as correlative rather than contradictory principles, it is logical to read the clauses as mirror-image prohibitions on government prescription and proscription, respectively, of the same thing—religious exercise." *Id.* at 808 (emphasis omitted).

142. For a discussion of how the exercise clause functions and how it differs from the establishment clause, *see* GARRY, WRESTLING WITH GOD, 128–40; Garry, *The Institutional*

Side of Religious Liberty, 2004 UTAH L. REV. at 1158–61, 1163–72 (2004).

143. Mark E. Chopko, *Religious Access to Public Programs and Governmental Funding,* 60 GEO. WASH. L. REV. 645,662 (1992). Preservation of religious institutional autonomy is one way of ensuring separation of church and state. *Id.*

144. *Id.* In *Wisconsin v. Yoder,* 406 U.S. 205 (1972), noting that the clauses work together as complementary protections for religious liberty, the Court wrote that "the Religion Clauses had specifically and firmly fixed the right to free exercise of religious beliefs, and buttressing this fundamental right was an equally firm, even if less explicit, prohibition against the establishment of any religion by government." *Id.* at 214.

145. Carl H. Esbeck, *Dissent and Disestablishment: The Church-State Settlement in the Early American Republic,* 2004 BYU L. REV. 1385, 1396 (2004).

146. Thomas C. Berg, *The Voluntary Principle and Church Autonomy, Then and Now,* 2004 BYU L. REV. 1593, 1597 (2004). The eighteenth-century notion of separation "was designed primarily to protect the vitality and independence of religious groups" and therefore "stood in marked contrast to a separationism founded on a suspicion of religion." *Id.*at 1594.

147. Richard John Neuhaus, *A New Order of Religious Freedom,* 60 GEO. WASH. L. REV. 620, 629 (1992). As Steven Smith argues, "[A] principle that forbids governmental invocation of religion may have the effect of rendering us tongue-tied when it comes to explaining our most basic political commitments," and this muffling of "the most basic matters is not a promising foundation for enduring political community." Steven D. Smith, *Nonestablishment under God? The Nonsectarian Principle,* 50 VILL. L. REV. 1, 11 (2005). Justice O'Connor's endorsement test actually results in a constriction of the political process, because it inhibits the workings and expressions of those political groups (religious believers) that might somehow cause other political groups or individuals (the nonreligious) to feel like social outsiders.

Chapter 8.
How the First Amendment Protects Individual Rights

1. *See* THE FEDERALIST NO. 10, 60 (James Madison) (Jacob E. Cooke ed., 1961).

2. *See* THE FEDERALIST NO. 51, 352 (James Madison) (Jacob E. Cooke ed., 1961).

3. McAffee, *Inalienable Rights,* 36 WAKE FOREST L. REV. at 747, 789 (2001).

4. *See Village of Willowbrook v. Olech,* 528 U.S. 562, 564 (2000) (stating that the equal protection clause secures protection against all "intentional and arbitrary discrimination").

5. *Lawrence v. Texas,* 539 U.S. 558, 579 (2003) (O'Connor, J., concurring). The clause was originally intended to prohibit and eliminate the widespread discrimination that existed in the South against former slaves after the Civil War. ERWIN CHEMERINSKY, CONSTITUTIONAL LAW 617 (2d ed., Aspen Publishers 2005).

6. WILLIAM E. NELSON, THE FOURTEENTH AMENDMENT: FROM POLITICAL PRINCIPLE TO JUDICIAL DOCTRINE 117 (Harvard Univ. Press 1988).

7. *See* 6 CHARLES FAIRMAN, RECONSTRUCTION AND REUNION, 1864–1888 at 1297 (Macmillan 1971); ERIC FONER, RECONSTRUCTION: AMERICA'S UNFINISHED REVOLUTION, 1863–1877 at 258–259 (Harper & Row 1988) (arguing that the Fourteenth Amendment was intended to combat violations of individual rights in the South).

8. JOHN HART ELY, DEMOCRACY AND DISTRUST: A THEORY OF JUDICIAL REVIEW 84 (Harvard Univ. Press 1980).

9. *See* Brian Smith, *Charles Demore v. Hyung Joon Kim: Another Step Away from Full Due Process Protections,* 38 AKRON L. REV. 207, 234 (2005). The fundamental rights for

which the equal protection clause mandates strict scrutiny include rights protected by the U.S. Constitution, such as the freedom of speech and religion. *See City of Cleburne, Tex. v. Cleburne Living Center,* 473 U.S. 432, 440. But the Court has been reluctant to extend strict-scrutiny review beyond those rights contained in the Constitution. Other than a few categories like voting practices and the treatment of indigents, the Court has generally rejected most claims that certain individual interests or rights are fundamental within the meaning of equal protection. *See Reynolds v. Sims,* 377 U.S. 533, 581 (1964) (applying strict scrutiny to a legislative scheme imposing unequal distribution of voting rights); *see also* Oliver Houck, *Standing on the Wrong Foot: A Case for Equal Protection,* 58 Syracuse L. Rev. 1, 32 (2007) (noting that the Court has rejected claims that welfare benefits and school funding schemes were fundamental within the meaning of equal protection).

10. *Massachusetts Board of Retirement v. Murgia,* 427 U.S. 307, 312 (1976). In *Washington v. Davis,* 426 U.S. 229 (1976), the Court found that a District of Columbia requirement that police officer candidates score a particular level on a written test ended up excluding African Americans disproportionately. *Id.* at 236–37. According to the Court, disproportionate effects were not enough to trigger strict scrutiny; instead, a facially nondiscriminatory statute would warrant strict scrutiny only if a racially discriminatory government purpose could be shown. *Id.* at 239.

11. These claims involve no legal values, such as common-law provisions or legislative intent; equal protection claims simply require judges to evaluate the reasonableness of the challenged categories. *See* William Araiza, *The Section Five Power and the Rational Basis Standard of Equal Protection,* 79 Tulane L. Rev. 519, 528 (2005).

12. *See* Richard H. Fallon, 54 UCLA L. Rev. 1267, 1303 (2007); *see also* Rubenfeld, *Affirmative Action,* 107 Yale L.J. 427, 427–29 (1997); *Johnson v. California,* 543 U.S. 499, 505 (2005).

13. Gregory P. Magarian, *The Jurisprudence of Colliding First Amendment Interests,* 83 Notre Dame L. Rev. 185, 234 (2007) (arguing that "the central question in the court's free speech analysis is whether a challenged regulation is neutral as to the content of speech"). Under a neutral First Amendment analysis, "[a] principled court is simply instructing the government to treat different speakers and viewpoints in an unbiased manner." *Id.* at 235.

14. *Id.* at 236.

15. Dorf, *Incidental Burdens,* 109 Harv. L. Rev. at 1250 (1996).

16. *See* Daniel Conkle, *The Path of American Religious Liberty,* 75 Ind. L.J. 1, 26 (2000); *see also Brown v. Board of Education,* 347 U.S. 483 (1954) (outlawing formal or deliberate segregation on the basis of race in public schools).

17. *Id.* at 28.

18. Magarian, *The Jurisprudence of Colliding First Amendment Interests,* 83 Notre Dame L. Rev. at 239.

19. *See Rosenberger v. Rector and Visitors of the University of Virginia,* 515 U.S. at 839.

20. Conkle, *Three Theories,* 85 N.C. L. Rev. 63, 66 (2006) (outlining "the problems of doctrinal clarity and judicial consistency" with substantive due process).

21. 497 U.S. 261, 278 (1990).

22. *See* 431 U.S. 494, 498 (1977).

23. 434 U.S. 374, 390–91 (1978).

24. 530 U.S. 57 (2000).

25. *Lawrence v. Texas,* 539 U.S. 558, 579–85 (2003).

26. For a longer discussion on whether a right of sexual intimacy should be found within the Constitution, *see* Donald H. J. Hermann, *Pulling the Fig Leaf Off the Right of Privacy,* 54 DePaul L. Rev. 909, 945–55 (2005).

27. McAffee, *Overcoming Lochner,* 42 U. Rich. L. Rev. at 597, 632 (2008).

28. *See Lloyd Corp. v. Tanner,* 407 U.S. 551, 558, 569 (1972).

29. *Id.*at 568.

30. *See Pacific Gas & Electric Co. v. Public Utilities Commission,* 475 U.S. 1, 5–7, 20 (1986). The Court has also protected the First Amendment freedom from being compelled to accommodate the viewpoint of others. In *Hurley,* the Court ruled that requiring private organizers of a St. Patrick's Day parade to allow a gay rights organization to participate was a violation of the First Amendment. 515 U.S. at 573–75. And in *Boy Scouts of America v. Dale,* the Court ruled that the Boy Scouts could not be forced to place a gay rights activist in a leadership position, imposing on the Boy Scouts a viewpoint the group did not want to express. 530 U.S. 640, 643–44 (2000).

31. 460 U.S. 575 (1983).

32. 505 U.S. 377, 386 (1992).

33. Despite the criticism that modern courts have over-applied the equal protection clause of the Fourteenth Amendment, there is little disagreement that it was certainly meant to apply to fundamental rights of the kind found in the First Amendment. *See* William Araiza, *Constitutional Rules and Institutional Roles,* 62 SMU L. Rev. 27, 42 (2009); Curtis, No State Shall Abridge 117–20 (Duke Univ. Press 1986) (arguing that the clause applies to fundamental rights, including those in the Bill of Rights).

34. *Wallace v. Jaffree,* 472 U.S. 38, 52–53 (1985).

35. *Everson v. Board of Education,* 330 U.S. 1, 15 (1947).

36. *Larson v. Valente,* 456 U.S. 228, 244 (1982).

37. 456 U.S. 228, 231 (1982).

38. *Id.* at 246. According to the Court, the registration exemption deliberately discriminated between different religious organizations. *Id.* at 247.

39. *See Comm. for Pub. Educ. & Religious Liberty v. Nyquist,* 413 U.S. 756, 782, 794 (1973).

40. *See, e.g., Mueller v. Allen,* 463 U.S. 388, 397 (1983) (approving of an aid program benefiting public and private school students).

41. 512 U.S. 687 (1994).

42. *Id.* at 706.

43. Douglas Laycock, *Theology Scholarships, the Pledge of Allegiance, and Religious Liberty: Avoiding the Extremes but Missing the Liberty,* 118 Harv. L. Rev. 155, 156 (2004). In establishment clause cases, government neutrality has become a governing principle. *Id.* at 158.

44. The no-aid principle held that no government assistance, however small, should be given to any religious activities or institutions. *See Everson,* 330 U.S. at 16. The nondiscrimination principle, however, stated that the government could not exclude individual religious believers, because of their faith, from receiving the benefits of public welfare legislation. *Id.* According to Laycock, the no-funding tradition "is a misinterpretation of the Establishment Clause, deeply rooted in historic anti-Catholicism," at least as applied to elementary and secondary schools. Laycock, *Theology Scholarships,* 118 Harv. L. Rev. at 185.

45. *See Zelman v. Simmons-Harris,* 536 U.S. 639 (2002); *Mitchell v. Helms,* 530 U.S. 793 (2000); *Zobrest v. Catalina Foothills School District,* 509 U.S. 1 (1993); *Bowen v. Kendrick,* 487 U.S. 589 (1988); *Witters v. Washington Dept. of Services for the Blind,* 474 U.S. 481 (1986).

46. *See Zelman,* 536 U.S. 639.

47. *See Mitchell,* 530 U.S. 793.

48. 392 U.S. 236, 243 (1968) (stating that "the law merely makes available to all children the benefits of a general program to lend schoolbooks free of charge").

49. 403 U.S. 672, 674–75 (1971).

50. 426 U.S. 736, 746–47 (1976) (suggesting that a refusal to permit religious schools to have access to these grants would make the state less than neutral).

51. 920 F.2d 1282, 1284–86 (6th Cir. 1990).

52. *Id.* at 1287.

53. 938 F.Supp. 1466 (Dist. Minn. 1996).

54. 534 F.3d 1245, 1250 (10th Cir. 2008).

55. *Id.* at 1259.

56. 508 U.S. 384, 387, 395 (1993).

57. 454 U.S. 263, 265 (1981).

58. *Id.* at 277.

59. *Widmar,* 454 U.S. at 273.

60. 515 U.S. 819, 822–23 (1995).

61. *Id.* at 824–25.

62. *Id.* at 831–32.

63. *Id.* at 839–40, 843–44.

64. *Id.* at 840. According to the Court, "A central lesson of our decisions is that a significant factor in upholding governmental programs in the face of establishment clause attack is their neutrality toward religion." *Id.* at 839.

65. 533 U.S. 98 (2001).

66. *Id.* at 102.

67. A neutrality approach has also allowed the courts to abandon the "no-aid" approach, which prohibited the flow of any governmental benefit to any religious organization. *See, e.g., Wolman v. Walter,* 433 U.S. 229 (1977); *Meek v. Pittenger,* 421 U.S. 349 (1975); *Comm. for Pub. Educ. v. Nyquist,* 413 U.S. 756 (1973). A strict no-aid reading of the establishment clause would require the exclusion of religious institutions from generally available government aid programs, and would thus constitute a "penalty" on the free exercise of religion. It was the no-aid approach that was "responsible for what is perceived to be irreconcilable tension between the Establishment Clause and the Free Exercise Clause." Thomas R. McCoy, *Quo Vadis: Is the Establishment Clause Undergoing Metamorphosis?* 41 BRANDEIS L.J. 547, 549 (2003).

68. 473 U.S. 402 (1985).

69. 521 U.S. 203, 228 (1997).

70. *Id.* at 231. As an example of this no-discrimination approach, the Fourth Circuit struck down a Maryland policy that funded secular colleges and some church-affiliated colleges, but not pervasively sectarian colleges. *Columbia Union College v. Oliver,* 254 F.3d 496, 504–8 (4th Cir. 2001).

71. 509 U.S. 1, 18 (1993).

72. 536 U.S. 639 (2002).

73. *Id.* at 662–63. In *Zelman,* the Court's finding that the Ohio program was one of true private choice was based upon the determination that the program is neutral toward religion, gives aid directly to a broad class of citizens without consideration of religion, and permits public and both religious and secular private schools to participate. *See id.* at 648–54.

74. *Id.* at 622.

75. In the lower court, it was found that 96 percent of the students participating in the voucher program were enrolled in religious schools. *See Simmons-Harris v. Zelman,* 234

F.3d 945, 949 (6th Cir. 2000), *rev'd,* 536 U.S. 639 (2002).

76. Conkle, *The Path of American Religious Liberty,* 75 IND. L.J. at 8 (2000).

77. 374 U.S. 203, 222 (1963).

78. 489 U.S. 1 (1991).

79. *Id.* at 5, 15. In the plurality opinion, Justice Brennan noted that "we in no way suggest that all benefits conferred exclusively upon religious groups or upon individuals on account of their religious beliefs are forbidden by the Establishment Clause unless they are mandated by the Free Exercise Clause." 489 U.S. at 18, n.8. But the Court could discern no "concrete need to accommodate religious activity" in this case. *Id.* at 18.

80. To Justice Blackmun, "a statutory preference for the dissemination of religious ideas offends our most basic understanding of what the establishment clause is all about and hence is constitutionally intolerable." *Texas Monthly v. Bullock,* 489 U.S. 1, 28 (1989).

81. *Corporation of the Presiding Bishop of the Church of Jesus Christ of Latter-day Saints v. Amos,* 483 U.S. 327 (1987). In *Amos,* the Court held that the government could exempt religious institutions from the religious antidiscrimination requirements of Title VII, thereby allowing them to favor members of their own faith in hiring for ministerial positions with the church. If it were not for this accommodation, the government would become deeply entangled with religiously sensitive church decisions and infringe on the free exercise rights of those church members.

82. 494 U.S. 872, 877–79 (1990).

83. *Id.* at 884–85 (1990). Thus, as long as the state does not deliberately single out a particular religious practice, any burdens on that practice will not violate the First Amendment. *See also Church of the Lukumi Babalu Aye, Inc. v. City of Hialeah,* 508 U.S. 520 (1993). In *City of Hialeah,* the Court struck down a city's ban on the ritual slaughter of animals, since the ban basically permitted all ritual slaughter except that practiced by a particular religious sect. 508 U.S. at 528, 542–45. The Court found that the law basically singled out for discriminatory treatment the religious practices of the Santerian sect, ruling that under *Smith* the free exercise clause will be enforced only where government intentionally targets religion with special burdens. *Id.* at 532–33.

84. *See Sherbert v. Verner,* 374 U.S. 398 (1963) (holding that a state could not refuse unemployment compensation to a Sabbatarian who is unavailable for work on Saturdays. *Id.* at 403–6) and *Wisconsin v. Yoder,* 406 U.S. 205, 213–36 (1972) (holding that a state could not require Amish children to attend high school).

85. In *Sherbert,* a Seventh-Day Adventist was denied unemployment compensation after having been fired from her job for refusing to work on Saturday. The Court held that a state unemployment law that only provided benefits to those willing to work on Saturdays violated the free exercise clause, because it could not be justified by a compelling state interest. 374 U.S. at 410. The Court focused on the fact that the state law required some individuals to violate a central belief of their religion so as to qualify for the state funding. *Id.* at 406. *Yoder* reaffirmed the *Sherbert* doctrine when it held that the free exercise clause prevents states from enforcing compulsory-school-attendance laws. 406 U.S. at 234. The respondent, an Amish man, claimed that religious beliefs exempted his daughter from such laws. *Id.* at 207–9.

86. *See Smith,* 494 U.S. at 876–90. Although the Court in *Smith* held that facially neutral statutes do not ordinarily violate the free exercise clause, it also reiterated that laws imposing special burdens on targeted religions are presumptively unconstitutional. 494 U.S. at 877.

87. *See Smith,* 494 U.S. at 886 (stating that free exercise exemptions are "a constitutional anomaly," unlike the "constitutional norm" of "equality of treatment").

88. Douglas Laycock, *Formal Substantive and Disaggregated Neutrality toward Religion,*

39 DePaul L. Rev. 993, 999 (1990) (arguing that formal neutrality would "prohibit classification in terms of religion either to confer a benefit or to impose a burden").

89. *Id.* at 1001–6.

90. Conkle, *The Path of American Religious Liberty,* 75 Ind. L.J. at 10.

91. Laycock, *Theology Scholarships,* 118 Harv. L. Rev. at 202.

92. 508 U.S. 520 (1993).

93. *Id.* at 535.

94. *Id.* at 535–36.

95. *See* Laycock, *Theology Scholarships,* 118 Harv. L. Rev. at 208–10.

96. *Id.* at 210. According to Laycock, "The protection for religious liberty under the *Smith-Lukumi* rules lies in their effect on the political process. Legislatures can impose on religious minorities only those laws that they are willing to impose on all their constituents." *Id.* And this essentially is the command of the equal protection doctrine.

97. 494 U.S. 872 (1990), 508 U.S. 520 (1993).

98. *Locke v. Davey,* 540 U.S. 712, 717 (2004).

99. *See* Laycock, *Theology Scholarships,* 118 Harv. L. Rev. at 214.

100. *See Locke v. Davey,* 124 S.Ct. 1307, 1315; *see also Rust v. Sullivan,* 500 U.S. 173, 192–93 (1991).

101. Robert W. Tuttle, *How Firm a Foundation? Protecting Religious Land Uses after Boerne,* 68 Geo. Wash. L. Rev. 861 (2000). Tuttle suggests that zoning ordinances that exclude religious uses while allowing similar secular uses are often deferentially reviewed by the courts, even though they appear to be facially content based. *Id.* at 894.

102. Alan E. Brownstein, *Protecting Religious Liberty: The False Messiahs of Free Speech Doctrine and Formal Neutrality,* 18 J.L. & Pol., 119, 148 (2002).

103. 481 U.S. 221, 228 (1987).

104. *See, e.g., Sable Communications v. FCC,* 492 U.S. 115, 126 (1989) (stating that content restrictions must promote a compelling government interest and be the least restrictive means of achieving that interest); *R.A.V. v. City of St. Paul,* 505 U.S. 377, 382 (1992) (stating the "content based regulations are presumptively invalid"); *Boos v. Barry,* 485 U.S. 312, 321 (1988) (stating that with content-based regulations courts will apply the "most exacting scrutiny").

105. *See, e.g., U.S. v. Playboy Entertainment Group,* 529 U.S. 803 (2000) (overturning restrictions on cable providers of sexually explicit programming); *Texas v. Johnson,* 491 U.S. 397 (1989) (striking down a flag-burning law); *Simon & Schuster Inc. v. Members of the New York State Crime Victims Board,* 502 U.S. 105 (1991) (striking down a law regulating the earnings of convicted criminals who write tell-all books about their crimes).

106. 398 U.S. 58, 63 (1970).

107. 408 U.S. 92, 102 (1972).

108. Geoffrey Stone, *Free Speech in the 21st Century: Ten Lessons from the 20th Century,* 36 Pepp. L. Rev. 273, 280 (2009).

109. *Id.* at 282.

110. *See, e.g., Ward v. Rock Against Racism,* 491 U.S. 781 (1989). The Court in *Ward* outlined a multipronged test for applying intermediate scrutiny: that the regulations be "justified without reference to the content of the regulated speech, that they [be] narrowly tailored to serve a significant governmental interest, and that they leave open ample alternative channels for communication of the information." *Id.* at 791. The "narrowly tailored" prong demands only that the statutory restrictions not be "substantially broader than necessary to achieve the government's interest"; they do not have to be the least restrictive means. *Id.* at 800; *see also Heffron v. International Society for Krishna Consciousness, Inc.,* 452 U.S.

640, 648 (1981) (upholding a law requiring that the distribution of literature at a state fair be conducted only from fixed locations, finding that the law satisfied intermediate scrutiny insofar as it served a significant government interest and left open ample alternative channels for communication of the information). Similarly, in *International Society for Krishna Consciousness v. Lee*, a regulation prohibiting society members from soliciting at airports was upheld. 505 U.S. 672 (1992). Intermediate scrutiny generally causes an invalidation of speech restrictions only when those restrictions end up banning or censoring the speech altogether, leaving no channels of communication open to it. *See City of Ladue v. Gilleo*, 512 U.S. 93 (1994) (overturning a law found to result in a near total ban on the display of signs on one's own property).

111. *See* Patrick M. Garry, *The First Amendment and Non-Political Speech: Exploring a Constitutional Model that Focuses on the Existence of Alternative Channels of Communication*, 71 Mo. L. Rev. 477, 485 (2007).

112. *See City of Renton v. Playtime Theaters*, 475 U.S. 41 (1986). Under the secondary-effects doctrine, a regulation is seen to be content neutral if it "serves purposes unrelated to the content of the expression . . . , even if it has an incidental effect on some speakers or messages." *Ward v. Rock Against Racism*, 491 U.S. 781, 791 (1989).

113. *See Hill v. Colorado*, 530 U.S. 703 (2000).

114. *See Hefron*, 452 U.S. at 640; *U.S. v. Kokinda*, 497 U.S. 720 (1990).

115. *See Turner Broadcasting System, Inc. v. FCC*, 512 U.S. 622, 643 (1994) (holding that the must-carry rules were content neutral and hence subject to the intermediate level of scrutiny, even though the rules imposed a direct burden on the freedom of cable operators).

116. 475 U.S. 41 (1986) (holding that an ordinance regulating adult theaters with the goal of reducing secondary effects "is completely consistent with our definition of content-neutral speech regulations as those are justified without reference to the content of the regulated speech.").

117. *Id.* at 41.

118. 427 U.S. 50, 52 (1976).

119. *Id.* at 82 (Powell, J., concurring).

120. *Id.* at 70.

121. *See, e.g.,* Frederick Schauer, *Speech and "Speech"—Obscenity and "Obscenity,"* 67 Geo. L.J. 899, 922 (1979); Cass Sunstein, *Pornography and the First Amendment*, 1986 Duke L.J. 589, 612–17.

122. 505 U.S. 377, 381 (1992).

123. 502 U.S. 105, 115–23 (1991).

124. *See Playboy*, 529 U.S. at 812 ("[T]he distinction between laws burdening and laws banning speech is but a matter of degree. The Government's content-based burdens must satisfy the same rigorous scrutiny as its content-based bans").

125. 518 U.S. 727 (1996).

126. 529 U.S. 803 (2000).

127. *Id.* at 845.

128. *Id.* at 842.

129. *Id.* at 846.

130. 503 U.S. 703, 723, 726 (2000).

131. *Id.* at 715–16.

132. *Id.* at 718.

133. *Id.* at 756.

134. *See Planned Parenthood v. Casey*, 505 U.S. 833, 876 (1992). In *Stenberg v. Carhart*, the Court struck down a Nebraska law outlawing partial-birth abortion as violating the

"undue burden" test. 530 U.S. 914 (2000). Such a balancing approach is also used in freedom of association cases, which involve conduct that facilitates expression. *See* Barry McDonald, *The First Amendment and the Free Flow of Information*, 65 OHIO ST. L.J. 249, 260 (2004). In these cases, the courts take into account the seriousness of the burdens on the freedom of expressive association before deciding on how strict or deferential a standard of review to apply to the law. *See, e.g., Clingman v. Beaver*, 125 S.Ct. 2029, 2035 (2005).

135. *See Ashcroft v. ACLU*, 542 U.S. 656 (2004); *Playboy*, 529 U.S. at 803.

136. *See Riley v. National Federation of the Blind*, 487 U.S. 781, 795–801 (1988) (imposing strict scrutiny after finding the law to be content based).

137. *See generally* Patrick M. Garry, *Defining Speech in an Entertainment Age: The Case of First Amendment Protection for Video Games*, 57 SMU L. REV. 139 (2004).

138. *See Interactive Digital Software Ass'n v. St. Louis County*, 329 F.3d 954 (8th Cir. 2003); *Video Software Dealers Ass'n v. Schwarzenegger*, 401 F. Supp.2d 1034 (N.D. Cal. 2005).

139. 336 U.S. 77 (1949).

140. *Id.* at 86–87.

141. *Id.* at 102, 81.

142. Courts have essentially assumed that the First Amendment requires opt-out. *See also Cohen v. California*, 403 U.S. 15, 26 (1971) (holding that, in the public square, listeners are presumed able to avert their eyes and ears from speech they find offensive and move on.); *Lamont v. Postmaster General*, 381 U.S. 301, 305 (1965) (holding that the government may not screen out sexually offensive materials in advance and require potential recipients to opt in); *Boler v. Youngs Drug Products Corp.*, 463 U.S. 60, 61 (1983) (holding that the federal government could not ban the unsolicited mailing of condom ads—a law that required opt-in).

143. In *Dial Info. Svcs. v. Thornburgh* and *Info. Providers' Coalition v. FCC*, the Second and Ninth Circuits ruled that the restrictions in the so-called Helms Amendment, 47 USC ⬚⬚ 223(b) et seq., did not violate the First Amendment. *Dial Info. Svcs. v. Thornburgh*, 938 F.2d 1535 (2d Cir. 1991); *Info. Providers' Coalition v. FCC*, 928 F.2d 866 (9th Cir. 1991).

144. *Red Lion Broadcasting Co. v. FCC*, 395 U.S. 367, 386 (1969).

145. *Kovacs v. Cooper*, 336 U.S. 77, 97 (1949) (Jackson, J., concurring).

146. *See* Jim Chen, *Conduit-Based Regulation of Speech*, 54 DUKE L.J. 1359, 1371–93 (2005).

147. *Id.* at 369, 378; *see also Ark. Educ. Television Comm'n v. Forbes*, 523 U.S. 666, 673 (1998).

148. *See Miami Herald Publishing Co. v. Tornillo*, 418 U.S. 241, 258 (1974) (striking down a state right-of-reply law applied to newspapers).

149. *See FCC v. National Citizens Committee for Broadcasting*, 436 U.S. 775, 779 (1978), where the Court upheld a ban on broadcast/newspaper cross ownership in the name of "the public interest in diversification of the mass communications media." 436 U.S. 775, 799 (1978). In justifying its decision, the Court stated that "efforts to enhance the volume and quality and coverage of public issues through regulation of broadcasting may be permissible where similar efforts to regulate the print media would not be." 436 U.S. at 800. As in *Red Lion*, the Court subjected structural regulation of the broadcast industry to a much lower scrutiny than similar efforts to regulate the print industry, thus using different baselines for the different media. *See Miami Herald Publishing Co. v. Tornillo*, where the Court invalidated a state right-of-reply law practically identical to the Fairness Doctrine, finding that the law unacceptably compromised a newspaper publisher's exercise of editorial control and judgment. *See* 418 U.S. 241, 258 (1974).

150. *FCC v. Pacifica Foundation*, 438 U.S. 726 (1978).

151. *Id.* at 748.

152. *Id.* at 749.

153. *Id.* at 748–49.

154. In *United States v. Southwestern Cable Co.*, 392 U.S. 157, 181 (1968), the Court held that the FCC had the power to regulate cable; however, the Court did not make clear exactly what constitutional model would be used to govern content regulations affecting cable. This failure to designate a specific standard of review of regulations governing cable continued in *City of Los Angeles v. Preferred Communications, Inc.*, 476 U.S. 488, 495 (1986). With cable, the Court has adopted an intermediate-scrutiny standard, which allows the government more room to regulate an industry that often possesses a monopolistic power over video programming in the markets it serves. *See Turner Broadcasting System, Inc. v. FCC*, 512 U.S. 622, 655 (1994) (*Turner I*); *Turner Broadcasting System, Inc. v. FCC*, 520 U.S. 180, 197 (1997) (*Turner II*).

155. *Turner Broadcasting System*, 512 U.S. 622, 641 (1994) (addressing the disparity in First Amendment treatment as reflected in *Miami Herald Publishing Co. v. Tornillo*, 418 U.S. 241 (1974) (conferring the most protective First Amendment status on the print media) and *Red Lion Broadcasting Co. v. FCC*, 395 U.S. 367 (1969) (granting a much less protective status to broadcasters).

156. *City of Los Angeles v. Preferred Communications, Inc.*, 476 U.S. 488 (1984).

157. *Turner Broadcasting System*, 512 U.S. 622, 662 (1994).

158. Glen O. Robinson, *The Electronic First Amendment: An Essay for the New Age*, 47 Duke L.J. 899, 935 (1998).

159. *Turner Broadcasting System*, 512 U.S at 633.

160. *Denver Area Educational Telecommunications Consortium, Inc. v. FCC*, 518 U.S. 727 (1996).

161. *Id.* at 744–45.

162. *Reno v. ACLU*, 521 U.S. 844, 868 (1997).

163. 535 U.S. 564, 594–95 (2002) (Kennedy, J., concurring).

164. *Id.* at 595. Many free speech activists, however, argue that constitutional doctrines should not treat each medium separately, that all the media should be treated uniformly, since they are all part of a larger system of public communication. For decades, free speech advocates have been pushing for all media technologies to have the same constitutional status as the print media. Ithiel Pool argued that media convergence and the democratizing aspects of the new media should bring about a convergence of constitutional treatment, and that under the First Amendment all media should be governed by the print model. *See generally* Ithiel de Sola Pool, Technologies of Freedom (Belknap Press 1983); Jeffrey Abramson, et al., The Electronic Commonwealth: The Impact of New Media Technologies on Democratic Politics 46, 57, 121–22 (Basic Books 1988). Yet while these advocates focus on likening cable and other technologies to print, in a regulatory and constitutional sense, they ignore the intrinsic differences in those media. What is so often ignored is that the different technologies have different ways of intruding and delivering unwanted speech or images. The reality still remains, for instance, that television is drastically different from print in both content and the way in which that content is delivered. Thus, perhaps the only standard that should be used to craft constitutional doctrines is not the technological features of the medium, but the ability of viewers to exert control over what content they are exposed to. As Denise Polivy argues, the Court should analyze speech restrictions according to the degree and type of filtering and exclusion that individuals (readers, viewers, listeners) can perform for the medium in question. Denise R. Polivy, *Virtue by Machine*, 29 Conn. L. Rev. 1749, 1791 (1997).

165. *See Minneapolis Star and Tribune Co. v. Minnesota Commissioner of Revenue,* 460 U.S. 575, 578 (1983).

166. *See* Patrick M. Garry, *The Democratic Aspect of the Establishment Clause,* 59 MERCER L. REV. 595, 597–600 (2008).

167. *Sherbert,* 374 U.S. at 409.

168. *Yoder,* 406 U.S. at 220.

169. *See Amos,* 483 U.S. 327, 338–40 (1987).

170. *Estate of Thornton v. Caldor,* 472 U.S. 703, 704 (1985).

171. *See id.* at 708–10.

172. 480 U.S. 136 (1987).

173. 452 U.S. 640 (1981).

174. *Id.* at 654–55.

175. *See* 460 U.S. 575, 585 (1983). In *Leathers v. Medlock,* the Court stated that the First Amendment scrutinizes only differential-taxation schemes that threaten to target particular viewpoints or speakers. 499 U.S. 439, 447 (1991). According to the Court, "differential taxation of speakers, even members of the press, does not implicate the First Amendment unless the tax is directed at, or presents the danger of suppressing, particular ideas."

176. 308 U.S. 147, 148 (1939).

177. A general ban on the distribution of all materials would be acceptable, despite the fact that such a ban would have an even more restrictive effect on individual-autonomy concerns. However, such a broader ban runs much less risk of the government's singling out or discriminating against certain types of speech.

178. *See* 521 U.S. 457 (1997).

179. *See* Garry, *The First Amendment and Non-Political Speech,* 72 MO. L. REV. 477, 514–20 (2007).

180. Cass Sunstein's four-part test for whether speech qualifies as "low value" is whether: (1) the speech is "far afield from the central concerns of the First Amendment" (which is the "effective popular control of public affairs"); (2) there are important "noncognitive aspects" of the speech; (3) "the speaker is seeking to communicate a message"; and (4) the speech is in an area in which the "government is unlikely to be acting for constitutionally impermissible reasons." Sunstein, *Pornography,* 1986 DUKE L.J. at 603–4 (1986). Stone's test states that low-value speech does not "primarily advance political discourse," is not defined in terms of "disfavored ideas or political viewpoints," has "a strong noncognitive" aspect, and has "long been regulated without undue harm to the overall system of free expression." Geoffrey Stone, *Sex, Violence and the First Amendment,* 74 U. CHI. L. REV. 1857, 1863–64 (2007).

181. *See Virginia State Board of Pharmacy v. Citizens Consumer Council,* 425 U.S. 748, 766–70, 773 (1976) (recognizing that only truthful, nondeceptive commercial speech about a lawful product deserves constitutional protection).

182. *See Time, Inc. v. Hill,* 385 U.S. 374, 387–88 (1966) (including within First Amendment coverage only the "false light" speech that pertains to matters of public concern and that is made without actual malice).

183. *See Cox Broadcasting v. Cohn,* 420 U.S. 469, 487 (1975) (recognizing that society has an interest in restricting speech that violates the "zone of privacy surrounding every individual"). The Court stated that an individual's "right to be free from unwanted publicity about his private affairs, which, although wholly true, would be offensive to a person of ordinary sensibilities" remains "plainly rooted in the traditions and significant concerns of our society." *Id.* at 489, 491.

184. *See New York v. Ferber,* 458 U.S. 747, 756–57 (1982) (stating that the governmental

interest in protecting children was "of surpassing importance"). The Court acknowledged that child pornography was "unprotected by the First Amendment." *Id.* at 764.

185. *See* Michael R. Siebecker, *Building a "New Institutional" Approach to Corporate Speech*, 59 ALA. L. REV. 247, 249 (making the case for the constitutionality of regulation of speech pertaining to financial securities).

186. 529 U.S. 277, 282–83 (2000).

187. *Id.* at 291.

188. 453 U.S. 490, 520–21 (1981).

189. *See* Stone, *Free Speech in the 21st Century*, 36 PEPP. L. REV. at 291.

190. 512 U.S. 43 (1994) (the justification of the law was to minimize visual clutter).

191. *See* Dorf, *Incidental Burdens,*109 HARV. L. REV. at 1250 (stating that "by definition, incidental effects do not burden the right").

192. *See* Patrick M. Garry, *A New First Amendment Model for Evaluating Content-Based Regulation of Internet Pornography*, 2007 BYU L. Rev. 1595, 1603–9 (2007).

193. As Stone points out, laws that have a direct effect have been subject to a more heightened scrutiny by the courts. Stone, *Free Speech in the 21st Century*, 36 PEPP. L. REV. at 297. The courts treat laws having direct effects on speech more harshly than laws having incidental effects because of the assumption that "laws that have only an incidental effect on speech are both less likely to be tainted by impermissible motivations and less likely to have a significant limiting or distorting effect on free expression." *Id.* at 298.

Conclusion

1. 454 U.S. 290 (1981).

2. *Id.* at 299–300.

3. 514 U.S. 334 (1995).

4. *Id.* at 357.

5. 536 U.S. 765 (2002).

6. 528 U.S. 377 (2000).

7. 424 U.S. at 20–21.

8. 424 U.S. 1 (1976).

9. 470 U.S. 480, 496 (1985).

10. 128 S.Ct. 2759 (2008).

11. 130 S.Ct. 876 (2010).

12. 518 U.S. 604 (1996).

13. 533 U.S. 431 (2001).

14. *Id.* at 464–65.

15. *Id.* at 449–50.

16. 548 U.S. 230 (2006).

17. *Id.* at 246.

18. *Id.* at 262.

19. Bradley Smith, *The John Roberts Salvage Company*, 68 OHIO ST. L.J. 891, 914 (2007).

20. 540 U.S. 93 (2003).

21. 551 U.S. 449 (2007).

22. 128 S.Ct. 2759 (2008).

23. 130 S.Ct. 876 (2010).

24. 130 S.Ct. at 909–10.

25. *Id.* at 913.

26. 130 S.Ct. at 889.

27. 435 U.S. 765 (1978).

28. Lillian R. BeVier, *Can Freedom of Speech Bear the Twenty-First Century's Weight?* 36 PEPP. L. REV. 415, 421 (2009).

29. Smith, *John Roberts Salvage Company,* 68 OHIO ST. L.J. at 893.

Index